e**x**treme sail

Oliver Dewar

FOREWORD BY DAME ELLEN MACARTHUR

PAVILION

CONTENTS

Foreword

To me sailing is a passion: an intoxicating ride along a path that is totally unpredictable, wild and powerful. But the sea needs to be respected. It has the ability to make you seem like the smallest object on the planet; it can toss you over with a flick of a wave and it has no compassion for its actions. It is this excitement that fuels my dedication to the sport of sailing.

At four years old I stepped on a boat with my aunt – it was to be a life changing experience. I loved the freedom of being out on the water; it was a totally new and exhilarating feeling. Of course, the more I learnt, the more my appetite for the challenge of the water grew, and by the time I was 18, sailing around Britain on my own in my 21ft boat *Iduna* – my fate was sealed. I continued to push the boundaries with each new project and sailing in the Mini Transat solo transatlantic race in 1997 led to the dream of the Vendée Globe – a legendary race that makes heroes of some sailors while claiming the lives of others. Twenty years after setting foot on a boat for the first time, I found myself in *Les Sables d'Olonne* preparing for the biggest race of my life so far. For

title page *A new perspective for world water-ski champion Patrice Martin behind Yvan Bourgnon's 60ft trimaran,* Rexona.

below *Ellen MacArthur takes a digital self-portrait with a companion during her record-breaking solo circumnavigation in 2004–5. MacArthur and trimaran* B&Q *were blasted by freezing hail at 51° South in the Pacific Ocean.*

4

most, the Vendèe Globe is the ultimate race in single-handed sailing – it pushes sailors to their very limits, mentally and physically, and tests every skill they have on the water. But as the saying goes, "to win, first you have to finish" and this is never more true than in this race. After 94 days at sea, I returned back to the same port that *Kingfisher* and I slipped away from in November 2000, having given everything to this race. It had been a roller-coaster ride but on the inside, I was still 'the same Ellen' – the girl with boundless enthusiasm for the sea and everything it has to offer.

After nearly ten years of professional sailing I continue to be grateful for the opportunities this sport has given me. In every race and every record attempt, I am given the opportunity to do better: to learn more and gain more understanding of this great sport and the environment to which it belongs. In my eyes, the Southern Ocean is one of the most beautiful environments on the planet. During the round-the-world record attempt on board the trimaran *B&Q*, I witnessed some incredible storms and, while at times I was concerned about how we would get through, I was also in awe at the beauty and power of the sea around me – sometimes dealing with the storm you are in is easier than the preparation and waiting in anticipation! As sailors we are privileged to be able to experience these oceans – the rawness and intensity – that have been shared by so few; more people have reached the summit of Everest than have raced non-stop around the world!

Sailing is a fantastic challenge; whether racing or cruising, there are many elements beyond our control, which bring a unique excitement and satisfaction. Although I have raced in many events, both fully crewed and solo, nothing is achieved without a real team effort. For me – and, I think for many who sail – to feel like an integral part of the crew or team; to work together getting to the finish line or getting through a storm brings the greatest sense of satisfaction.

Ultimately, the sea is my home – it is where I feel most content. I know that sailing is a passion that many people all over the world share. It is that passion and enjoyment that takes us out on to the sea. This book opens up that world, taking a look at all the major yachting events around the globe: from inshore to offshore, from solo to crewed – all illustrated by a collection of stunning photos.

I hope you enjoy this book – may it go with you wherever you sail!

Dame Ellen MacArthur MBE

Skipper trimaran *B&Q*

www.ellenmacarthur.com

Ocean, n. A body of water occupying about two-thirds of a world made for man – who has no gills.

Ambrose Bierce (1842–c.1914), *The Devil's Dictionary*

Introduction

It can be argued that setting out to sea in any vessel before accurate navigation methods evolved in the mid-1700s was extreme and to be avoided. For many, this logic holds true today, regardless of advances in boat design, technology and onboard communication systems. But what drives some men to venture into the remote, watery deserts of the planet? Any attempt to answer this question requires a brief study of man's history afloat.

Early offshore sailing was stimulated exclusively by trade and settlement, beginning with the Greek and Roman expeditions to India and China during the Hellenistic period (323–31 BC), and continuing, at around the time of Christ's birth, with Polynesian rafts filtering east across the Pacific Ocean, reaching Easter Island and Hawaii sometime between AD300–400. In about the year AD1,000, Norse sailors left Europe, calling into Iceland before briefly settling in North America, while during the thirteenth and fourteenth centuries, Marco Polo sailed throughout Asia and Ibn Battuta visited the Islamic countries of Africa, Europe and the Far East. By the early fifteenth century, fleets of Chinese junks were regularly crossing the Indian Ocean returning home with exotic treasures and curiosities for Emperor Ming. As navigation, chart making and shipbuilding practices improved, sailors travelled over increasing distances.

The true size of the planet and oceans, however, remained a mystery until the Golden Age of Exploration in the late fifteenth and sixteenth centuries. Christopher Columbus crossed the mid-Atlantic in 1492 (500 years after Leif Eriksson crossed the northern Atlantic), 'discovering' the New World and igniting an intense era of trans-oceanic sailing; Portuguese ships streamed south along the dark, mysterious coast of Africa and around the Cape of Good Hope into the Indian Ocean. Meanwhile, Spanish expeditions headed west into the Atlantic, then down the coast of South America and into the Pacific: both nations dispatching sailors to dangerous, diseased, uncharted areas of the globe in the name of god, glory and gold.

Since the fleet led by Ferdinand Magellan (c.1480–1521) first circumnavigated the globe, sailors have continued to risk their lives at sea, although in more recent times, some have done so without the desire to colonize, convert or pillage remote areas of the planet. In 1968, Sir Robin Knox-Johnston completed the first single-handed, non-stop circumnavigation of the globe. In the log of this journey he claimed (during a brief bout of introspection), "I was sailing around the world simply because I bloody well wanted to – and, I realized, I was thoroughly enjoying myself." Conversely, Knox-Johnston's

> Surely oak and threefold brass surrounded his heart who first trusted a frail vessel to the merciless ocean?
>
> Horace (65–8 BC), Roman poet

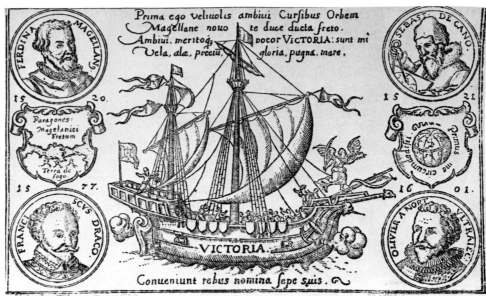

Prima ego velivolis ambivi Curfibus Orbem
Magellane nouo te duce ducta freto.
Ambivi, meritoq, vocor VICTORIA: sunt mi
Vela, alæ, precium, gloria, pugna, mare,

FERDINAN. MAGELLAN.

1520.

Paragones:
Magelanici
Fretum

Terra de
fogo

1577.

FRANCI SCVS DRACO.

VICTORIA.

Conueniunt rebus nomina fepe suis.

SEBAST. DE CANO.

1521.

1601.

OLIVIER A NORT. VLTRAIEC.

No. Exploration 1500-15?   THE FIRST SHIP TO CIRCUMNAVIGATE THE WORLD.   PICTURE COLLECTION

direct contemporary, the legendary French circumnavigator, Bernard Moitessier (1925–1994), suggested a more spiritual and poetic spur for wandering the oceans, saying: "You do not ask a tame seagull why he needs to disappear from time to time towards the open sea. He goes, that's all."

Whatever inspires men to sail beyond the limit of normal human endurance, a diverse cultural legacy remains: for many Anglo-Saxon sailors the sea represents a challenge to be endured and conquered, yet for their French counterparts, the sea is often considered a supreme, primeval force of nature connecting man with his soul. One of the aims of *Extreme Sail* is to reveal the environment that has generated this range of conviction.

Furthermore, this book aims to unite the various modern disciplines within the sport: inshore and offshore, big boats and dinghies, cruising and racing. Although many insist that the sea binds together all levels and sectors of the sport in a salty, marine brotherhood, this belief is misguided. Many inshore racing crews regard offshore sailors as courageous Neanderthals, while these ocean-racing primates view their shore-based relatives as delicate, coastal flowers. Many cruising

above *A representation of Ferdinand Magellan and his ship,* Victoria, *during the world's first circumnavigation, 1519–1522.*

yachtsmen consider racing crews to be arrogant speed freaks who, in return, often treat cruisers as mossy-bottomed obstacles cluttering a race course (in reality, the only consensus among sailors is the belief that large motor yachts should be treated with contempt). *Extreme Sail* attempts to demolish the maze of partitions that exist within the sport.

Finally, the images in *Extreme Sail* aim to find a thread of common, seafaring purpose – to establish a link between the mutinous, superstitious pioneers of Magellan's voyage and modern sailors on their racing thoroughbreds bristling with satellite technology.

above *Sir Robin Knox-Johnston approaches the end of the first non-stop single-handed voyage around the world in his 32ft ketch,* Suhaili, *after 313 days at sea.* Suhaili *averaged 4.04 knots during the 30,123-mile circumnavigation. Note that the self-steering system at the stern has been destroyed.*

right *Technology has changed the character of the sport, but not the nature of the ocean or man's endurance. Australian skipper Nick Moloney puts Open 60,* Skandia, *to the test in the run-up to the 2004–5 Vendée Globe.*

1

Inshore

- WHAT'S IT ALL ABOUT?

- THE RULES AND WHAT
  TO DO WITH THEM

- IN THE BEGINNING…

What's it all about?

There are two distinct styles of inshore sailing: you can cruise, or you can race. Cruising generally involves leaving Point A and arriving at the desired destination, Point B, ahead of a fixed deadline, such as high or low water, lunchtime, a pre-arranged cocktail hour, before the supermarket closes or before onboard relationships break down irretrievably. Between Points A and B, a yacht's skipper and crew must negotiate the natural variables of wind, tide, depth and current and remain aware of any man-made hazards; other sailing yachts, commercial shipping, submerged wrecks or structures, and motorboats. Whether you are cruising off Martha's Vineyard or the Galapagos Islands, these basic principles apply.

Inshore racing, however, involves leaving Point A at precisely the same time as a number of other yachts, then visiting Points B, C, D, E and F before arriving at Point G. Reaching the destination and finishing a race safely is crucial, but to do this quickly and ahead of any other yachts is a fundamentally important goal. Achieving this objective successfully requires years of practice and experience and can absorb huge sums of money. This sector of sailing, though, is a unique arena where racing novices can compete alongside, or against, professionals; America's Cup grandees and Olympic legends may find themselves approaching a racing mark at the same time as an inexperienced weekend sailor whose grasp of the Racing Rules of Sailing is minimal. Although these circumstances can prove stressful and, occasionally, expensive, they are unrivalled in sport and add colour and excitement to every inshore race or regatta.

The global appeal and diversity of inshore racing is vast. On any given stretch of coastline anywhere in the world, evidence of competitive sailing is usually to be found. This can range from off-duty fishermen in East Africa to financial analysts enjoying a corporate hospitality regatta

> Though no scientific corollary has yet been published, sailors, as people, tend to be frighteningly Jekyll-and-Hyde-like. Some of the nicest guys on land can be the meanest !&*?s on the water
>
> Dave Perry, yachtsman and author
> (from *Winning In One-Designs*)

previous page *Designed for solo or two-handed offshore marathons, Orma 60 trimarans provide a surreal spectacle when fully crewed and powered-up for inshore races.*

left *Corinthian sailing at its most extreme – rounding Gurnard Ledge buoy west of Cowes. X One-Designs have been competing on the Solent for nearly 100 years and with seventy-nine entries the class provided the biggest racing fleet at Skandia Cowes Week 2005.*

in European waters: polar opposites, culturally, but connected by sport. The annual New Year's Day dhow race circumnavigating the island of Lamu off Kenya is raced in boats that have changed little in design over the past 500 years, while the world's biggest regatta, Skandia Cowes Week, held every August off the southern coast of England, attracted over 1,000 entries in 2005. Although the eight days of racing at Cowes Week are a high-profile showcase for the latest innovations, the intent, approach and competitive atmosphere is identical to the mariners of the Kenyan coastline. Strategy, technique and testosterone dominate both events and post-race debriefings are indistinguishable; eavesdrop on a conversation over mango juice in Lamu after a dhow race and the themes will be interchangeable with a beer-tent debate in Cowes. Interestingly, there is one onshore habit – a language, even – that is common to yacht racers globally, known as 'Karate Sailing'; an activity involving the use of hand-chopping movements to illustrate the tacks and gybes of opposing boats and which often involves using an empty bottle as a windward mark.

At Cowes Week, start line infringements are recorded on CCTV and computer software assists in setting individual courses for the forty different classes, but technological arrogance is inappropriate. It should be noted that the largest and most fiercely competitive racing class during Britain's premier regatta is the ancient X One-Design (XOD) first produced in 1909; seventy-nine of these 20ft keelboats raced in 2005 and these heavy, wooden vessels are wetter and slower than any craft of Lamu.

above *A momentary loss of concentration can turn a day out racing into a whole new world of pain.* Carabistouille *receives a Cowes Week reminder that inshore racing is not always plain sailing.*

next page *The extreme glamour of the Costa Smeralda adds to the attraction of big boat racing at regattas based in Porto Cervo, Sardinia.*

You haven't won the race, if in winning the race you've lost the respect of your competition

Paul Elvström, Danish yachtsman and

winner of four Olympic sailing gold medals

The rules and what to do with them

For many sailors, yacht racing represents temporary freedom from shore-based routine set in a fiercely competitive environment. It is, therefore, essential that the sport be governed by a set of rules. The use and application of these laws reveal two distinct species of racing yachtsman: those who will race within the rules and use their knowledge and skill to win through tactical excellence, and those who will occasionally attempt to race outside the rules. The choice of flouting the racing rules may be driven by a number of factors; the high stakes of prestige, publicity, money and ego can all contribute to this decision. It would be inappropriate in *Extreme Sail* to explain the rules in any depth, but a brief glance at the most important aspects will assist in understanding the appeal and emotional intensity of inshore racing.

There are essentially two types of sailing rules within the Racing Rules of Sailing (RRS): the 'technical' rules and 'human' rules. Both varieties are vital to racing and are frequently revised by the International Sailing Federation (ISAF) to keep pace with a sport that is constantly developing. In addition, a yacht will be subject to class rules, which apply to everyone racing a particular type of boat, and 'Sailing Instructions', which apply to every competitor in each individual race series or regatta.

The overall aims of the RRS are to promote safety, equality and sportsmanship in yacht racing and ensure that any person or yacht infringing these rules should receive a penalty. The 'technical' rules govern all the variables that can arise when boats are racing: rights of way, propulsion methods and the complex definitions employed in competitive sailing. 'Human' rules offer directions on conduct and behaviour when racing, including the recent introduction of anti-doping laws. From 100ft maxi yachts competing offshore in the Mediterranean to radio-controlled model boats racing on small, urban ponds – these rules apply equally to every racing yacht from the moment the preparatory signal for her race has been made. Any punishment for an infringement is either carried out during the race, when the offending yacht undertakes an immediate, pre-arranged penalty manoeuvre, or in front of an independent protest committee provided by the race organisation. In the latter case, a jury of racing experts will make a judgement if any protest is contested (i.e. the alleged offender denies breaking the rules) or a yacht fails to take a penalty manoeuvre while racing.

Possibly the most fundamental 'technical' rule involves 'overlap': a right-of-way and overtaking principle that causes more debate than all the other rules within the RRS combined. Another heavily argued point is Rule 42 (RRS 2005–2008), which is concerned with 'propulsion'

opposite *Race leaders bunch together in a gybing match downwind off St Tropez during the Dragon class 75th anniversary regatta in 2005.*

above *Onboard blood pressures rise as views on overlap and right of way are exchanged between IRC boats at the Spi Ouest regatta 2005.*

above *Race yacht or circus act? A Dragonfly's nimble crew rearrange their complex multi-trapeze system during the Centomiglia on Lake Garda, Italy.*

and the use of illegal and repetitive actions by the crew to assist the movement of a yacht racing in light winds. The rule includes guidelines on such exotic tricks as 'fanning', 'flicking', 'pumping' and 'torquing' and what a crew should do if they suspect an opposing boat of entering the mysterious 'yellow light area' (an occasion when a yacht's crew may be on the verge of repeating a dubious and potentially illegal motion). Rule 42.2(c) goes even further and prohibits the activity of 'ooching': this involves one or more of the crew running from the aft end of a becalmed boat, then abruptly halting near the bow and, thereby illegally propelling the yacht forwards. To anyone unfamiliar with yacht racing these examples from the RRS illustrate both the lengths to which sailors will go to win races and the importance of understanding the complex language and definitions in the sport.

The 'human' rules, however, are more understandable – superficially. Rule 2 of the RRS concerns 'Fair Sailing' and requires that yachts and their crews "shall compete in compliance with recognized principles of sportsmanship and fair play." This rule relies on a sailor's personal integrity and a traditional interpretation of Rule 2 prohibits intimidation on the racecourse. For example, the skipper of a yacht with no right of way (on port tack) may begin dishonestly yelling

"Starboard!" at a yacht who has the right of way (on starboard tack) and who is under no obligation to alter her course to avoid the approaching yacht and her screaming helmsman. Due to inexperience, panic, inexpert knowledge of the rules or purely wishing to avoid being rammed, the innocent yacht may throw itself into a manoeuvre away from the potential danger zone and lose valuable ground. Some sailors will regard this action as the height of gamesmanship and a valid necessity born of competition – part of the psychological struggle between sportsmen. This intentional misuse of a right-of-way rule, though, transcends ideas of "sportsmanship and fairplay" and may result in the transgressor being penalised under Rule 69 'Allegations of Gross Misconduct'. Section 69.2(a) of the rule states that a race authority may act and punish a yachtsman upon hearing "a report alleging conduct that has brought the sport into disrepute." This noble sentiment is intrinsic to sportsmanship and the purity of the sport, but may be invoked as an effective way of silencing any embarrassing, awkward criticism of a competitor, a race organisation or a racing authority and is open to misuse.

below *Some obsessive-compulsive behaviour is allowed within the Racing Rules of Sailing (RRS). A Spi Ouest regatta crew attempt to reduce waterline drag with some last minute housework shortly before the start gun.*

In the beginning…

So, how did this variation and complexity start? The roots of inshore yacht racing are found in the town of Cowes on the northern tip of the Isle of Wight, just two miles off the southern coast of England. Here, on a narrow stretch of water called the Solent, the sport was established as an exclusive and fashionable pastime of the very rich. Self-regulated by membership-only yacht clubs and dominated by the Royal Yacht Squadron (RYS), yacht racing languished in a gentle atmosphere of carefully manicured club lawns and revolved around bonnets, baronets and black tie balls. A popular misconception surrounding Cowes is the belief that the magnificent yachts of the late nineteenth century, and their owners were entirely responsible for popularising the sport. Certainly, paintings and photographs of these elegant craft powering along under clouds of canvas are evocative and enduring. This supremely confident period is typified by the 1893 tussle between *Britannia*, belonging to the Prince of Wales and launched the previous year, and the American yacht *Ivanhoe*. In one particular race, the British yacht clutched victory on the final beat, defeating her faster nemesis and prompting the era's senior yachting journalist, Brook Heckstall-Smith, to comment: "*Britannia* had beaten her [*Ivanhoe*] to windward, and somehow or other we never had any fear of an American sloop in British waters again…" (clearly the loss of the America's Cup forty-two years earlier had left a deep scar).

At the time, such admiration was not unanimous. Professor Sir Walter Alexander Raleigh (1861–1922), a direct descendant of Britain's swashbuckling, codpiece-clad hero, bristled: "The so-called yachtsmen of Cowes, it seems, have champagne lunches in the Solent, and then spread canvas and take two hours' run when the breeze is fair and light… They meet the same people at Cowes as they meet later at grouse … different clothes and the same well-fed, carefully exercised bodies, the same bored minds tired of wondering whether passion will ever come their way."

Although Raleigh had a point, the situation was rapidly changing. For while the membership portcullis at the RYS was raised only to admit those with the bluest blood or biggest wallet, the less high born were busy in half decked boats crewed by two or three people, such as the 1-Rater, ½-Rater and 2½-Rater classes. Through the proliferation of these smaller boats, the Solent claimed its early status as a centre for sailing and, soon, affordable yacht racing spread to America and the Continent. This period, the 1880s and 1890s, produced a shrewd anecdote that still has resonance:

Big boat professional skipper: "Would you care to take the helm, Sir?"
Big boat owner: "Thanks, Captain, but I take nothing between meals."

above *Represented racing up the Solent towards Cowes in 1893, Britannia epitomizes an era of massive sailing yachts and their noble owners. During a sailing career spanning forty-three years, the yacht competed in 635 races, winning 231 and taking second and third in 129.*

In 1936, after the death of her final owner, George V, Britannia *was towed into deep water off the southern tip of the Isle of Wight and scuttled in accordance with the late king's wishes.*

The most tangible evidence of this period is to catch a glimpse of the huge classic yachts that still compete in inshore races around the world. Partially restored or totally rebuilt, they recall an era of elitism and private financial commitment to yacht racing that is unmatched today. The passion for these marine masterpieces, though, remains unchanged and while the racing may be more sedate in terms of speed than modern yachts, the competitive rivalry at classic regattas is fanatical; these yachts are far more than expensive, attractive toys for self-indulgent millionaires.

The Royal Yacht Squadron: The hardest club in the world to get into or away from. Ladies who are permitted to enter the RYS grounds are required to speak quietly and to wear stockings, though it is hard to believe that a Member of the Squadron would ever look with sufficient interest at a lady's legs to see whether she was wearing stockings or not.

From a glossary of technical sailing terms by Patrick Boyle, c.1938

left *A crewman is sent aloft on* Adix *during the Voiles des St Tropez regatta in the South of France. A great part of the expense in classic yachting is paying for a competent and acrobatic crew.*

right *Built in 1933,* Velsheda *required thirty crew for racing. Rescued from a mud berth in southern England in 1984, she now appears at many classic regattas around the world and won all three races in the 'Spirit of Tradition Class A' at Antigua Classic Week 2005.*

2

The America's Cup Challenge

- A SPORT ON ITS OWN

- WHY, WHEN AND
  WHO'S WHO?

- THINGS TO DO ON AN
  AMERICA'S CUP YACHT

- HOW TO WIN

A sport on its own

There is little point attempting to combine the America's Cup Challenge (ACC) with any other division of sailing; the event stands alone and the personalities, the racing environment, the boats and the objectives of the competitors are unique. Through intense media coverage, the ACC is the most publicly accessible sailing event on earth, but it is also one of the most misunderstood arenas of yachting. Detractors will claim that the ACC is little more than a handful of multi-millionaires and their over-paid teams indulging in a private regatta. Indeed, the event's long and often controversial history continues to astonish ACC enthusiasts and this, coupled with the immense amounts of money and subsequent glamour this naturally generates, will always attract criticism. However, even the most cynical observer must concede that the America's Cup is never dull.

In 1992 the Kansas billionaire, Bill Koch, took over the role of defending the ACC from foreign raiders and keeping the cup on American soil. Koch is attributed with commenting: "The America's Cup is a race of management, money, technology, teamwork and – last and incidentally – sailing"; a memorable soundbite that quickly become a rallying cry for yachting purists. The truth, however, is far more complex. The ACC is about passion and this manifests itself in a number of forms: competitiveness, skill, ego, avarice and devotion – essentially, all the components and emotions that exist in yachting, but to an extreme degree.

left British yachtsmen were reluctant to race a mysterious challenger from America until press accusations of cowardice forced a contest. Consequently, the '100 Sovereigns Cup', inexplicably changed by the victors to the '100 Guinea Cup', disappeared to America and the world's greatest yacht racing challenge was born.

above, right Almost half the crew of K-Challenge crowd the foredeck for a spinnaker drop in Marseilles during the opening Louis Vuitton Act of the 2007 America's Cup.

previous page The best view in the house during a fleet race in Valencia. A 'windseeker' will be sent aloft in light airs to identify areas of breeze on the racecourse by spotting bands of ripples or wavelets on the water's surface.

The America's Cup is the most important sailing competition and one of the most famous sporting events in the world. In sport, there will always be a winner and a loser. That's where the beauty of it resides.

Biotech millionaire, Ernesto Bertarelli, shortly after winning the
America's Cup Challenge in 2003 with *Alinghi*

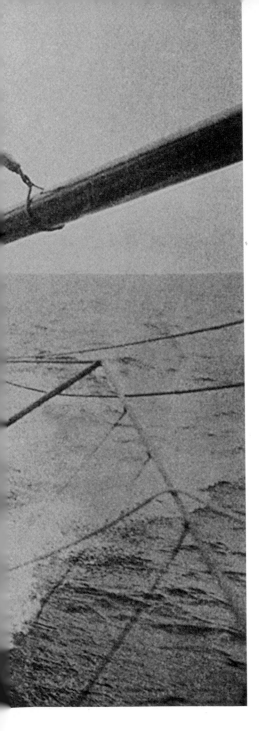

Why, when and who's who?

A quick study of the challenge's history since the Cup's inception in 1851 is necessary to fully grasp why the ACC is a legendary event and how its modern format has evolved. Knowledge of the historical and contemporary personalities involved will help explain why the names of many ACC heroes and villains are spoken in soft tones of respect, or never mentioned at all. Finally, the following timeline may help a spectator forgive – or at least comprehend – the ACC some of its litigious and less wholesome aspects.

HIGHLIGHTS IN THE HISTORY OF THE ACC:

1851 How dare they?

The schooner *America* crosses the Atlantic to Great Britain. Initially, the yacht's fearsome reputation deters competition until a journalist from *The Times* newspaper shames British yachtsmen into accepting the challenge, deriding them for allowing "the illustrious stranger to return with the proud boast to the New World that she had flung down the gauntlet to England, Ireland, and Scotland, and not one had been found to take it up."

It works, and a race is arranged around the Isle of Wight organized by the Royal Yacht Squadron (RYS) offering a 'Cup of 100 Sovereigns' – now known as the '100 Guinea Cup' – to the victor. *America* competes in the race on behalf of the New York Yacht Club (NYYC) and defeats a fleet of fourteen prime British yachts to win the trophy. The victors return to New York offering the cup to the NYYC in 1857, as a 'Deed of Gift' with the intention that it should represent "a perpetual challenge cup for friendly competition between nations". The America's Cup is born.

1870 Have a nice day... and goodbye!

The first British challenger arrives in America, but James Ashbury on *Cambria*, representing the Royal Thames yacht Club (RTYC), has no success racing against fourteen American yachts, finishing 10th out of 15 on corrected time.

1871 Sulking over the silverware

Ashbury returns to challenge with a customized racing yacht, *Livonia*, built for the express purpose of winning the cup, but refuses to race more than one opponent. Lawyers become involved and the NYYC eventually concedes, but provides four candidates to race against *Livonia* while retaining the right to choose their defending yacht on each morning of racing. The American yachts *Columbia* and *Sappho* triumph and a bitter Ashbury returns to Britain. The multi-defence format is abandoned and Match Racing is introduced to the ACC.

1885 Thank you so much!

Sir Richard Sutton and Genesta challenge for the ACC and win the first race after the defender, *Puritan*, is disqualified from racing for a rule infringement. Sutton, however, forfeits this victory, claiming: "We have come here to race, not to parade victory on our own." American yachtsmen praise Sutton for this show of sportsmanship and then swiftly defeat *Genesta* in the following two races.

1895 Are we all playing the same game?

The Earl of Dunraven and *Valkyrie III* are beaten in the first race and immediately accuse the American opponent, *Defender*, of sailing outside the measurement rules of the ACC: an accusation that is dismissed. During the second race, *Valkyrie III* manoeuvres to avoid a spectator boat and rams *Defender*. Dunraven continues sailing and wins the race, but is disqualified for the earlier collision. On the third race, Dunraven sails to the start line but abandons the race and returns to Britain publicly accusing the defenders of cheating.

1899–1930 Long-suffering Lipton

During this period, Sir Thomas Lipton – a grocer, rubber and tea plantation owner, and self-made millionaire – launched five unsuccessful challenge

previous page *British tea-baron, Sir Thomas Lipton, made five challenges for the Cup between 1899 and 1930. The foredeck crew on his first America's Cup yacht, Shamrock, keep an eye on a fearless and agile photographer.*

above *In 1983, the unbeatable Aussie combination of businessman, Alan Bond with skipper, Jean Bertrand and yacht designer, Ben Lexcen, took the Cup from America for the first time in 132 years with 12 Metre, Australia II.*

next page *The gloves come off in the five-minute, pre-start period during Race 1 of the Louis Vuitton semi-finals in Auckland. Intimidation, forcing a penalty on your opponent and an advantageous position for the first leg are paramount. One World (USA-67) went on to beat Prada.*

Break her (Shamrock IV) up, Bob, and burn her in your fireplace! I never want to see this boat again

Sir Thomas Lipton to Bob Jacob (owner of a New York shipyard) after failing to win the America's Cup in 1920 on his fourth and penultimate attempt

attempts with a series of yachts called *Shamrock*. His nemesis in the ACC was the outstanding American helmsman, Charlie Barr. At 82 years old, Lipton made his final challenge for the cup on *Shamrock V* as the ACC moved its base from New York to Newport, Rhode Island and was outclassed by Harold Vanderbilt on the advanced J Class yacht, *Enterprise*.

1934 Protests and pay disputes
British aircraft designer and manufacturer Sir Tommy Sopwith challenges with the super-fast J Class yacht, *Endeavour*, and provides a serious threat for the defender, Vanderbilt, and his amateur crew on *Rainbow*. Sopwith wins the first two races, but a disallowed protest against *Rainbow* and a crew striking for a salary increase prevent him from achieving victory.

1937 *Ranger*, the unstoppable racing machine
Unnerved by the strength of Britain's challenge in 1934, Vanderbilt swore to defend the cup effectively. The result was a super-J Class beast of a boat: *Ranger*, a yacht designed after rigorous tank and wind tunnel testing, and built using the latest materials and technology. The ACC had entered a new era and Sopwith's second challenge with *Endeavour II* stood little chance of success. After the victorious defence, Vanderbilt questioned this leap in racing yacht design: "Was *Ranger* so good that she killed the class and scared off the others?"

1958 And after the break…
ACC racing recommences after a 21-year suspension. In the austere post-World War II period, J Class-sized budgets became unsustainable and the International 12 Metre Class was introduced, reducing ACC yachts from 65ft (19.81m) to 44ft (13.41m), effectively cutting down crew numbers and build costs.

1983 An Australian shake-up
The Louis Vuitton Cup (LVC) series is introduced as a method of selecting a challenger to face the defender in the ACC. *Australia II* proves to be unbeatable and wins the challenger series. The Australian team introduces the 'modesty skirt' hiding the yacht's radical winged keel behind a screen each time she is lifted from the water. Dennis Connor defends for America with *Liberty* and the seven races of ACC are tight with the score at 3-3 before the final race. During Race 7, *Australia II* overtakes *Liberty* on the final upwind leg and removes the Cup from America for the first time in 132 years.

1987 Connor to the rescue
Dennis Connor challenges on behalf of the San Diego Yacht Club with *Stars & Stripes*. The highly motivated team easily defeat *Kookaburra III* in Fremantle, Australia, and the cup returns to America. This edition of the ACC is the debut for New Zealand, challenging with *KiwiMagic*.

1988 Court cases + catamaran = Cup chaos

New Zealand banker, Michael Fay, exploits a loophole in the 'Deed of Gift' to launch a 'rogue challenge.' After a legal squabble over the legitimacy of the challenge, the Supreme Court in New York rules that the ACC should be raced and Fay arrives in America with a 90ft (27.43m) monohull, *New Zealand*. Connor and the San Diego Yacht Club respond with *Stars & Stripes*, a 55ft (16.76m) catamaran and the competitors return to court as the *New Zealand*ers insist that their opponent should race in a similar design of yacht. The court insists that the challenge should continue and Fay's team are beaten by the faster, American multihull.

1992 Finally, a formula

The standardized America's Cup Class of yacht is introduced. Bill Koch heads the defence with *America3* and successfully triumphs over the Italian challenge from *Il Moro de Venezia*, skippered by American Paul Cayard.

1995 The Blake and Coutts phenomenon

New Zealand win 42 races from 43 starts with *Black Magic* during the LVC. The Kiwi partnership of Sir Peter Blake and Russell Coutts defeat Dennis Connor and *Young America*. The ACC leaves San Diego for the Southern Hemisphere again.

2000 A Kiwi clean sweep

A decisive ACC victory for *Team New Zealand* with Blake and Coutts beating Italy's *Luna Rossa* 4–0: the Cup remains in Auckland. Confidence on board *Team New Zealand* is so high that Coutts hands the helm to his 26-year-old understudy, Dean Barker, for the final race.

2003 The tycoon frenzy

Russell Coutts and Brad Butterworth leave the New Zealand camp to join Ernesto Bertarelli and his new Swiss team, *Alinghi*. During the four months of racing in LVC, *Alinghi* scores 23 wins from 26 starts, defeating *Oracle BMW* of the American software mogul Larry Ellison. During the ACC, *Alinghi* faces the defender, *Team New Zealand* and the Kiwi team suffer severe gear failure, forcing them to retire from two races, leaving *Alinghi* to win the ACC with a clean sweep of 5-0. The cup heads back to Europe for the first time in 149 years.

2007 The 32nd ACC: The next 'Act'

The incumbent Swiss yacht club, Société Nautique de Genève (SNG), is challenged by the Golden Gate Yacht Club and the 32nd ACC begins. Bertarelli and his team choose the Spanish town of Valencia as the location and create a new three-year format of races. The Swiss team's former skipper, Russell Coutts, leaves *Alinghi* and is forbidden to compete in the cup for any of the teams. The ACC attracts eleven challengers with debut appearances from the Republic of South Africa and China.

It is a business and we, in England, who sail our yachts because we love sailing, can never win the America's Cup until we make it a business too

Sir Tommy Sopwith after defeat in two consecutive America's Cup Challenges

Things to do on an America's Cup yacht

Current ACC yachts race with a crew of seventeen: each team will divide the duties onboard according to the skills and strengths of the crew, but a 'typical' set-up for a yacht would be:

1/2. Tactician/Strategist

The intelligence-gathering core of the 'afterguard' (the generic term for the collection of expertise at the aft end of a boat). They will assess information from the Helmsman, Navigator and sail Trimmers, then combine this with their own observations of wind direction and the yacht's position relative to the competition and formulate a strategy for the race. The real talent is to successfully juggle immediate tactics and the effect these will have later in the race.

3. Navigator

Passes position information to the Helmsman, Strategist and Tactician.

4. Helmsman

Often the skipper of the boat, he has the overriding decision on tactics and must ensure the boat is sailing at its optimum speed and is manoeuvring effectively. On some ACC yachts, there may be two helmsmen: one for starting the race and a second for sailing the course. "A skipper's role is managing director on board," maintains Chris Dickson, skipper of *BMW Oracle* for the 2007 ACC. "I need accurate information in a timely fashion, presented in a clear way to enable the right decision to be made."

5. Traveller

Controls the mainsheet traveller dictating upwind speed.

6. Runners

Work the running backstays and controls the mast bend. In constant communication with Helmsman and Trimmers to maximize sail shape and the subsequent boat speed.

7. Mainsail Trimmer

Responsible for the position of the mainsail. Works with the Helmsman to maintain the maximum speed on every point of sail.

8. Mainsail Grinder

Controls the winch pedestal – or 'coffee grinder' – for the mainsail. Works directly to the commands of the Mainsail Trimmer.

opposite *Two crewmen on the current Cup defender,* Alinghi, *prepare to drop the jib while a third inspects the 'sewer': the most uncomfortable and stomach-churning place to find yourself on any racing yacht.*

below *Concentration for trimmer, Lorenzo Mazza, and tactician, Torben Grael (in black hat) on Italy's* Prada Challenge, *during the 2002 Louis Vuitton Cup quarter finals in the Hauraki Gulf, New Zealand. For the most efficient sheeting angles, a working jib sheet is loaded on to the winch 'wrong way round'.*

next page *Nerves of steel, an accurate watch and an advanced sense of balance for the bowman of French America's Cup contender,* K-Challenge, *as they take on the defender,* Alinghi, *at the start of Louis Vuitton Act 2 off Valencia in October 2004.*

Men in a ship are always looking up, and men onshore are usually looking down

John Masefield (1878-1987), poet and novelist

9/10. Headsail Trimmers

Directly control the upwind and downwind headsails and the critical 'height' (ability of sailing close to the wind) of the boat and overall speeds when sailing off the wind.

11/12. Grinders

Work the winch pedestals for the headsail sheets and all the halyards. They grind to the commands of the Headsail Trimmers during tacks and gybes and to the orders of the Mast and Pit for hoisting sails. Consistently in demand during a race, the job is physically demanding and Grinders are often the largest crewmembers on board. Usually they will be members of the informal Federation of Grinders (FOG) who, with the FDU (see below), represent the 'grunt' element of an ACC yacht.

13. Mast

His extra weight and strength on the halyards speeds sail hoists. During sail drops and gybing manoeuvres he will assist the foredeck crew.

14. Pit

Controls operations at the front of the boat co-ordinating sail changes and will assist the Grinders. He is also a link between the afterguard and the foredeck crew.

15. Sewer

As part of the foredeck crew, he will assist on deck during sail changes and manoeuvres, but his primary function is to re-pack and stow sails after a drop and prepare sails pre-hoist. Although he will receive help from the Mast, Pit and Mid-bow, he will spend extended periods alone below decks in cramped, damp and – when the boat is being driven hard – nauseous conditions.

16. Mid-bow

Acts as back-up to the Bowman and will assist Sewer, Pit and Mast when needed. Requires agility, stamina, a thick skin and an ability to follow orders without question.

17. Bowman

Possibly the busiest position on an ACC boat – brains and brawn combined. At the beginning of a race he must keep the Helmsman informed of the distance to the start line via hand signals and continue to advise the afterguard of any overlaps throughout the race. An error or misjudgement can fatally jeopardize a race. He is responsible for connecting sheets and halyards to the headsails during sail changes and is in sole charge of the outboard end of the spinnaker pole. He is usually the appointed spokesman of a yacht's Foredeck Union (FDU) with a membership comprising Mid-bow, Mast, Sewer and occasionally – but not always – Pit.

How to win

With a three-lap race course of slightly less than nineteen nautical miles, the 32nd ACC aims to provide close racing, regardless of differing crew quality between teams, and should prevent a competitor with a superior boat design from dominating on pure speed capabilities. The windward-leeward legs are of restricted length to reduce the chance of a faster design developing an unassailable lead and disappearing over the horizon, while the course covers enough distance to ensure that a yacht with an exceptionally skilled crew will not tyrannize an opponent on tactics alone. All very democratic… in theory.

An ACC race can be split into three sections: the Start, the Windward legs and the Leeward legs – totally distinct territories offering many different, tactical opportunities.

Start: Ten minutes before the start of a race as the yachts ready themselves near the starting area, a warning gun will be fired. This is a signal for crews to transfer any unwanted sails and equipment on to speedboats standing by. As the shore crew remove this excess weight from the yacht, the afterguard will be receiving final data from their dedicated weather analysts and last minute instructions from the team's coaches.

Five minutes before the start, a second gun is fired signalling the 'Pre-Start' period. The yachts are now forbidden any further outside assistance and a communication blackout is imposed. This period is an opportunity for a team to force their opponent into an error or a rule infringement and destroy their confidence while striving to gain the most favourable start. Although one of the greatest skills of a helmsman is the ability to steer his yacht across the start line milliseconds after the cannon fires, the primary objective is to seize an advantageous position for the

right *New Zealand feel the squeeze from* +39 Challenge *and* Luna Rossa Challenge *(*Prada*), two of Italy's three challengers for the 2007 America's Cup.*

When you start to beat the big boys, you have to be prepared and get a lawyer

Magnus Holmberg, skipper of Sweden's *Victory Challenge* on being disqualified after winning Louis Vuitton Act 5 in June 2005

upwind leg to the first windward mark. Gaining this objective provides the excitement immediately before the start as the yachts dance around each other, jousting for pole position. One of the final reports passed to the afterguard before the pre-start will have been an evaluation of any likely change in wind direction during the first leg. Crossing the start line first is not always an asset – determining the first wind shift is crucial.

Windward: The leading boat on an upwind leg will normally have the advantage. The team can bury the trailing yacht in their wind shadow and pin them down by mirroring each manoeuvre as the chasing yacht attempts to break free and find fresh breeze away from the turbulent, 'dirty air' in the wake of the lead boat.

The second and third windward legs, however, allow the trailing yacht to break clear of the leader. Instead of having both yachts round the same leeward mark, they pass through a gate of approximately six boat lengths in width at the leeward limit of the course; one yacht turns to port and the other to starboard. Splitting from the lead yacht and sailing upwind in clear air alters the entire complexion of the race.

Leeward: Sailing downwind, the trailing boat is able to disrupt the leader's advantage and – if the boats are close – control the race through use of their wind shadow and overlap. In the 32nd ACC, the final leg to the finish line is leeward and the final result can be overturned in the closing minutes of a race.

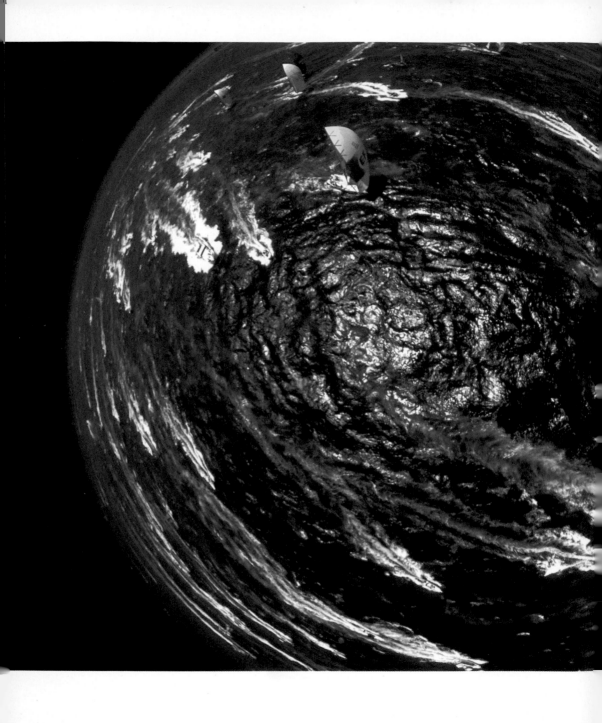

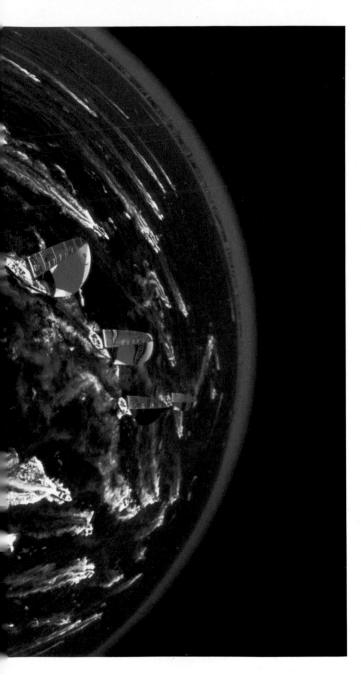

3

The Volvo Ocean Race

• THE BIG ONE

• OFFSHORE MADNESS?

• DEEP SEA STORIES

The big one

previous page *The fleet leaves Fort Lauderdale, Florida, during the 1997–98 Whitbread Race. A succession of protests, resignations and a disqualification dominated the seventh edition of the race.*

The Volvo Ocean Race – as the former Whitbread Race has been known since 2001 – captures public imagination more than any other round-the-world sailing event. This is due, in part, to well managed media surrounding the race and access to the competitors at nine stopover ports during the circumnavigation. An offshore race can often alienate spectators when the fleet of yachts are at sea for long periods in a remote environment that few yachtsmen have ever experienced. The intense tactics, the constant evaluation of weather systems and fanatical attention to sustaining high speeds can seem alien to the lay-sailor. However, the Volvo Ocean Race is, above all, about human endeavour and hardship; almost all sailors can connect in some way with the teams battling gales in distant oceans and for this reason, it is frequently the stories from the race, rather than the overall results, that enthral the land-based spectator.

Advances in technology have not softened the challenge facing teams in the 2005-06 Volvo Ocean Race. The ability to compress onboard video footage and stream these images ashore from the high latitudes of the Southern Ocean does not diminish a hostile and potentially lethal environment. Likewise, weather data fed to the race yachts and a 24-hour satellite tracking system logging the fleet's course around the globe are essential, but these features are little more than modern novelties when conditions deteriorate on a deep-ocean racing yacht.

Freeze-dried food, satellite connections with onshore medical staff, high-tech foul weather clothing and a carefully calculated calorie intake, boosted for the colder legs of the race, were unknown to competitors in the earlier editions of the event. Today's Volvo Ocean Race sailors may benefit from better communications and more enlightened ideas on personal safety and onboard conditions, but the pressure to race hard is more powerful than ever. Corporate sponsorship, professionalism and the media spotlight combine to push teams to their limit in yachts customized to break speed records.

right *Rothmans buries her bow during the 1989–90 Whitbread race. Skippered by Britain's Lawrie Smith, the yacht finished 4th in a fleet of 21 entrants and recorded a blistering average speed of 19.9 knots over a 90-minute period on Leg 2 between Uruguay, South America, and Fremantle, Australia.*

No man will be a sailor who has contrivance enough to get himself into jail;
for being in a ship is being in jail, with the chance of being drowned [...].
A man in jail has more room, better food, and commonly better company.

Samuel Johnson (1709–1784), English writer, critic and landlubber

Offshore madness

During the 1960s, ocean racing became the chosen sport for sailors seeking fresh offshore challenges. In 1967, Sir Francis Chichester completed the first single-handed circumnavigation of the world, stopping only once in Australia, while two years later, Sir Robin Knox-Johnston became the first solo sailor to circle the planet non-stop in The Golden Globe Race. In France, meanwhile, Eric Tabarly was awarded the Legion of Honour by President Charles de Gaulle for his victory in the 1964 OSTAR single-handed race across the North Atlantic, but no event existed for yachtsmen craving fully crewed ocean racing.

The prospect of a round-the-world yacht race aroused intense scepticism. At this time, fewer than ten private yachts had rounded Cape Horn, while the Golden Globe Race of 1968 saw only one competitor finish from eight entrants and produced a catalogue of disasters, capsizes and a mid-Atlantic suicide. Who would underwrite and organize such folly?

The ocean-going environment of hardship, danger and endurance had a provocative appeal for at least one section of the seafaring community: the Royal Navy. In association with British brewing giant Whitbread, the Navy formulated a framework for the first fully crewed, competitive, circumnavigation. On 8 September 1973, seventeen yachts from seven nations with a total of 167 crew started the first Whitbread Round The World Race off Portsmouth, southern England.

The race has always provided drama and, sometimes, tragedy; the modern Volvo Ocean Race continues to attract world class sailors and a global following. From the earliest editions of the race it became clear that the Whitbread was an exceptional challenge and it continues to generate extraordinary stories of courage, determination and ingenuity. The race may also be one of the few sporting events where competitors have been arrested on suspicion of espionage and a yacht has been disqualified for carrying radioactive waste!

left *The bowman of* Amer Sports One *wrestles with the spinnaker's tack fitting as the yacht powers downwind during the 2001–02 Volvo Ocean Race. A total of three sailors were lost overboard during the first Whitbread race in 1973–74 and crew safety is a constant anxiety for competitors in deep-ocean events.*

next page *Volvo 60,* Assa Abloy, *surfs as her crew cling on during a power reach in the 2001–02 Volvo Ocean Race. The stress loads on the yacht's mast, rigging, sails and fittings must be constantly monitored to prevent breakages and maintain the delicate balance between speed and boat preservation.*

Deep sea stories

A summary of the human drama, turmoil and theatrics in the Whitbread and Volvo races from 1973 to 2002:

1973–74: A dangerous and deadly debut

Italian yacht *Tauranga* suffers sail damage in 50-knot winds during Leg 2 of the race between Cape Town, South Africa, and Sydney, Australia. Crewman Paul Waterhouse heads to the foredeck and is knocked unconscious as he is thrown to the deck: lying on the jib, a second gust picks up the sail and Waterhouse is flung overboard. The crew are unable to locate him.

Less than a week later, French ketch *33 Export* is caught in a gale. Massive waves sweep the 60ft yacht's decks and crewman Dominique Guilett is washed overboard when his harness snaps. Guilett becomes the second fatality of the race.

After leaving Sydney on Leg 3 bound for Rio de Janeiro, Brazil, Bernie Hosking is thrown overboard from *Great Britain II* during a storm that nearly dismasts the 77ft ketch. On Leg 1, Hosking was lost overboard en route to Cape Town and the crew recovered him, but the Pacific Ocean refused to give the yachtsman up.

Winner: *Sayula II* (Mexico)

1977–78: Luck, injuries and extreme bravery

On the second leg of the race, between Cape Town and Auckland, New Zealand, Bill Abram is flung over the side of *Heath's Condor* while not attached by a safety harness. The crew immediately lose sight of Abram behind tall waves, but a group of albatross are spotted circling in the distance. The object of their interest is a very fortunate Abram who is soon recovered by his crewmates.

On *Great Britain II*, Nick Dunlop is trapped when the spinnaker guy becomes wrapped around his waist. Before the line is cut, the force generated by the sail squeezes Dunlop until the blood vessels in his eyes rupture. Any attempts to move Dunlop produce screams of agony, but he sustains no permanent injuries.

In the Roaring Forties on Leg 3 between Auckland and Rio, *33 Export* broaches and Eric Letrosne fractures a leg when he is slammed into the guardrails. The crew radio Dr Jean Louis Sarbarly on the nearby yacht, *Japy-Hermes*, and after a diagnosis over the VHF, Sarbarly braves freezing Southern Ocean water, swims across to *33 Export* and treats Letrosne.

French yacht *Pen Duick VI* is disqualified from the race when it is found that her heavy keel is weighted with depleted uranium (twice as heavy as lead).

Winner: *Flyer* (Netherlands)

below: *Shortly before the finish of Leg 2 of the 1985–86 Whitbread,* Lion New Zealand *collided with a whale. With serious damage to the rudder, skipper, Peter Blake nursed the yacht to the Auckland finish line arriving in 4th place.*

The sea is dangerous and its storms terrible – but these obstacles have never been sufficient reason to remain ashore.

Ferdinand Magellan (c.1480–1521), Portuguese explorer and circumnavigator

1981–82: Dismastings and double agents

As the yachts head down through the Atlantic on Leg 1, New Zealand entry *Ceramco NZ* dismasts 150 miles north of Ascension Island. They continue racing with a jury rig and arrive in Cape Town in 18th place (out of 26).

South African crew racing on the Italian yacht *Vivanapoli* are arrested on suspicion of espionage when the boat is boarded by personnel from an Angolan gunboat. The Italian embassy eventually secures their release from prison.

On Leg 2 between Cape Town and Auckland, *33 Export* dismasts and diverts to the remote and barren Kerguelen Islands in the high latitudes of the Indian Ocean to make repairs.

Spanish entry *Licor* dismasts on Leg 3 in a 60-knot Pacific Ocean gale. The crew continue under jury rig and sail round Cape Horn to the next stopover in Mar del Plata, Argentina. *Gauloises II* also dismasts on Leg 3, but the yacht retires to Tahiti.

With a comfortable lead on the final leg of the race, *Flyer* runs aground on the notorious Shingles Bank within a few miles of the finish. The crew succeed in freeing the yacht on an ebb tide and sail the final twelve miles to Portsmouth.

Winner: *Flyer* (Netherlands)

below *Swedish entry,* The Card, *suffered a broach in the Indian Ocean's high latitudes during Leg 2 of the 1989–90 race. Skipper Dr. Roger Nilson used the onboard tool kit to make a cast for the broken arm of a French crewmember injured when the yacht was knocked flat.*

above *Whitbread 60,* Tokio, *was dismasted off the coast of Brazil during the 1993–94 Whitbread Race and headed into the port of Santos. Chris Dickson and his crew repaired the mast within thirty-six hours before setting back out to sea and sailing to rejoin the fleet in Fort Lauderdale, Florida.*

1985–86: Scuba diving and mast climbing in the Southern Ocean

Atlantic Privateer dismasts 500 miles from Cape Town on Leg 1 and her jury rig fails soon afterwards forcing the crew to sail the boat under engine power. *Drum* suffers drastic delamination in vicious gales shortly after crossing the Equator and a hull inspection in South Africa reveals that the keel is in danger of falling off the bottom of the boat.

Three days into Leg 3 between Auckland and Punta del Este, Uruguay, *NZI Enterprise* breaks her mast in two places and retires to the Chatham Islands.

A spinnaker sail bag is swept off the deck of *Drum* and becomes tangled around the propeller. Crewman Magnus Olsson, climbs into scuba gear and dives over the side attached to a tether, but is knocked unconscious by the stern of the pitching boat and the crew haul him back onboard. Olsson is uninjured and the bag is eventually removed by dragging a line along the yacht's hull until the obstruction is snagged.

Ed Danby is sent to the top of the mast on *Lion New Zealand* to retrieve a spinnaker that is flying from its halyard only. The attachment of the bosun's chair fails and Danby is left clinging to the top spreaders until a second crewman is hauled aloft and brings him down to deck level.

Winner: *L'Esprit d'Equipe* (France)

1989–90: Tragedy onshore and offshore

The first all-women crew enter the race with *Maiden*, skippered by Britain's Tracy Edwards.

Two deaths occur onshore during the stopover at the end of Leg 1 from Southampton to Punta del Este, Uruguay: Alexei Grishschenko, co-skipper of the Russian entry, *Fazisi*, commits suicide and Janne Gustaffson, a crewmember of *The Card*, is killed in a motorcycle accident.

On the second leg from Uruguay to Fremantle, Australia, a crewman on *Fortuna Extra Lights* is washed overboard. Although he is not wearing a safety harness, his radio locator enables the crew to recover him.

In the Indian Ocean, *Creightons Naturally* loses two crewmen overboard in two consecutive crash gybes. Bart van den Dwey is located after forty-five minutes in freezing water and Tony Phillips is found after a further quarter of an hour. Three hours of CPR fail to resuscitate Phillips.

After rounding Cape Horn, the keel falls off Finnish yacht, *Martela OF*, as she sails north along the coast of South America. The crew manage to send a 'Mayday' before the yacht inverts totally and the radio equipment fails. *Merit* and *Charles Jourdan* divert to the stricken yacht's position and rescue the crew from an upturned hull.

Winner: *Steinlager 2*

1993–94: Tough crews and tender boats

Two classes race; the larger Maxi class and the Whitbread 60 (W60).

Heading west across the Atlantic from Southampton to Punta del Este, Spanish yacht *Fortuna* dismasts early in Leg 1 and the team retire from the race. The yacht's skipper, Lawrie Smith, takes over the top spot on *Intrum Justicia* at the Uruguayan stopover.

On the longest, second leg from South America to Fremantle, *NZ Endeavour*, skippered by Grant Dalton, broaches and snaps her mizzen mast. Italian W60, *Brooksfield*, breaks her rudder shaft and 3 tons of water pour through the gaping hole below the waterline. The crew send an SOS and Dennis Connor's *Winston* and Smith's *Intrum Justicia* immediately divert to the sinking yacht's position. Twelve hours after the distress signal, the first yacht to reach *Brooksfield* is French entrant, *La Poste*, skippered by Eric Tabarly. *La Poste* remains on standby in 60-knot winds until two US Navy ships rendezvous mid-ocean and escort the mortally wounded yacht to port.

The attrition of the race begins to show on Leg 5 between Uruguay and Fort Lauderdale, Florida, as many of the W60 fleet suffer severe delamination, causing a dangerous weakening of the hull. British entrant *Dolphin & Youth* diverts to Rio, fearing that the boat will disintegrate, while *NZ Endeavour* and *La Poste* make temporary repairs and continue to the US. Chris Dickson's W60, *Tokio*, is spared delamination, but dismasts and is forced to head for the Brazilian port of Santos. In thirty-six hours, Dickson's crew repair the broken mast and head for America.

Winners: Maxi class: *New Zealand Endeavour*
W60 class: *Yamaha* (Japan/New Zealand)

above *No frills down below for the female crew of* EF Language *in the 2001–02 Volvo Ocean Race. In the limited space aboard a VO60, crew must 'hot-bunk': a crewmember coming off watch will crawl into the recently vacated bunk of a crewmember heading on deck for their turn on watch.*

above *Learning not to flinch when tons of ice-cold water pour aft along the decks is an essential asset to an offshore helmsman.*

1997–98: Big names and big trouble

The last edition of the race to bear the Whitbread title and the longest with nine legs in total, including short, sprint passages.

There is an early setback for Norwegian *Innovation Kvaerner*, when her generator explodes within sight of the Southampton start line.

Rudder damage on *BrunelSunergy* after striking a whale in the Atlantic forces the team to head for Recife, Brazil, to make repairs. Generally light winds and slow speeds on the 7,350-mile first leg to Cape Town cause food shortages on a number of boats. However, Lawrie Smith and British entry *Silk Cut* produce a record breaking 24-hour run of 417.2 miles. The yacht betters this record on Leg 2 sailing 449.1 miles at an average speed of 18.7 knots.

American skipper Paul Cayard wins Leg 1 on *EF Language*, silencing critics who believed that his success and experience in the America's Cup would be worthless in an offshore race.

Two boats cause controversy in the South African stopover; Chris Dickson resigns as skipper of *Toshiba*, commenting: "I would be letting myself down by continuing the campaign." Rumours of friction between

Dickson and the team's project manager, Dennis Connor, circulate. Also, the un-sponsored US entry of Dr Neil Bath pulls out due to lack of funding.

At the end of Leg 2 in Fremantle, Australia, two further team changes take place: the skipper of Dutch entry, *BrunelSunergy*, steps down after finishing last in the first two legs and is replaced by Olympic medallist Roy Heiner. Soon afterwards, co-skipper of *Chessie Racing*, Mark Fischer, resigns. When asked to comment on the tense atmosphere aboard the yacht, Fischer explained curtly: "On any boat during the heat of competition you get some normal friction between skipper and crew."

On the first 2,250-mile 'sprint' of the race, Leg 3 between Fremantle and Sydney, *Innovation Kvaerner* discovers potentially disastrous damage to the yacht's mast. Skipper Knut Frostad radios his shore team and a helicopter drops a repair kit to the yacht.

During the second 'sprint' leg between Sydney and Auckland, Dennis Connor joins the crew on *Toshiba* racing against his America's Cup rival, Paul Cayard, on *EF Language*. Connor protests against Cayard for failing to switch on his navigation lights after dark, claiming that this gave *EF Language* a tactical advantage in concealing her position. A protest jury is flown to New Zealand and Connor's claim is judged to be invalid.

Leaving the protests and intrigue in Auckland, the yachts head into the Southern Ocean for Leg 5 to São Sebastião, Brazil. Both *Silk Cut* and *EF Education* (sister ship to Cayard's *EF Language*) suffer mast and rigging failure 2,000 miles from the nearest land and are forced to limp cautiously to the Argentine port of Ushuaia, north-east of Cape Horn.

In Brazil, it is discovered that *Toshiba* started her engine and engaged reverse gear to free the yacht from a bed of kelp wrapped around the keel. Before crossing the finish line, the crew replaced a security seal specifically fitted by race officers in Auckland to reveal any evidence of the yacht's propeller shaft turning. As the team failed to inform the race committee of this action and even omitted to record the incident in the boat's log, *Toshiba* is disqualified from Leg 5.

Further protests marred Leg 7 between Fort Lauderdale and Baltimore when *EF Education* protest against *Toshiba* for failing to execute a 720° penalty turn after a port/starboard incident. The race jury uphold the protest and Connor's navigator, Andrew Cape, resigns describing the Whitbread as "a hard race and I have not especially enjoyed it."

A series of protests threatened to disrupt the final leg from La Rochelle, France, to Southampton, but – possibly weary of squabbling after a long and controversial race – all claims and procedures are dropped.

Winner: *EF Language* (Sweden)

2001–02: Less arguing and more racing

Re-named the Volvo Ocean Race, the event signifies a leap in offshore competitive sailing. Fierce rivalry is reflected in close racing and the outbreak of egos and internal politics witnessed in the previous race are avoided. Ocean racing enters a newer, faster and intensely combative era.

Winner: *Illbruck* (Germany)

left *Volvo 60* Illbruck *– winner of the 2001–02 Volvo Ocean Race – glides past the lighthouse in Gothenburg, Sweden.*

4

Offshore Fully Crewed

The Fastnet Race

The biennial Fastnet Race is far from being the longest offshore racing event: the Cape Town to Rio Race traverses the South Atlantic covering 4,000 miles and the gruelling Trans-Pacific Yacht Race from Los Angeles to Honolulu, Hawaii, lasts between seven and eight days – over twice the usual length of the Fastnet. Nonetheless, the event has always been considered a *grand cru* offshore yacht race.

The Notice of Race for the 608-mile (978km) course is simple: "Cowes – Fastnet Rock – Plymouth", taking the racing fleet south-west from the start line off Cowes. After the yachts compress and bunch between Hurst Point and The Needles marking the end of the confined, opening stage of the race in The Solent between the Isle of Wight and mainland Britain, they head into the English Channel. The passage along Britain's southern coast takes the race past the headlands of Anvil Point, Portland Bill, Start Point and The Lizard before leaving Land's End to starboard and heading into the Celtic Sea. Yachts then head north-west for 180 nautical miles of open water to the lighthouse clinging on to Fastnet Rock off the southern tip of Ireland. Once round the rock, yachts head back across their outward route, rounding Bishop Rock Lighthouse to the south of the Isles of Scilly – 30 miles off Land's End – and on to the final leg and the finish line in Plymouth.

The history of the Fastnet contributes to its legendary status. Originated in 1925, the race appealed to amateur British yachtsmen and the early races were remarkable for the high level of retirements from the course: evidence of inexperienced crews, ancient and poorly equipped yachts and a tough route. During the 1930s, American and French yachts joined the racing fleet and quickly upstaged the British entrants, bringing a new spirit of competition to the event. Although the race is held in August – a period of high pressure and traditionally light winds – a gale during the 1931 Fastnet battered the fleet and one crewmember was lost overboard: a catastrophic episode, but a feature that firmly established the race as a rite of passage for offshore sailors.

The Fastnet Race won a senior place in sailing folklore during the disastrous 1979 edition of the event. During a brutal storm, the fleet of 303 yachts was smashed by hurricane-strength winds and monstrous seas. In total, twenty-four yachts were abandoned of which five sank and although fifteen sailors lost their lives, the extraordinary skill of rescue services resulted in 136 men and women being plucked from yachts and liferafts. The tragedy of the race and sheer terror and might of this storm is conveyed by the account of 17-year-old yachtsman, Matt Sheahan, sailing on his father's yacht, *Grimalkin*. Sheahan survived the gale in a liferaft although his father David was lost overboard – his body carried downwind away from the stricken yacht.

previous page *Slamming to windward across the Bass Strait, 47ft (14.3m)* Ausmaid *heads south to Tasmania in the 1997 Sydney–Hobart Race. Conscious of the wild conditions yachts can encounter offshore in the Bass Strait, entry documents for the race must include a "colour photograph of the boat under sail no older than twelve months and suitable for search and rescue purposes".*

opposite *Fastnet Rock off the southern tip of Ireland. For nineteenth-century Irish immigrants sailing to America, the rock was the final glimpse of home and became known as 'Ireland's Teardrop.' The lighthouse is now the mid-point turning mark of the biennial Fastnet Race – a rite of passage for offshore sailors.*

We heard the radio messages from the aeroplanes saying: "I've done my square search. I haven't found you, but DON'T WORRY – we'll be back and WE WILL FIND YOU!"

Robin Aisher, skipper of *Yeoman XXI*, in a BBC interview after his crew and yacht survived

the tragic 1979 Fastnet Race

"Sometimes events are so big and get so out of control as to make you feel minuscule. Something deep within you realizes that there's absolutely nothing you can do about it. You almost go beyond a state of fear. The whole thing was completely and utterly overwhelming."

A tangible legacy of the 1979 race exists in the stringent qualifications and safety requirements demanded by the race organizers, the Royal Ocean Racing Club (RORC). To enter the Fastnet Race, a yacht's skipper and half of her crew must have already completed a 300-mile offshore race or a non-stop, offshore cruising passage of the same length. In addition, a first aid certificate is mandatory for two crewmembers on each yacht and half the crew must have received training in the use of liferafts. Ominously, all competitors must submit their 'Next of Kin' details before starting the race.

opposite *The death toll during gales in the tragic 1979 Fastnet Race reached fifteen. Trailing warps and sea anchors, the eighth and final crewmember waits to be hoisted from a badly stricken yacht.*

below *The challenge of the Fastnet Race attracts a broad range of entrants. Three different nationalities squeeze past the Needles, thirteen miles west of the start line during the early stages of the 2005 race.*

The Sydney–Hobart Race

The 628-mile route of the annual Sydney–Hobart Race could easily appear in a luxury cruise brochure. Yachts leave Sydney Harbour on 26 December at the height of the Southern Hemisphere summer and sail across the 150 miles of the Bass Strait separating mainland Australia from the island of Tasmania. The race continues south past the stunning scenery of Tasmania's east coast until reaching Tasman Island and turning west into Storm Bay with a further 40 miles to the final destination at the city of Hobart. After rounding an old whaling station called Iron Pot, 11 miles of sailing along the Derwent River brings you to Battery Point in the island's capital city. However, this is the only feature that the brutal race shares with spending the Christmas holidays on a liner.

The Sydney–Hobart Race and its older, northern equivalent, the Fastnet Race, have a similar appeal for sailors. The event is open to a wide range of boats and attracts a broad spectrum of yachtsmen from serial ocean racers to offshore novices. The thrill of a passage

through open ocean is topped by close racing along the coast of Tasmania and a vibrant welcome at the destination port. A perfect combination, perhaps, were it not for the narrow, shallow obstacle of the Bass Strait: an infamous and savage sea area littered with shipwrecks from the nineteenth century. The strait continues to wreak havoc with modern racing yachts as they sprint across this turbulent link separating the vast Indian Ocean from the plunging depths of the Tasman Basin. The Sydney–Hobart has a chilling history of destructive storms, damaged yachts and human fatalities. A gale during the 1984 edition of the race caused one death and compelled 104 of the 150 entrants to retire. Four years later, 119 yachts crossed the start line in Sydney Harbour and thirty-eight opted to retire before reaching Hobart. In 1993 a four-day gale sank two yachts and forced sixty-four entrants to retire.

While Northern Hemisphere yachtsmen regard the 1979 Fastnet Race as an offshore bogey-man, towering waves six storeys high and winds reaching 70mph during the 1998 Sydney–Hobart Race caused a catastrophic loss of life. In horrific conditions, seven boats were abandoned of which five sank, including the 52ft (15.8m) *Winston Churchill*, a veteran of the first Sydney–Hobart Race in 1945. Chris Winning, the yacht's skipper, described the horror after being recovered:

"The worst thing of the whole affair was that after we got into the liferaft and became separated from the others, the damned thing capsized twice on these great seas at night which is bloody frightening, let me tell you."

The sea is feline. It licks your feet –
its huge flanks purr very pleasant
for you; but it will crack your bones
and eat you, for all that, and wipe
the crimsoned foam from its jaws
as if nothing had happened.

Oliver Wendell Holmes (1809-1894), American physician and writer

previous page *After crossing the 150-mile wide Bass Strait, Sydney–Hobart yachts slide down the east coast of Tasmania and under 'the organ pipes' at Cape Raoul.*

above *Size is important, but it cannot guarantee a comfortable ride – the crew on 80ft (24.4m) maxi* Nicorette *braves the weather rail on the 2002 Sydney–Hobart. A big swell and high winds in the Bass Strait produced waterspouts and a severe pounding for the race fleet.*

opposite *The Sydney–Hobart 2004 claims a victim –* Yendys *hurtles past the liferaft of capsized and abandoned maxi yacht,* Skandia Wild Thing *off the coast of Tasmania.*

Twenty-four fixed-wing aircraft and six helicopters armed with heat-seeking equipment joined in a desperate hunt for sailors in a search area extending over 4,000 square nautical miles, successfully rescuing fifty-five yachtsmen. It is purely due to the speed, skill and bravery of the rescue services that the tragic death toll was limited to six.

The 1998 Sydney–Hobart Race illustrates that advances in technology, communications and – most importantly – weather forecasting cannot guarantee safety at sea or provide a protective scientific buffer of knowledge against the elements. Winner of the first race in 1945, the 34ft (10.3m) yacht *Rani* took a little over eleven days to complete the course with the skipper and crew spending much of the race stuffing bedding and blankets into gaping holes in the hull as the yacht's pine planks worked loose. Fifty-four years later, a water-ballasted, purpose-built racing machine, *Nokia*, sped from Sydney to Hobart in one day and twenty hours. The speed and durability of racing yachts has increased over time, but sailors still face an element that continues to show little respect for technological sophistication.

The Global Challenge: a ticket to ride

In 1971, Sir Chay Blyth became the first man to sail around the world non-stop west-about – against the prevailing winds and currents. Sailing downwind around the globe has always been the preferred route and Blyth's decision to beat upwind through hostile oceans into the endless waves rolling around the planet was not a popular choice. However, since his pioneering circumnavigation, Blyth has persuaded over 650 people to follow the perilous and uncomfortable 'wrong direction' route and pay a considerable amount of money for this honour.

The Global Challenge provides a 29,000-mile circumnavigation race for twelve, identical, 72ft (21.9m) yachts crewed by amateur yachtsmen with a professional skipper on board each boat. After crossing the start line off Portsmouth, England, the fleet spends just under nine months ploughing to windward with stopover ports in Argentina, New Zealand, Australia, South Africa, USA and France before returning to the UK and crossing the final finish line. There are few similarities between the Global Challenge and the Volvo Ocean Race, although both events involve a fully crewed circumnavigation and promote themselves as "the toughest yacht race in the world". Boats in the Volvo Ocean Race are stripped-down, super-light racing machines crewed by professionals with the sole purpose of circling the globe in 'the right direction' as fast as possible. Global Challenge yachts are wide and solid with the strength and capability to carry an amateur crew around the world 'the wrong way'.

The cost of joining the Global Challenge is another fundamental difference: £28,750 (approx. US$51,800 or 42,150Euros) will secure a place for the entire circumnavigation in the 2008–09 edition of the race and the event attracts crew from a diverse, international spectrum. Housewives, lawyers, students, company directors and plumbers have raced around the world with no prior sailing experience other than a pre-race training programme provided by Blyth's organisation. While the price of a place on board a Global Challenge yacht includes plenty of headroom and space with the use of a hot water shower in the freezing Southern Ocean, it also incorporates sailing through notoriously treacherous oceans with a collection of strangers. Mid-Atlantic gales, numbing cold, constant discomfort and exhaustion are tough to handle when sailing with an experienced, professional crew, but encountering extreme offshore conditions on board a yacht crewed by novices with predominantly land-based backgrounds is even more demanding.

Without doubt, lifelong bonds of friendship are forged through shared hardship during the Global Challenge. During the 2004–05 race, two crew on competing yachts became engaged over the VHF radio. This proposal is highly romantic and possibly unique, although the rules demand that the radio is left 'open' throughout the race and this deeply personal moment was eavesdropped upon by all 216 sailors in the twelve-boat fleet.

opposite *Constant discomfort, freezing conditions and a permanent adrenaline rush face Global Challenge crews during their 29,000-mile, nine-month, pay-as-you-go circumnavigation.*

next page *A Global Challenge crew succeeds in hoisting their fluorescent storm jib as the yacht pounds through the turbulent wind funnel of Cook Strait between North Island and South Island, New Zealand.*

69

He that would go to sea for pleasure, would go to hell for a pastime.

A sailing proverb

How many crew?
The Transat Jacques Vabre

The double-handed Transat Jacques Vabre race fills a gap in the Open class competitive calendar. Held every two years, the race is restricted to 60ft (18.28m) and 50ft (15.24m) Open class monohulls and multihulls. Normally, these yachts compete in fully crewed inshore races or race single-handed in transatlantic events. However, put two sailors on an IMOCA (International Monohull Open Class Association) or ORMA (Open Racing Multihull Association) 50- or 60-footer, and a new type of sailing evolves.

Open class solo sailors are an independent breed: pairing two of these solitary ocean wanderers on the same boat and challenging them to race from France to Brazil presents a unique set of circumstances. French trimaran ace Loïck Peyron explains:

"The difficulty [in a double-handed transatlantic race] is that you tend to push the boat to her limits as if there were a full crew on board, when in reality there are just two soloists."

This situation produces a thrilling spectacle for the spectator – greedily absorbing tales from the race track via television or the Internet – as the yachts hurtle into the Atlantic at full pace on the edge of control. In addition, the race starts in November, obliging the fleet to head immediately into strong winds from deep, low pressure systems charging towards Europe, before the yachts hook on to the trade winds and head for the equator. All the components for an epic contest are fused in the Transat Jacques Vabre.

above *The two crewmembers racing a 60ft trimaran are constantly active and alert for the two weeks at sea during the Transat Jacques Vabre race. Heavy commercial traffic in the English Channel and November gales in the Bay of Biscay can mean no sleep or hot food for the initial four days of racing as the yachts fly south towards the Equator. Jean-Luc Nelias and Loïck Peyron sailed* Belgacom *across the finish line taking 2nd place in 2003, completing the transatlantic race in less than twelve days.*

opposite top *Capable of beam reaching at 30 knots in 20-knot wind speeds, hand steering is essential. While autopilots can function effectively in flat water, a rapid human response is needed to control the boat, follow the 'wave train' and maximize speed in rough conditions.*

opposite bottom *Arguably the most extreme offshore sailing machines on the planet, ORMA 60 trimarans wait in the French port of Le Havre for the start of the 5,000-mile Transat Jacques Vabre race from France to Brazil. Meticulous pre-race preparation is vital to ensure the boats can be pushed hard through the North and South Atlantic.*

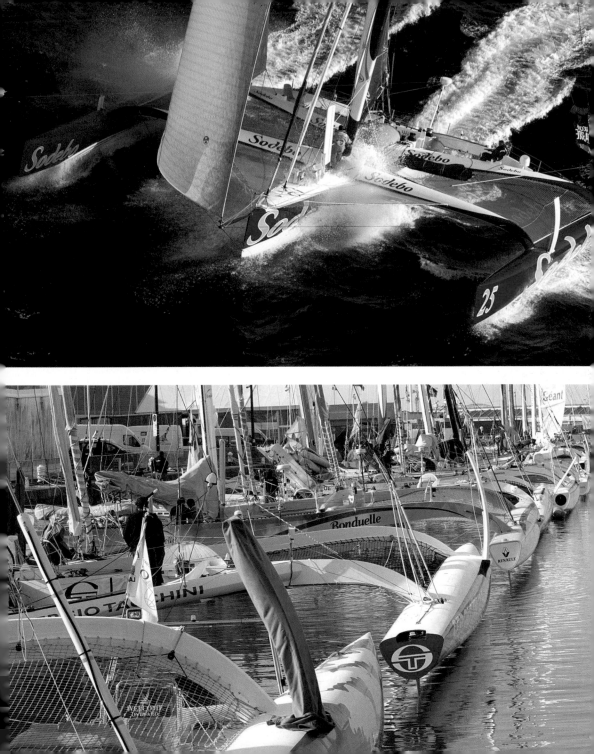

A race anatomy

Straight into the action: The race leaves Le Havre on the north coast of France over two days: the monohulls and 50ft trimarans are sent off first with the faster 60ft multihulls starting a day later. Heading west along the English Channel, the first hurdle will be the bulk of commercial traffic streaming down the coast. This hazard increases during the first night at sea as the fleet approach Ushant, the western extremity of France and a busy junction for shipping heading north and south along the continental coast.

Turning the corner into an early ambush: Once past Ushant, the Bay of Biscay can form a dangerous trap for the yachts. Cutting a fine line south across Biscay to clip Cape Finisterre – the western tip of Spain – competitors risk being forced deep into the bay by westerly winds and swells rolling in from the Atlantic. Misjudging the track across the bay can force yachts to tack north-west and escape into open waters as the more prudent boats slip past Finisterre and head towards the Azores archipelago; for some boats and crews the initial four days can be the most demanding part of the race. Rough weather and vital early tactical decisions place immense pressure on man and machine, preventing crews from developing any offshore racing rhythm of sleeping and eating.

Trade Winds and tactics: The boats will soon increase speed as they link with the North Atlantic trade winds off the coast of Portugal, sailing downwind, pushed south by the north-west breeze. The two Atlantic archipelagos of the Canary Islands and the Cape Verde Islands off the coast of Africa are crucial stages of the race: threading through the islands or sailing to leeward can leave a boat stalled in windless conditions. Heading close inshore may also increase the risk of a night-collision with small local fishing boats, many of which carry no navigation lights.

Down in the Doldrums: Before crossing the equator and heading into the Southern Hemisphere, the racing fleet must traverse the Doldrums – an area where good judgement can produce massive gains. The Doldrums area is a constantly shifting band of light and fickle winds interspersed with savage squalls. Racing crews will have been studying satellite weather information for this area since shortly after crossing the start line, as finding the narrowest section of the Doldrums and ensuring a swift transition southward, is supremely important. Evaluating meteorological data for the area is notoriously difficult and poor judgement or inaccurate weather forecasting can leave a yacht drifting slowly south with slack sails.

Drag racing to the finish: Once through the Doldrums barrier, the monohulls will head west towards Brazil, hooking into the south-east trade winds. Downwind speed and pushing the boat hard become the

above *The intense competition and rivalry of the Transat Jacques Vabre race pushes both man and machine to the limit. Inaccurate weather data, a minor tactical error forced by fatigue, gear failure or plain bad luck can result in disappointment and – occasionally – disaster.*

determining factor of the race. At this stage, thorough pre-race preparation of the boat becomes critical to enable the crew to drive the boat hard with the maximum sail area. Any equipment failure during this high-speed drag race towards the Brazilian coast can prove catastrophic and vital time will be lost as the crew is forced to slow down and make repairs. A 60ft monohull will complete the 4,500-mile race in approximately sixteen days and is likely to average speeds of 11 knots.

After exiting the Doldrums, the 60ft multihulls are sent further south to round the remote mid-Atlantic turning mark of Ascension Island before heading west to the finish line off Salvador de Bahia. Capable of average speeds hovering around 15 knots, the ORMA multihulls will still complete the extended 5,000-mile race course one or two days ahead of the leading monohull.

5

Solo
Sailing
Pioneers

• THE PIONEERS

• THE GOLDEN GLOBE

The pioneers

Joshua Slocum (1844–1909) consistently rejected any idea that his round-the-world, single-handed voyage on *Spray* was an historic, pioneering journey. The proud and professional commercial sailor regarded the three-year circumnavigation between 1895 and 1898 as an exercise in seamanship and offshore tourism: "If the *Spray* discovered no continents on her voyage, it may be that there are no more continents to be discovered. To find one's way to lands already discovered is a good thing and *Spray* made the discovery that even the worst sea is not so terrible to a well-appointed ship." The Canadian yachtsman's summary ignores extraordinary drama encountered during a voyage that included outrunning pirates off Gibraltar and successfully repelling two canoes filled with barefooted Indians in the Straits of Magellan by covering the 36ft sloop's decks with carpet-tacks.

Thirty years later, French sailor Alain Gerbault (1893–1942), a World War I fighter pilot, socialite and tennis maestro, arrived in Le Havre on the northern coast of France having completed a five-year, solo circumnavigation in *Firecrest*. The length of Gerbault's voyage reflects a strong relationship with the ocean, the independence that a yacht provides and the access this allows to remote, 'uncivilized' areas of the planet. While absorbing the beauty and culture of the Pacific Islands, Gerbault spent time mixing with exiled fellow countrymen and mysterious misfits scattered throughout French Polynesia. He also delayed departure if the chance of playing any sport arose; Gerbault defeated all his tennis opponents in Bermuda, Ascension Island and Durban, South Africa, while joining rugby games in Samoa and football matches in both the Cape Verde Archipelago and on Réunion, east of

I realized that I could not hope to arrive in time for the tennis tournament at Wimbledon.

Alain Gerbault's only regret after his five-year, solo circumnavigation (from *In Quest of The Sun*)

below *Chichester's 1966–67 circumnavigation followed the route used by clipper ships, sailing with the prevailing winds and currents from west to east around the world. Before his voyage on Gypsy Moth IV, only nine small yachts had circumnavigated the world via Cape Horn taking three years on average: Chichester's one-stop marathon took nine months.*

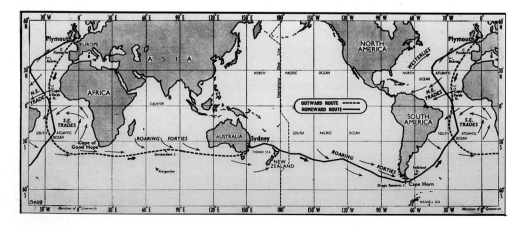

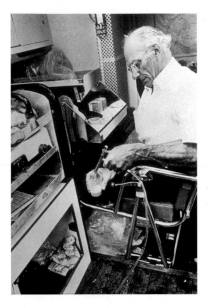

sailing *Gypsy Moth III* from Plymouth, England, to Newport, Rhode Island, and between 1966 and 1967 he completed a solo circumnavigation of the globe – including one stop over in Australia – on *Gypsy Moth IV*.

The entire concept for Chichester's circumnavigation had been audacious. When *Gypsy Moth IV* set off on her voyage, fewer than ten yachts had circumnavigated the world via Cape Horn at the tip of South America. At the time, the longest recorded solo ocean passage was 7,500 miles, sailed by Argentine yachtsman Vito Dumas, from Cape Town to New Zealand during World War II: Chichester's first leg between England and Australia would double this distance. He was also 64 years old and had recently suffered carcinoma of a lung – circumstances that caused a chilling prediction in the *Daily Express* newspaper by clairvoyant Marjorie Staves: "Lone yachtsman Francis Chichester is doomed to failure in his attempt to sail around the world. He will give up due to lack of physical strength."

Chichester's outstanding achievement and ceaseless humour when sailing a boat that he frequently cursed for her "vicious faults" and described as "about as unbalanced or unstable a boat that there could be", inspired a generation of sailors. This tough and resilient yachtsman was not exempt from fear, although it appeared in an unexpected form. On the second leg of the circumnavigation, from Australia to Britain, *Gypsy Moth IV* was hailed by an oil tanker after rounding Cape Horn and heading north-east into the South Atlantic. Chichester's log entry for this incident illustrates the effects of extreme isolation on even the most independent and indomitable spirit: "To my disgust I found that this first contact with people was making me tremble… three months' solitude is strong medicine."

above *Chichester was assisted by hand-pumped Whitbread beer during his round-the-world voyage on board* Gypsy Moth IV. *Spotted loading supplies of gin on to the yacht before setting off on from Plymouth, he commented: "Any damn fool can navigate the world sober. It takes a really good sailor to do it drunk."*

opposite Gypsy Moth IV *rounds Cape Horn in 1967 during a gale. Sir Francis Chichester was amazed – and annoyed – at the presence of the Royal Navy ice patrol ship,* HMS Protector *at the Horn: "I cursed* Protector *for hanging about, especially as I noted that she looked steady enough to play a game of billiards on her deck."*
(from Gypsy Moth Circles The World*)*

Full rig, smoking [jacket],
smart new trousers, black shoes etc.
the only slip-up is that I left
my bow-tie behind.

Sir Francis Chichester's log on
Gypsy Moth IV records dressing for
dinner on his 65th birthday in
the Doldrums after twenty-one
days alone at sea

The Golden Globe

On 20 July 1969, Neil Armstrong and 'Buzz' Aldrin became the first men to walk on the Moon. The two astronauts spent a total of twenty-one hours on the Moon's surface collecting rock samples and transmitting images and audio back to Earth. A year earlier, nine men set off to race non-stop, single-handed around the planet using navigation techniques that had changed little since the eighteenth-century voyages of Captain James Cook. In an era before GPS (Global Positioning System) and the wide range of meteorological information that is currently available via fax, radio and satellite, the sailors in the 1968 Golden Globe Race represent the purest form of ocean racing.

While modern ocean racers can speak with their families, shore teams or the media on satellite phones and are constantly tracked by Argos beacons installed on board, Knox-Johnston and his fellow yachtsmen depended on unreliable radio sets with patchy coverage for communication and human contact. The absence of satellite tracking and infrequent – or non-existent – radio communication with the competitors meant that the yachtsmen were effectively 'invisible' for extended periods. Often their location and existence was only revealed through chance sightings by deep-sea fishermen or commercial vessels sailing the ocean's shipping lanes. This isolation and information vacuum had a number of consequences: those onshore following the race could only guess whether the sailors were alive, the competitors had no idea where their opponents were and, finally, the situation provided an opportunity for foul play.

The Golden Globe is an important milestone in ocean racing and the same conditions and problems faced by the nine pioneering yachtsmen still affect modern sailors. A brief study of the characters and their experiences during this race demonstrates that solo sailing has always been the most extreme section of the sport:

In 1966, a pair of British soldiers rowed across the Atlantic in a 20ft open boat; two years later, the two men, John Ridgway and Chay Blyth, entered the Golden Globe. Both Ridgway and Blyth sailed twin-keeled, 30ft sloops designed for coastal cruising and were unsuited to ocean racing. Ridgway's *English Rose IV* began to develop serious structural problems in the Atlantic Ocean, forcing an early retirement to the port of Recife, Brazil. With no previous sailing experience, Blyth sailed *Dysticus III* south through the North Atlantic and across the Equator before his self-steering gear failed. After discovering that his fuel supply had been contaminated with seawater, Blyth headed for the island of Tristan da Cunha in the middle of the South Atlantic and received assistance from a fuel tanker anchored off the remote settlement. Noting in his log: "It was my voyage of discovery, and what I discovered was me," Blyth headed for South Africa and retired from the race.

The former British submarine commander Bill King built the 42ft, junk-rigged schooner, *Galway Blazer II*, specifically for a circumnavigation, but a knock-down and total inversion in mid-Atlantic damaged her masts and King sailed to Cape Town and out of the race. The experienced Italian solo sailor Alex Carazzo built 66ft *Gancia Americano* for long distance solo sailing, but stomach ulcer problems and continuously vomiting blood as he sailed through the Bay of Biscay forced Carazzo to retire to Portugal. French yachtsman Loïck Fougeron sailed to the Cape Verde Islands and handed his flea-ridden cat to a local fisherman after she ate through electric cables on board 30ft *Capitaine Browne*. Continuing south, Fougeron was caught in a severe gale and decided to head for Cape Town and retire from the Golden Globe.

The strangest story from the race concerns the British electronics engineer Donald Crowhurst and *Teignmouth Electron*. Crowhurst sailed his 40ft plywood trimaran across the Atlantic towards Brazil, frequently telegraphing record-breaking daily runs and high speeds in Morse code to the race organisation. However, *Teignmouth Electron* did not leave the Atlantic, although her skipper regularly sent radio messages claiming positions throughout the Southern Ocean and even duplicated a false log book plotting his course around the world. After calling into a Brazilian port to make repairs, Crowhurst headed towards England and the finish line, but his deteriorating mental state drove him to suicide in the mid-Atlantic: *Teignmouth Electron* was found drifting in calm seas by a freighter. One of the final entries in Crowhurst's log gives a good indication of his disturbed state of mind:

"my great god who has
revealed at last to his son
not only the exact nature
of his reason for games but
has also revealed the truth of
the way of the ending of the
next game that

It is finished-
It is finished

IT IS THE MERCY"

Sailing a nearly identical trimaran to Crowhurst's, the Royal Navy officer Nigel Tetley succeeded in sailing *Victress* through the world's most fearsome oceans and into the Atlantic. Heading through the North Atlantic towards England, disaster struck when the bow of the multihull's port float fell off. Although a watertight bulkhead prevented the float from filling with water, the detached section had smashed the centre hull's

above *The world's first solo, non-stop circumnavigators are reunited in Paris, eighteen years after the Golden Globe race. The late Bernard Moitessier (right) set sail to save his soul, while Sir Robin Knox-Johnston stormed around the world to prove a point.*

bow and water was pouring into the yacht. Tetley grabbed the radio: "Mayday, Mayday, Mayday. This is sailing yacht *Victress* at Latitude 39° 10' North, Longitude 24° 30' West. I am sinking and require assistance. Mayday, Mayday, Mayday." A Dutch ship immediately replied and Tetley climbed into his liferaft as *Victress* sank to the bottom.

The inspiration to compete in such a dangerous, physically and mentally demanding event differed for all the competitors. 28-year-old British Merchant Marine captain Robin Knox-Johnston was driven by adventure, patriotism and admiration for the circumnavigation of Sir Francis Chichester, saying: "Once Chichester had shown that this trip was possible, I could not accept that anyone but a Briton should be the first to do it, and I wanted to be that Briton." The stimulation for 45-year-old French yachtsman and author, Bernard Moitessier, is less distinct, but resembles the desires of Alain Gerbault and his search for personal freedom. Moitessier, however, was vocal in his dislike for the 'civilized' world and raged in his log book against its "false gods, always lying in wait, spider-like, eating our liver, sucking our marrow."

While Knox-Johnston battled through the Southern Ocean on his solid teak 32ft ketch *Suhaili*, Moitessier wrestled with his personal demons and a consuming love affair with nature on board 39ft steel-hulled *Joshua*. Passing Cape Horn, Knox-Johnston scrawled "Yippee!!!" in his log book and celebrated the momentous occasion by unwrapping his Aunt Aileen's fruitcake, while – chasing hard – Moitessier was moved to poetic prose: "*Joshua* drives towards the Horn under the light of the stars and the somewhat distant tenderness of the moon… I no longer know how far I have got, except that we long ago left the borders of too much behind." Entering the Atlantic was a defining moment for Moitessier and as Knox-Johnston continued north-east towards the finish line and victory, the mystical Frenchman turned south-east to the tip of South Africa and into the Indian Ocean. Off Cape Town, *Joshua* sailed close to a British oil tanker and Moitessier used his handheld catapult to shoot a final message on to the ship's deck: "My intention is to continue the voyage, still non-stop, towards the Pacific Islands, where there is plenty of sun and more peace than Europe."

I am continuing non-stop because I am happy at sea
and perhaps because I want to save my soul.

Bernard Moitessier's final message to the Golden Globe race organisation

Offshore Solo

The OSTAR

In 1960 four Britons and one Frenchman raced single-handed from Plymouth, England, to New York for a 'Half Crown' wager (approx. twenty-five pence) and the OSTAR (*Observer* Single-handed Transatlantic Race) was born. Organized by the Royal Western Yacht Club in Plymouth and held every four years, the race is open to professional and amateur sailors in a variety of boat sizes, both monohulls and multihulls. Today, the race still maintains its 'Corinthian' element and legendary status, attracting sailors from around the world to an event known as 'La Transat Anglaise'.

Although the spirit of the first OSTAR remains, the race has undergone many name and rule changes throughout its history, including moving the finish from New York to Newport, Rhode Island. What remains unaltered, however, is the ferocious attrition rate as the racing fleet heads west into the Atlantic. The event's history is littered with sinking or abandoned yachts and courageous rescue and salvage attempts. Possibly the most astonishing tale from the OSTAR concerns the sinking of the 30ft monohull *Hyccup* after an attack by whales in 1988. The yacht's skipper, David Sellings, climbed into a liferaft and was spotted by a Nimrod aeroplane. Later, via radio from the rescue ship, Sellings recounted the experience:

"On the first night, I saw several whales in the distance. The next night I heard them grunting and squealing like pigs in a trough. They were clearly talking to each other and bringing other whales in. They went away and came back next morning. This time there were more of them, probably fifty or sixty, they kept coming closer, making an awful lot of noise and pushing tight up against the boat. There were two distinct bumps and that was it. The rudder was smashed and they had disabled the ship."

Although the sinking of *Hyccup* is sinister and unique, the retirement rate has hovered around the 50 per cent level for the past two editions. Further patterns that reflect the development of solo sailing emerge from the results of the OSTAR: the French dominance of the sport and a period of dramatic advances in boat design. These improvements and the introduction of professional offshore sailors saw the transatlantic race time slip below twenty days and then fall below the ten-day barrier by 2000. During the 1976 OSTAR, 42 per cent of the racing fleet was forced to retire and two skippers were lost: this tragedy generated a focus on safety measures and the casualty rate subsequently dropped while the yachts continued to slash days from the OSTAR race record. Finally, the retirement rate from the most recent OSTAR in 2005 is identical to the attrition percentage during the 1968 edition of the race and indicates a return to the event's 'Corinthian' roots with the participation of adventurous, amateur sailors.

Q: What caused you to retire?

A: Knocked down in Force 11, thrown overboard, harness held, injured shoulder, torn main, torn jib, main compass broken, all electronic instruments out, batteries lost acid, VHF gone.

Q: By whom were you rescued?

A: Made port under own steam.

Colin Drummond, skipper of *Sleuth Hound*, in his retirement questionnaire form after the 1976 OSTAR

previous page *French trimaran ace Loïck Peyron flies off the start line of the 2002 Route du Rhum on Fujicolor. Huge seas and high winds devastated the ORMA 60 trimaran fleet forcing a majority of the yachts to retire. Peyron's multihull began to break up as he drove hard into the North Atlantic.*

above *Sir Francis Chichester leans against the mast of* Gypsy Moth III *shortly before the start of the 1964 OSTAR discussing tactics with the only French entrant, a naval lieutenant, Eric Tabarly (far right). Chichester had won the inaugural OSTAR four years earlier taking 40 days to cross the Atlantic: Tabarly won the 1964 race in just 27 days aboard his 44ft ketch,* Pen Duick II. *Having crossed the finish line, Tabarly let slip that his self steering gear had failed after eight days at sea. President de Gaulle awarded the new French sailing legend with the Legion of Honour.*

The OSTAR roll of honour and casualty list 1960-2005:

1960 OSTAR (Plymouth-New York)
Winner: Sir Francis Chichester (GBR) *Gypsy Moth III*
Time: 40d 12h 30m
Total of 5 competitors at the start. 100% of fleet finishes the race

1964 OSTAR (Plymouth-Newport, Rhode Island)
Winner: Eric Tabarly (FRA) *Pen Duick II*
Time: 27d 03h 56m
Total of 15 competitors at the start. 93% of fleet finish the race
Details: 1 yacht retires

1968 OSTAR
Winner (monohull): Geoffrey Williams (GBR) *Sir Thomas Lipton*
Time: 25d 20h 33m
Winner (multihull): Bill Howell (AUS) *Golden Cockerel*
Time: 31d 16h 24m
Total of 35 competitors at the start. 51% of the fleet finish the race
Details: 1 yacht disqualified, 12 retire, 4 abandoned or sunk

1972 OSTAR
Winner (multihull): Alain Colas (FRA) *Pen Duick IV*
Time: 20d 13h 15m
Winner (monohull): Jean-Yves Terlain (FRA) *Vendredi Treize*
Time: 21d 05h 14m
Total of 55 competitors at the start. 72% of the fleet finish the race
Details: 10 yachts retire, 1 abandoned

1976 OSTAR
Winner (monohull): Eric Tabarly (FRA) *Pen Duick VI*
Time: 23d 20h 12m
Winner (multihull): Mike Birch (Canada) *The Third Turtle*
Time: 24d 20h 39m
Total of 125 competitors at the start. 58% of the fleet complete the race
Details: 40 yachts retired, 6 abandoned or sunk, 5 finish outside the race time limit, 2 skippers lost

1980 OSTAR
Winner (multihull): Philip Weld (USA) *Moxie*
Time: 17d 23h 12m
Winner (monohull): Kazimierz Jaworski (Poland) *Spaniel II*
Time: 19d 13h 25m
Total of 90 competitors at the start. 80% of the fleet complete the race
Details: 4 yachts abandoned or sunk, 12 retire, 1 disqualified

1984 Carlsberg
Winner (trimaran): Yvon Fauconier (FRA) *Umupro Jardin V*
Time: 16d 22h 25m
Winner (catamaran): Marc Pajot (FRA) *Elf Aquitaine II*
Time: 16d 12h 18m
Winner (monohull): Warren Luhrs (USA) *Thursday's Child*

Time: 16d 22h 27m
Total of 91 competitors at the start. 70% of the fleet complete the race
Details: 19 yachts retire, 8 sunk or abandoned

1988 Carlsberg
Winner (trimaran): Philippe Poupon (FRA) *Fleury Michon*
Time: 10d 09h 15m
Winner (catamaran): Bruno Peyron (FRA) *VSD*
Time: 12d 23h 20m
Winner (monohull): Jean Yves Terlain (FRA) *UAP 1992*
Time: 17d 04h 05m
Total of 95 competitors at the start. 76% of the fleet complete the race
Details: 17 yachts retire, 5 sunk or abandoned

1992 Europe 1 Star
Winner (multihull): Loïck Peyron (FRA) *Fujicolor*
Time: 11d 01h 35m
Winner (monohull): Yves Parlier (FRA) *Cacolac d'Aquitaine*
Time: 14d 16h 01m
Total of 66 competitors at the start. 83% of the fleet complete the race
Details: 3 skippers retire through injury or fatigue, 1 dismasting, 1 capsize, 1 collision with debris

1996 Europe 1 Star
Winner (multihull): Loïck Peyron (FRA) *Fujicolor II*
Time: 10d 10h 05m
Winner (monohull): Gerry Roufs (FRA) *Groupe LG2*
Time: 15d 14h 50m
Total of 69 competitors. 56% of the fleet complete the race
Details:

2000 Europe 1 New Man Star
Winner (trimaran): Francis Joyon (FRA) *Eure et Loire*
Time: 09d 23h 21m
Winner (monohull): Ellen MacArthur (GBR) *Kingfisher*
Time: 14d 23h 01m
Total of 69 competitors. 56% of the fleet complete the race
Details: 4 yachts dismasted, 3 retire with associated mast problems, 4 retire with autopilot and self steering gear failure

2005 Faraday Mill OSTAR
Winner (multihull): Franco Manzoli (ITA) *Cotonella*
Time: 17d 21h 41m
Winner (monohull): Steve White (GBR) *Olympian Challenger*
Time: 20d 5h 24m
Total of 35 competitors. 51% of the fleet complete the race
Details: 1 dismasting, 1 retires with injured skipper, and 15 retire with rigging and equipment failure

The Transat

Organized by the professional racing team Offshore Challenges Events, The Transat 2004 provided a North Atlantic 'sprint' for 50- and 60-foot monohulls and multihulls between Plymouth, England, and Boston, Massachusetts. On 31 May, thirty-seven solo sailors crossed the start line off Penlee Point in blustery and rough conditions that were to continue for the majority of the 2,800-mile course. The early stages of the race along the southern coast of England were brutal: 20-knot headwinds forced constant tacking and manoeuvring within the tightly packed fleet preventing skippers from snatching any rest during their first night at sea.

As the second North Atlantic depression began gathering size and momentum to the west of the fleet, a period of light winds and thick fog hampered progress. This period of light, shifting breeze demanded constant sail trimming and lowered the morale of many skippers already exhausted by three days of beating to windward. The predicted 35-knot winds rolling eastwards were preceded by confused seas and the majority of the racing fleet headed north to avoid the headwinds on the bottom edge of the depression spinning anti-clockwise towards them. Timing the weather system's progress would be crucial for the leading multihulls; judging the exact moment to bear away south-west from the centre of the depression to sail fast downwind was a key moment of the race.

All of the ORMA 60 trimaran fleet escaped from the high winds of the low pressure system without capsizing, but not without incident. Alain Gautier, skipper of *Foncia*, described passing through the eye of the storm on his satellite phone: "The night was hard when we passed the centre of the low pressure with rough sea and wind increasing to around 45 or 50 knots. I was on starboard [tack] for one hour and, suddenly, in two minutes it was Armageddon – the mainsheet broke and the boom flew out, breaking four of the battens. I have to drop the mainsail, but in 45 knots... it's not easy."

The 60ft monohull fleet was not so fortunate. Sailing under storm-jib only, Jean-Pierre Dick and Open 60 monohull *Virbac* rolled through 360° in 50-knot winds and 6–7m waves approximately 100 miles from the centre of the depression. Dick was down below when the yacht rolled and survived uninjured, but the yacht's mast was broken in three places. With the structural integrity of the hull intact, the French

powering his yacht's canting keel mechanism in the opening hours of The Transat 2004. Many skippers would have retired from racing before entering the fierce North Atlantic weather ahead, but Golding chose to continue. For 2,800 miles

he used a perilous method of overpowering Ecover *and "laying her on her ear" to drop the keel to leeward. Golding could then tack the boat leaving the keel on the windward side. His plan succeeded and* Ecover *took monohull line honours.*

skipper declined any offers of outside assistance from other competitors and began constructing a jury rig from the stump of his mast. Three days later, the 60ft monohull *PRB*, skippered by Vincent Riou, dismasted and two hours later – sixty miles to the north-west – Franco–Swiss skipper Bernard Stamm activated his distress beacon when the keel detached from his 60ft monohull *Cheminees Poujoulat-Armor Lux*, 360 miles west of St. Johns, Newfoundland. All three yachts and skippers involved in the mid-Atlantic catastrophe survived: Stamm was rescued from his upturned hull by the crew of a small tanker and later salvaged his yacht with an ocean-going tug based in Newfoundland, while Riou, Dick and their yachts were towed back to France.

High drama continued as yachts approached the American coast. Thick fog, fishing vessels, icebergs and drilling platforms in the Flemish Cap and Grand Banks areas off Newfoundland proved a hazard for the fleet. The most dramatic incident occurred on *Sodebo*, the ORMA 60 trimaran skippered by Thomas Coville. Travelling at 22–23 knots in a wind building to 35 knots, Coville was preparing to take in his third reef when the boat collided with something. Winching in the reef and facing aft to protect himself from constant spray, Coville was catapulted across the cockpit and knocked unconscious. The French skipper called the race organization after regaining consciousness: "I do not know how long I was unconscious for. It might have been seconds or a few minutes.

above *Thomas Coville was knocked unconscious on* Sodebo *during the single-handed Transat 2004 when a whale became wedged between the daggerboard and rudder of the 60ft trimaran's starboard float. Collisions with whales and debris cause a dramatic number of retirements in offshore racing. Coville recovered to take second place in the ORMA multihull class.*

opposite *The ORMA 60 fleet start The Transat 2004 heavily reefed due to the squalls and boat-breaking seas off Plymouth. After the first night of racing, Michel Desjoyeaux on trimaran,* Géant, *declared: "I'm too old to take all these waves". Nonetheless, Desjoyeaux led the multihull fleet through the North Atlantic, taking line honours in Boston.*

Every wave made me cringe as the ear-splitting sound of carbon slamming against the ocean was taking its toll.

Conrad Humphreys, skipper of *Hellomoto*, feels the effects of a mid-Atlantic depression during The Transat 2004

I couldn't see or hear anything. Then there was a sound and a sharp pain in my temple, which made me look around. I could see the boat was in good shape and the mast too. I stood up and touched my head... thankfully I had been wearing my survival suit and its neoprene hood protected me."

Having confirmed that he was uninjured, Coville wanted to investigate the condition of *Sodebo* and discover what had caused the impact: "The boat had stopped... or nearly. I took a light to check the daggerboard... for me the race seemed over. In the fluorescent part of the water I could see a large white object around the daggerboard. I dropped the mainsail and the jib and lifted the daggerboard beyond its normal limit with a halyard. As I did this, I felt the boat break free and we were off again." Trapping a whale – if it was a whale – between the daggerboard and rudder failed to stop Coville continuing the race and finishing in 2nd place, just two hours behind winner Michel Desjoyeaux on *Géant*.

Racing was equally close at the head of the IMOCA 60 monohull fleet. Hampered by the failure of his canting keel's hydraulic motor within hours of the start, Mike Golding on *Ecover* finished 1st, beating Swiss skipper Dominique Wavre on *Temenos* in 2nd, and New Zealand's Mike Sanderson on *Pindar Alphagraphics* in 3rd. The trio had stayed within thirty miles of each other for the final 1,400 miles of racing.

Route du Rhum

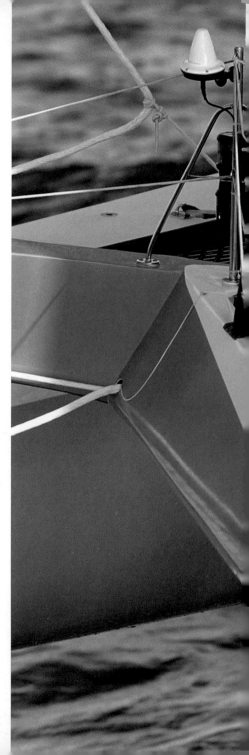

Covering 3,600 miles from the French port of St Malo to Point-à-Pitre, Guadeloupe, in the eastern Caribbean and raced by monohulls and multihulls, the Route du Rhum is arguably the toughest, most demanding single-handed transatlantic event. Held every four years since the inaugural race in 1978 and originally created to challenge the British-run OSTAR, the 'Rhum' attracts solo sailing's elite and produces extraordinary levels of competition between participants. The race has also yielded two outstanding female victories in what is a male-dominated area of offshore sailing. French yachtswoman, Florence Arthaud, won the 1990 edition of the race and Britain's Ellen MacArthur took line honours in 2002, becoming the first monohull sailor to beat the Route du Rhum's multihull fleet.

The 2002 Route du Rhum will always be remembered for the catastrophic disaster rate in the ORMA 60 fleet as fifteen of the original eighteen multihulls entered in the race either capsized or suffered damage that forced retirement. Although none of the skippers were lost overboard, the 2002 edition of the race illustrated that pushing a trimaran hard on the limit of control is highly dangerous. Only the skill of the sailors involved and the strength of their boats averted tragedy. Starting a Northern Hemisphere race in the stormy conditions usually experienced in November adds to the risks involved. Consequently, the 2006 Route du Rhum is scheduled to start in October.

A timeline of the 2002 Route du Rhum's multihull victor, Michel Desjoyeaux of France, demonstrates why 'Le Professeur' is possibly the world's ultimate solo sailor:

November 10: Eighteen 60ft trimarans cross the start line off St Malo.

November 11: Desjoyeaux makes a three-hour pit stop in a bay outside Brest harbour to rectify autopilot problems on *Géant* and repair broken mainsail battens.

November 12: To avoid a deep depression, Desjoyeaux heads west to keep above the weather system. While many in the trimaran fleet suffer 80 knots of wind, *Géant* records wind speeds of 40–45 knots.

November 13: Desjoyeaux sails through a second depression under bare poles (no sails).

November 15: On hearing reports that two trimarans similar to *Géant* have suffered wave impact damage to the forward beams connecting their hulls, Desjoyeaux rendezvous with this shore team on the island of Porto Santo, north-east of Madeira. After a 15-hour stop over for repairs, the multihull leaves port and continues racing.

November 19: Leading the remaining four trimarans, Steve Ravussin capsizes *Technomarine* and Desjoyeaux takes pole position. The French skipper remarks: "I have been parachuted into the lead by the misfortune of others. This is maybe not ideal."

November 23: *Géant* crosses the finish line after 13 days and 8 hours' racing. Desjoyeaux completed the race at an average speed of 14.2 knots.

Sailing a monohull single-handed, you are racing. Sailing a trimaran single-handed, you are risking your life.

Loïck Peyron,
solo trimaran skipper

left *British skipper Sam Davies, on the 32ft Figaro Beneteau* Skandia, *was one of only three women competing in a fleet of 46 boats during the 2005 Solitaire Afflelou Le Figaro. Raced in identical yachts, The Figaro is a demanding mix of inshore and offshore solo sailing with stop over ports in France, Spain and Ireland. Close racing and constant sail trimming causes extreme levels of sleep deprivation among skippers.*

previous page *Michel Desjoyeaux crosses the single-handed transatlantic 2002 Route du Rhum finish line off Guadeloupe on ORMA 60 trimaran,* Géant. *The protective screen around the helming pod provides vital protection from spray constantly flying aft through the trampoline netting strung between the yacht's hull and floats. Desjoyeaux's multihull victory in the 2002 Route du Rhum and his earlier monohull win in the 2000–01 Vendée Globe were followed by trimaran triumph in the 2004 Transat as "Le Professeur" claimed the laurels for solo sailing's 'big three'.*

below *French skipper Jérémie Beyou won the final leg of the Solitaire Afflelou Le Figaro on* Delta Dore *sailing from Cork in southern Ireland to Port Bourgenay, France. Beyou took 51 hours to sail 496 miles alone across some of the busiest shipping lanes in the world. This victory clinched an overall win for the 1,460-mile race.*

The annual Figaro season of offshore solo races is a proving ground for aspiring single-handed sailors. The race series provides a balance between inshore and offshore racing and has been dominated by French solo sailors since the inaugural race in 1970. A list of Figaro victors reveals the pedigree of sailing talent required to win this race: Christophe Augin (1986), Laurent Bourgnon (1988), Jean Le Cam (1994, 1996 and 1999), Alain Gautier (1989) and Michel Desjoyeaux (1992 and 1998).

The 2005 edition of the race involved four separate legs raced between ports in France, Spain and Ireland covering just less than 1,500 miles at sea. Racing identical 32ft yachts, the skippers are forbidden satellite communication systems and must rely on weather information from faxes and radio broadcasts. The communications ban includes satellite phones and competitors can only converse via VHF. The Figaro is raced through the busiest commercial shipping lanes in the world along the Bay of Biscay and across the English Channel: this feature adds to the sleep deprivation experienced by skippers already racing hard and close in a tightly packed fleet.

99

inset left *French skipper, Sebastien Gladu, prepares supper on Transat 6.50, Armor Lux. In addition to 100 litres of water and 35 kilos of food, the cramped interior must serve as storage for the yacht's sails, a liferaft, medical supplies, spare parts and the small amount of electronics carried onboard a Mini Transat yacht. A bucket serves as both bathroom and washroom.*

Mini Transat

The Transat 6.50 is the smallest boat in the 'Open' class with a reputation for radical, fast designs demanding endurance and nerves of steel from their skippers. The class was an English innovation as a cheap alternative to the single-handed OSTAR race where bigger boats required budgets and sponsorship deals unavailable to solo sailors trying to break into the sport. Today, the Mini Transat racing circuit is a predominantly French event, although well funded projects from outside France are re-establishing a foothold within the class.

The Mini fleet is divided into two sub-sections; 'protos' (custom-built boats) and 'series' (production models), but both the categories are very similar in size. During the longest race in the Mini calendar, skippers will spend around twenty-eight days in the Atlantic on a boat that is no bigger than an inshore dinghy. The conditions on board are minimalist and cramped in a racing machine that is designed for speed, with no concessions for comfort. The sail area on a Mini is out of proportion with the boat's size: the mast is a little under twice the length of the hull and a three-metre bowsprit almost doubles the length of the boat, enabling a sail area of around 100 square metres. Recent designs incorporate a bowsprit that swivels around a fitting on the yacht's stem, allowing the spar to be swung out from the boat like a switchblade. Wisely, the class organisation has forbidden their use on the start line and the long poles must be stowed inboard to prevent any carnage in the early stages of a race.

Mini Transat boats are an example of high technology applied to the purest form of solo sailing. While the class is seen as a testing ground for new designs, the skippers are allowed only a few relatively low-tech gadgets onboard. An autopilot is obviously a fundamental requirement and this self-steering system is powered by solar panels. These vital screens are usually mounted on brackets over the stern to limit the risk of damage and reduce any potential power loss through shadows cast by the sails. The yachts are allowed GPS to aid navigation, but Internet communication is forbidden. Although weather information can be received by long-range SSB radio, the skippers are not permitted to transmit on this equipment and all voice communication is limited to short-range VHF radio. This ocean racing communications blackout is unique to the Mini class and skippers on bigger, 40–60ft 'Open' boats can maintain contact with family and shore teams via satellite phones and email. After a transatlantic Mini race, it is difficult to stop the skippers from talking once they have crossed the finish line and post-race press conferences are often the liveliest in the sport.

above *It takes approximately four paces to walk from bow to stern on a Transat 6.50. For four weeks during the Mini Transat race from La Rochelle, France, to Salvador de Bahia in Brazil, this dinghy-sized, offshore rocket is home. The skippers are only allowed to transmit on short-range VHF radio, and apart from a brief stop over at Lanzarote in the Canary Islands, contact with the outside world is minimal.*

7

Solo
Round
The
World
Races

- THE VENDÉE GLOBE

- VELUX 5 OCEANS RACE

The Vendée Globe

The concept of the Vendée Globe is simple: sail around the world alone, non-stop, without any outside assistance. In reality, the race is arguably the toughest sporting challenge known to man. Held every four years, the event is based in the town of Les Sables d'Olonne on the Bay of Biscay in the Vendée region of France and attracts the world's solo sailing elite.

After the 2000–01 edition of the Vendée Globe, entry was limited to Open 60 yachts: high-tech, super-light, carbon fibre racing machines using the latest developments in boat design and manufacture. Sailing skill and owning a fast, new yacht are not enough to successfully complete this race: impeccable boat preparation, self-motivation, endurance and courage are required to survive the hostile environment of the Southern Ocean and the relentless racing pace of the 23,000-mile circumnavigation.

A key feature of the Vendée Globe is the rule forbidding outside assistance. This removes the opportunity for a competitor to receive aid or materials from a third party, effectively preventing a skipper from docking alongside a quay or another vessel and obtaining spare parts dropped from ships or aircraft. For this reason, a skipper must be talented in all aspects of boat management. Being an accomplished sailor, navigator and meteorologist is insufficient – a skipper must possess the ability to operate as boatbuilder, plumber, electrician, rigger and sailmaker.

Every edition of the race is rich with stories of extraordinary willpower, but the dogged determination to nurse a damaged yacht around the world is typified by French yachtsman, Jean-Pierre Dick in 2004–05:

Just eleven days into the race, his yacht, *Virbac-Paprec*, developed problems with the vital gooseneck fitting connecting the boom to the mast. The following day, J-P Dick was forced to dive under the boat and remove a long length of line and debris from around the yacht's keel. Then, shortly after crossing the Equator, a lashing on the gennaker tack failed. As the huge headsail thrashed around in strong winds, it ripped the stainless steel pulpit from the foredeck leaving large holes and a vital repair project for the skipper. Heading into the Indian Ocean, the engine failed leaving Dick unable to charge the batteries and run the vital electronic systems and autopilot. Deciding to rely on solar panels for electricity, the skipper chose to continue racing with the prospect of hand steering for six or seven hours at a time. Running under reduced power, the autopilot became unable to steer in heavy conditions and the boat broached, burying her boom underwater and breaking the gooseneck fitting. After sixty-one days at sea, the yacht's boom broke in the depths of the Southern Ocean, 1,200 miles west of Cape Horn. Dick made temporary repairs and rounded the world's southernmost cape six days later. In the South Atlantic he completed the boom repairs and made a final dive below the boat to remove a huge bed of kelp wrapped around the keel before finishing the race in 6th place after ninety-eight days at sea.

previous page *American skipper Brad van Liew won every leg of the 2002–03 Around Alone for Class II on Open 50,* Tommy Hilfiger-Freedom America. *Pictured off Tauranga, New Zealand, van Liew deploys his asymmetric spinnaker: on many solo sailing yachts the spinnaker is hauled up the mast in a 'sock' that is then lifted allowing the sail to fill. The spinnaker can be quickly 'snuffed' by pulling the sock downwards over the sail… in theory.*

opposite *Michel Desjoyeaux won the 2000–01 Vendée Globe taking 90 days to race Open 60,* PRB, *around the planet. After crossing the finishing line, "Le Professeur" reflected on the race: "This single-handed trip around the world is an incredible page in your life history: it adds years to your age, it makes you more mature and throws things into perspective."*

next page left *Engine failure on board Jean-Pierre Dick's Open 60,* Virbac, *in the Indian Ocean left the French skipper with no method of charging his batteries to run the yacht's electrical systems. Dick chose to continue racing using the power generated by solar panels to run the vital autopilot. Sailing with a dramatically reduced power supply, Dick was forced to hand steer for 6–7 hours at a time for over half the 2004–05 Vendée Globe circumnavigation.*

One cannot come home from a Vendée Globe without bearing any marks. Several months will undoubtedly be necessary for me to come back to my normal life ashore. The Deep South let me through this time. The real enemy in this voyage is firstly the sea itself.

Christophe Auguin, French winner of the 1996–97 Vendée Globe

The good thing about spending New Year's Eve in the middle of the ocean is that the cops can't chuck me in jail

Australian skipper, Nick Moloney, prepares for celebrations on
Open 60 Skandia during the 2004–05 Vendée Globe

opposite *Ellen MacArthur shot into the global limelight after finishing 2nd in the 2000–01 Vendée Globe, crossing the finish line off Les Sables d'Olonne, France, 24 hours after race winner, Michel Desjoyeaux. Her achievement stunned the offshore racing community and merited one of the highest accolades in solo sailing – a nickname – 'La Petite Anglaise'.*

Since the first edition of the Vendée Globe in 1989–90, the event has been filled with drama and extraordinary examples of seamanship. In 1992, the first Briton to enter the race, Nigel Burgess, was found drowned off Cape Finisterre just four days after the start when gales forced many skippers to return to Les Sables d'Olonne with damaged boats. During the 1996–97 race, Raphaël Dinelli was plucked from his liferaft by British sailor Pete Goss after the Frenchman's yacht, *Algimouss*, capsized in the Southern Ocean. In the same patch of ocean, Thierry Dubois from France and English yachtsman Tony Bullimore were pulled from their stricken yachts by the Australian Navy. Another Vendée tragedy of the same year was the loss of Gerry Roufs whose yacht, *Groupe LG*, was found drifting upside down off the coast of Chile, South America, six months after the race organization lost contact with the Canadian sailor.

The following race in 2000–01 produced extreme levels of ingenuity as Yves Parlier single-handedly repaired the broken mast of 60ft Aquitaine *Innovations* while anchored off a Pacific island before continuing to race halfway round the world. Disaster struck Catherine Chabaud late in the same race when *Whirlpool* dismasted as the French yachtswoman approached the continent. In the same year, a young English entrant, Ellen MacArthur, astonished the solo sailing community by finishing in 2nd place.

The recent Vendée Globe in 2004–05 yielded the fastest and most exciting edition of the event as yachts sped round the world breaking all previous race records. Although additional Southern Ocean waypoints were introduced for this edition of the race to keep the fleet north of the predicted ice limit, the yachts flew through a barrier of icebergs and fog between New Zealand and Antarctica at the 'halfway' point in the circumnavigation. The intense competition throughout the fleet and between the leading three boats in particular forced the skippers to push themselves and their yachts to the limit for the entire length of the Pacific and Atlantic Oceans, driving the battered boats hard until the finish line.

above *After 28 days at sea, Open 60, Hellomoto, broke the tip of her starboard rudder on floating debris after a high speed collision in the South Atlantic during the 2004–05 Vendée Globe. Her skipper, Conrad Humphreys, nursed the yacht to a mooring off Simonstown in False Bay near the Cape of Good Hope, South Africa. Without infringing race rules governing assistance by a third party, the British skipper single-handedly replaced the damaged rudder with a spare carried onboard and continued racing.*

previous page right *When Mike Golding rounded the Cape of Good Hope, he was 800 miles behind the lead yacht in the 2004–05 Vendée Globe. Thirty-one days later, after 10,000 miles of Southern Ocean racing, the British skipper had reduced this deficit to 113 miles as* Ecover *rounded Cape Horn. Golding modestly commented: "The boat's the star of the show." A further 7,000 miles later, the keel dropped off the bottom of Golding's yacht within sight of the finish line: he managed to sail the remaining 50 miles taking third place and becoming the first yachtsman to finish an offshore race without a keel.*

Velux 5 Oceans Race

Raced in customized Open 60 and 50 yachts, the single-handed 2006 Velux 5 Oceans race is descended from the 1982–83 BOC (British Oxygen Corporation) Challenge and pre-dates the Vendée Globe by seven years. The race also includes a number of stop-overs – usually three or four – and the yachtsmen are allowed to seek outside assistance and pull into port, although this incurs a time penalty. Many solo sailors believe that the Velux 5 Oceans (ex-BOC Challenge, ex-Around Alone Race) pushes boats harder than in the Vendée Globe as the skippers are able to rely on shore teams patching the yachts back together after they have been thrashed across the oceans.

Certainly, yachts take a beating in the race and the opportunity to seek assistance offshore during the 30,000-mile circumnavigation is often invaluable. In the 2002–03 Around Alone Race, the 60ft yacht *Hexagon* broke her boom in a Pacific Ocean gale and her New Zealand skipper, Graham Dalton, arranged to rendezvous with his shore crew off the coast of Tierra del Fuego, just north-east of Cape Horn. His team repaired the damage and Dalton continued racing although he dismasted a few days later off the coast of Patagonia. During the same race, two yachts diverted to Port Stanley in the Falkland Islands for repair work and one yacht motored into the port of Ushuaia in Argentina having dismasted off Cape Horn.

Although the winner of the first BOC Challenge, Philippe Jeantot, went on to found the non-stop Vendée Globe in a quest for the ultimate solo sailing experience, the 1982–83 race gave a clear, early warning of the dangers inherent in offshore solo sailing. An incident on Leg 3 between Sidney and Rio de Janeiro proved to be a template for a very similar disaster in the Vendée Globe fourteen years later.

In huge following seas the 41ft (12.5m) yacht, *Skoiern III*, pitch-poled violently, burying her bow and instantly dismasting. The yacht's foredeck hatch was ripped from its hinges and icy water poured into the boat at such a rate that the pressure change popped the ears of her French skipper, Jacques de Roux. Bleeding and semi-concussed, the former submariner grabbed his yellow Argos distress transponder, moved the large emergency button to 'transmit' and started pumping water out of the boat.

Pitch-poling a yacht and dismasting is catastrophic when sailing close inshore, but the forward somersault performed by *Skoiern III* took place in the most desolate area of the Pacific Ocean. The French yachtsman was sinking 2,400 miles east of the southern tip of South Island, New Zealand, and 2,200 miles west of Cape Horn. The nearest speck of land was Pitcairn Island, 1,800 miles due north. Two hours after De Roux activated his distress beacon, its signal reached the Argos

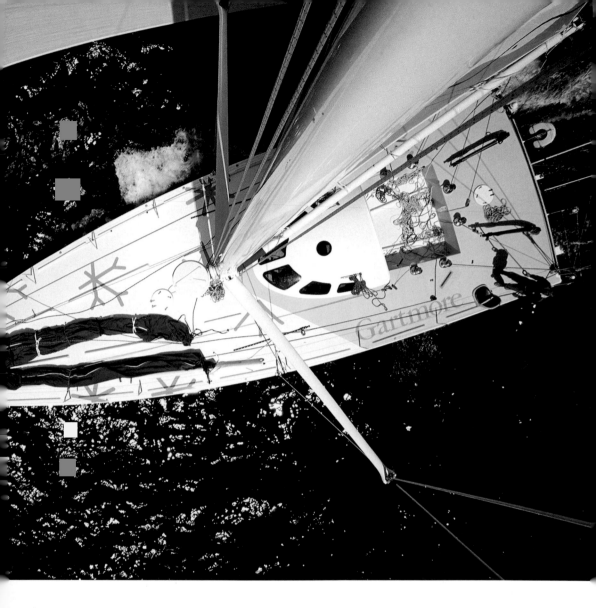

above *Josh Hall and Open 60* Gartmore *during the single-handed, 1998–99 Around Alone (formerly the 'BOC Challenge' and now the 'Velux 5 Oceans Race'). Stop-over ports during the circumnavigation allow skippers to push their boats hard across the Atlantic, Indian, Pacific and Southern Ocean in the knowledge that a professional shore crew will repair any damage. Sometimes, the boats are pushed too hard: Hall lost his 82ft mast on Leg 3 and diverted to the Chatham Islands, 420 miles due east of Christchurch, New Zealand.*

decoding station in Toulouse, France, and a network of ham radio enthusiasts immediately began the task of contacting the BOC yachts closest to *Skoiern III*. With the nearest commercial shipping lane thousands of miles to the north, it was clear that any rescue attempt would have to be undertaken by fellow competitors. After twelve hours of constant calling, a radio ham reached 52ft (15.65m) *Perseverance of Medina*, skippered by British yachtsman, Richard Broadhead, positioned approximately 300 miles east of *Skoiern III*. Broadhead turned his yacht around and headed into the wind and huge seas, making only 5 knots of boat speed and hampered by thick fog.

Forty-seven hours after being alerted, Broadhead arrived at the Argos position of *Skoiern III*, but there was no sign of the yacht. Could De Roux have survived for three days? The British skipper went below to radio for a position check, unaware that the dismasted yacht was only 50 yards away, hidden behind a tall swell rolling down from the west. De Roux, however, had spotted *Perseverance* and leapt about on deck shouting and waving his arms and let off seven flares to attract Broadhead's attention although his rescuer was already below decks concentrating on his radio set. Hours later, Broadhead reappeared from below and his eyes were caught by a white flash two miles away: a

above left *Thierry Dubois, displays complete faith in his autopilot as he charges into Salvador de Bahia, Brazil, on* Solidaire *at the finish of Leg 4 during the 2002–03 Around Alone. Light winds and slow progress frustrated Dubois as he approached the Brazilian coastline and the French skipper set fire to a stuffed toy of a kiwi – a souvenir from the New Zealand stop over – in a desperate sacrifice to the wind gods. The race organisation became alarmed when Dubois threatened to shoot himself unless the wind increased: fortunately,* Solidaire *carries no firearms.*

above right *Franco-Swiss skipper, Bernard Stamm, took Class 1 (60ft) line honours on every leg of the 2002–03 Around Alone and consistently sailed* Bobst Group-Armor Lux *with the throttle wide open, whatever the sea conditions. Stamm arrived in New Zealand at the finish of Leg 3 with a six-foot section of carbon fibre peeling from the starboard side of his hull after crossing the Indian Ocean. On the following leg to Brazil, he was forced to make a swift pit stop at Port Stanley in the Falkland Islands to repair damage to the yacht's keel after rounding Cape Horn.*

scrap of sail on the French yacht's stump of a mast. In building seas the transfer was difficult and the two yachts collided a number of times before De Roux leapt from the deck of *Skoiern III* as Broadhead made his fourth pass, mistiming the jump but managing to grab the guardrails as *Perseverance* rolled away from the sinking yacht. Broadhead describes the scene:

"He was absolutely knackered. He just hung there by his armpits over the top of the lifelines and if the two boats had come together again, he would have lost his legs."

Four hours after the rescue, De Roux's Argos beacon ceased sending a signal: *Skoiern III* had sunk in 4,000 metres of freezing water. Three days later, *Perseverance* made a mid-ocean rendezvous with a French Navy ship and De Roux was transferred aboard in exchange for a hamper of food and a plentiful supply of wine.

8

For The Record

- HOW TO BREAK
A SAILING RECORD

- FROM A TO B AND BEYOND

- THE JULES VERNE TROPHY

- THE FASTEST WOMAN
ON THE PLANET

How to break a sailing record

The diversity within sailing provides the World Sailing Speed Record Council (WSSRC) with a complex task. Record attempts are sub-divided by three main factors: 1) the type of yacht, 2) the number of crew, 3) the distance covered.

1 The enormous variety of yachts attempting to break records produces a long menu of options: IMS (International Measurement System), IOR (International Offshore Rule), ULDB (Ultra Light Displacement Yachts), trimarans, catamarans, monohulls, etc. A separate division is provided for "a vessel with powered sailing sytems": hydraulic or electrical winches and halyards or other mechanical systems that will assist in sailing a yacht. However, the highest speeds on the water have been recorded by windsurfers, and this sector of sailing demands a unique set of rules.

2 The number, sex and nature of the crew sailing a yacht allows multiple records for a similar discipline or route. Fully crewed, single-handed and 'single-handed by a disabled sailor' records exist for circumnavigation speed attempts and this is reproduced in passage records (between two locations) and inshore sailing.

3 Seventy per cent of the Earth's surface is covered by water supplying a limitless range of locations for sailing record attempts. The WSSRC's guidelines for a speed record state that any attempt should be between "fixed points of land, fixed navigational beacons or other charted objects fixed to the land or seabed". Exceptions are made for 'straight-line', windsurfing speed records held over a 500-metre course or over one nautical mile (1,852 metres) and offshore, mid-ocean, 24-hour run records, which are recorded by GPS.

previous page *In 1909, the pioneering aviator, Louis Blériot, flew across the Channel in 37 minutes: Alain Thébault and crew set out to beat this record in February 2005 on the radical hydrofoil,* L'Hydroptère. *Averaging 33.3 knots, the team took three minutes off Blériot's time between Dover and Calais.*

below *In 2005, yachtswoman, Hilary Lister, became the first quadriplegic sailor to cross the English Channel single-handed. Using the 'sip and puff' method, Lister helmed her 26ft Soling,* Malin, *by blowing onto an instrument panel through a rubber hose, crossing from Dover to Calais in 6 hours and 13 minutes. Although the boat had been specially adapted for Lister, she experienced such discomfort that a supply of painkillers was attached to her right shoulder within reach of her lips.*

above *Described as a "classy creation" by her skipper, Bruno Peyron, catamaran* Orange II *broke the Jules Verne Trophy record for a fully crewed circumnavigation in 2005 when she sailed round the world in 50 days 16 hours 20 minutes 4 seconds.*

From A to B and beyond

A few examples of the less well-known sailing records illustrate the range responsibility held by the WSSRC:

Oldest single-handed transatlantic crossing:
Stefan Szwarnowski (GBR) aged 77 years on *Tawny Pipit* in 1989. 72 days

Longest series of non-stop circumnavigations:
Jon Saunders (AUS) on *Perry Endeavour* in 1986–88. Three circumnavigations, 1 westabout, 2 eastabout. 657 days

Fastest sailing speed over one nautical mile:
Bjorn Dunkerbek on a windsurfer in 2004. 34.44 knots

First disabled, single-handed circumnavigation:
Vincent Lauwers (AUS) on *Vision Quest* in 2000. 233 days

The Gold Race (New York – San Francisco, via Cape Horn):
Yves Parlier (FRA) and crew on *Aquitaine Innovations* in 1998. 57 days

Melbourne – Osaka (two-handed):
Grant Wharington and Scot Gilbert (AUS) on *Wild Thing* in 1995. 26 days

Montego Bay, Jamaica – Lizard Point, Cornwall:
Tony Bullimore (GBR) and Fedor Konyukhov (RUS) with nine crew, on *Scarlet Sails* in 2003. 16 days

The Jules Verne Trophy

The Jules Verne Trophy is named after the French writer and author of *Around The World In 80 Days*: a story charting the circumnavigation adventures of the fictional character, Phileas Fogg. The event is open to any size of yacht, has no limitation on crew numbers and involves sailing non-stop, around the planet, starting and finishing on a line stretching between Lizard Point and the French island of Ushant at the western entrance to the English Channel. To date, the Jules Verne has been attempted by huge multihulls capable of maintaining high speeds for extended periods.

opposite *Gale force winds lashed catamaran, ENZA, in the final miles of her Jules Verne Trophy circumnavigation. Sir Robin Knox-Johnston, Sir Peter Blake and crew sailed around the world in just under 75 days.*

below *American aviator, balloonist and serial record breaker, Steve Fossett and his crew, smashed the transatlantic sailing record on 125ft (38.1m) Cheyenne in 2001.*

Jules Verne Trophy holders:

1993–94
Bruno Peyron (FRA)
Explorer (catamaran)
79 days

1994–95
Robin Knox-Johnston (GBR) and Peter Blake (NZ)
Enza (catamaran)
74 days

1997
Olivier de Kersauson (FRA)
Sport Elec (trimaran)
71 days

2002
Bruno Peyron
Orange (catamaran)
64 days

2004*
Olivier de Kersauson
Geronimo (trimaran)
63 days

2005
Bruno Peyron
Orange II (catamaran)
50 days

*Round-the-world racing was hit by controversy in 2004–05 when American yachtsman, Steve Fosset, sailed the route of the Jules Verne in 58 days on *Cheyenne*. Fosset chose not to pay the 30,000 euros entry fee required for a Jules Verne Trophy challenge and his record attempt was not recognized, although the WSSRC ratified his circumnavigation as a world record.

The fastest women on the planet

On 7 February 2005, British yachtswoman, Ellen MacArthur, sailed her 22.9-metre trimaran, *B&Q*, across the finish line between Lizard and Ushant completing a non-stop, solo circumnavigation in 71 days 14 hours 18 minutes 33 seconds to become the fastest person to sail alone around the world. MacArthur's entire voyage was paced against the previous record holder, Francis Joyon, who had set an exceptional time on a larger and far older trimaran, *IDEC*. When the legendary French yachtsman smashed the existing solo circumnavigation time by 21 days, many considered that the record would remain unbreakable for years to come.

The achievements of both Joyon and MacArthur are outstanding, but the two attempts were approached with very different methods. Joyon's record attempt was undertaken with a minimal budget on a yacht designed for fully crewed racing: a yacht that had already circumnavigated the world as Olivier de Kersauson's *Sport Elec* during a Jules Verne Trophy attempt seven years earlier (Joyon also used de Kersauson's ancient mainsail). MacArthur's immaculately managed and fully funded campaign was launched with a new, state of the art trimaran bristling with technology. The methods of communication also differed widely between these two skippers. After finishing his round the world trip, Francis Joyon became agitated by clamouring media attention and the throng of journalists crowding round *IDEC* on the pontoons in France and commented wearily: "A boat is a way of seeing and experiencing the oceans, NOT a method of communication." Conversely, Ellen MacArthur is supremely skilled in engaging armchair sailors and conveying the thrills, terror and hardship of circumnavigating the globe single-handed and recording the extraordinary power and beauty of the sea.

> I often thought about Ellen when she was in some difficult patches with winds and squalls violently pouring down on the boat

Francis Joyon, shortly after Ellen MacArthur beat his solo circumnavigation record

A selection of Ellen MacArthur's comments from her record breaking solo circumnavigation:

"Everything is flying around the cabin - I have to hold on to something the whole time to stop being flung across the boat... I've had my head smashed against the hull a few times by the violent motion."
Encountering 30-knot winds in the South Atlantic after 15 days at sea

"It's like sailing over mountains... it's like driving an all-terrain vehicle very fast over mountains."
At 43° South, shortly after rounding the Cape of Good Hope and entering the Indian Ocean

"The beauty of those immense, rolling waves is endless and there is a kind of eternal feeling about their majestic rolling that will live on forever."

Heading further south after 23 days at sea

"To be surfing at 25-28 knots in that amount of breeze in those waves, to be handling as well as she did - I was just absolutely over the moon with her performance... it was fantastic."
Passing north of the Crozet Islands 20 hours ahead of Joyon's record

"I've been stressed all night - so stressed. I've got a cracking headache, hardly had any sleep and I've been so stressed my tongue's come out in ulcers."
Christmas Day in 35–45 knots

"There are birds around me - that's always a sign of an iceberg. There's thick fog; I can't see more than a few boat lengths in front of me. This is pretty scary..."
New Year's Eve after 34 days alone at sea, 670 miles south-west of New Zealand

"I dragged myself off the floor where I was huddled in my oilskins under a fleece blanket and looked to the sky to see yet another demon black cloud."
After 40 days at sea, preparing for a monstrous storm west of Cape Horn

"It is going to hit us. We can't get away from this one..."

Christmas Eve in the Southern Ocean as a massive low-pressure system hurtles towards the trimaran

"We're still 10,000 miles from home. We're in a boat that's getting tired, a skipper that's getting tired – mentally and emotionally zonked."
Approaching a dangerous level of fatigue after foul weather in the Southern Ocean

"I've put everything in – my heart, my soul, my flesh, my blood, just everything. I've never pushed this hard."

MacArthur slips 10 hours behind Joyon's record as wind speeds drop to below 4 knots in the South Atlantic

"Main halyard is creaking, everything is groaning, runners are stretching and there's nothing I can do. I've tried slowing down, I've tried speeding up... I've tried everything, but the fact is we've got mountains heading towards us. This God-damned low that's been sat on our nose."
Headwinds slow progress on day 49 north-east of the Falkland Islands in the South Atlantic

"I feel like I've been beaten up this morning... stiff as hell and moving around with the speed and elegance of an arthritic robot."
Having completed two mast climbs to repair damage after 22,000 miles of sailing

"We're getting a bit closer everyday, bit by bit. As long as the wind keeps blowing we'll make it home one way or the other... as long as we don't do anything stupid."
Passing the Cape Verde Islands in the North Atlantic and pulling back a two-day lead over Francis Joyon's record

"I cannot articulate how I feel, I doubt I shall ever be able to express what this trip has put me through, or continues to put me through."
On the 69th day at sea, light winds west of Spain hinder progress and threaten the record attempt as B&Q nears the finish line

"We had a few really big waves in the night – I was virtually thrown out of the bunk by one that broke right over the boat filled the cockpit... It was good I had the door shut."

The final night at sea approaching the finishing line of Ushant. Ellen MacArthur beats Francis Joyon's record by 1 day and 8 hours.

"Going to be lucky to come through this without breaking something or capsizing, to be frank, because it's already really rough and it's going to get really, really rough. The waves are going to be absolutely huge and we're going to be going straight across them which is the worst thing you could possibly do. I'm really worried."
Rounds Cape Finisterre heading into the Bay of Biscay with the prospect of Force 8–9 winds

9

Extreme
Cruising

Swinging the lantern

Offer to show a friend or colleague photographs of a recent cruising holiday and the reaction can be short-term indulgence or a brief period of tolerance. Like wedding pictures, snaps of a cruising holiday can be formulaic: the crew drinking cocktails in the cockpit, children playing in the yacht's dinghy, golden sand fringing a clear-water lagoon, the boat heeling over under sail with the owner helming, etc. It is very difficult to convey the thrill of cruising on a yacht through photographs alone. How can a picture transmit the sense of adventure and freedom gained when sailing a yacht, the feeling of independence and mobility or the friendships made while at sea or in port? For this reason, cruising's verbal tradition and the ability to discuss sailing and boats in extraordinary detail for prolonged periods is an integral component of the sport: a skill known as "swinging the lantern".

All successful yachtsmen – both racing and cruising – must be proficient in the telling of yarns: a talent that can be studied and learnt in pubs, bars and yacht clubs at every sailing destination on the planet. The ability to entertain fellow yachtsmen or impressionable cruising novices with sailing tales is vital, but a sailor should also be confident in contributing to any conversation on navigation, boat handling, yacht maintenance, local customs and the global price of spare or replacement parts. Wander along a marina pontoon anywhere in the world and the sound of cruising yachtsmen swapping stories accompanies the 'clink' of loose halyards slapping against aluminium masts.

Heaven protects children, sailors and drunken men

Mid-19th century proverb

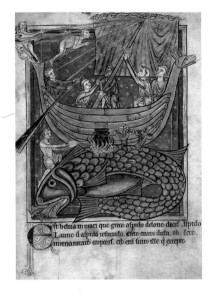

previous page *Eric Tabarly's yacht,* Côte d'Or, *in 1987 sailing past two 'pinnacle' bergs 10 miles south of Newfoundland.*

above *Modern history's most committed cruising yachtsman, St Brendan of Ardfert. The Irish monk and his crew sailed around the North Atlantic during the 6th century searching for the 'Land of Delight'. Unlike St Brendan, modern yachtsmen are unlikely to encounter man-eating fish, gryphons, fire breathing dragons, raving hermits, talking birds and "various monsters of the deep".*

opposite top *The Lemaire Channel between Booth Island and the mainland Antarctic Peninsular is aptly named 'Kodak Valley'.*

opposite bottom *Steel-hulled yacht* Seal *has a close encounter with an iceberg in Greenland's Nuuk fjord system. A majority of the North Atlantic's bergs originate from 100 glaciers along the country's western coast.*

The do's and don'ts of cruising

For the novice sailor, stepping into the alien environment of a cruising yacht can be a tense experience. The observant beginner will quickly appreciate that going sailing involves a range of equipment that is not normally encountered on dry land. It soon becomes apparent, also, that sliding gracefully through crystal clear waters demands considerable co-ordination, a comprehensive knowledge of the sea and a degree of advanced planning: an understanding of these features will enhance the enjoyment of cruising. Every cruising yacht operates under a different regime, but in most cases the skipper wields supreme authority on board: a sailing yacht is not a true democracy. If the owner or skipper is of the variety who enjoys humorous plaques, a small sign screwed in a visible position on the boat declaring that "The Skipper is Always Right" (or similar) will inform all crew as to the nature of command on the forthcoming cruise.

On many boats the crew will be given a briefing before departure and this may often answer important questions or concerns for the novice cruiser. It is impossible to investigate all aspects of sailing or cruising in an informal, pre-sail chat, but the basics on safety, the route, a destination (if any) and the weather that is likely to be encountered are significant factors. Further information can be acquired by talking with experienced members of the crew without distracting the yacht's skipper who will usually be absorbed in running the boat. Very large books have been filled with advice and instructions on cruising, but a few fundamental guidelines can prove invaluable for the beginner on his first outing:

Boarding a yacht:

Footwear is crucial in making a favourable first impression. **Don't** wear hard-bottomed shoes or black soles as both can leave easily traceable tracks on teak or fibreglass decks. **Do** check the soles of your shoes for chewing gum and other street grime. On many boats, a basket or box will be located on deck: this is not evidence of a ship's cat, but indicates that shoes should be removed.

If the boat is 'rafted' in a marina and it becomes necessary to cross another yacht to reach your cruiser, it is customary to walk around the front of the intervening boat's mast, never through the cockpit. **Don't** stumble through a yacht's cockpit uninvited as this breaches cruising etiquette and infringes unwritten territorial rules.

Once on board, **don't** throw your luggage on to the largest, most comfortable bed. This 'bunk' or 'berth' is likely to be reserved for the skipper or owner and such presumption will cause acrimony. It is often best to place your bag in a visible position that does not obstruct crew movement and hope that a berth will soon be allocated. In addition, **don't** begin unpacking your belongings immediately: space is at a premium on board and observing experienced crew activity is essential to learn the art of stowing gear.

"There is a type of yachtsman whose boat is so full of things – mostly junk – that there is scarcely room to move about. Such a boat will be congested with such objects as old condemned ropes, leaky oil cans, discarded portions of Primus stove, empty boxes, picture postcards, broken shackles, paint tins with small deposits of hardened paint on the bottom…"

Patrick Boyle, from *Sailing in a Nutshell*, published 1938

At sea:

Do pay special attention to the boom (the horizontal spar attached to the rear side of the mast at the bottom of the mainsail). Depending on the helming and communication skills of the skipper, this object can sweep across the boat without warning and deliver a blow to the head that may prove fatal. When sailing, **don't** sit on any static ropes or pieces of deck gear: a boat requires constant attention and ropes and equipment are liable to suddenly move at alarming speeds. This can result in unpleasant rope burns to the buttocks or the loss of fingers.

above *Queuing for fuel, queuing for supplies at the supermarket, endless paperwork issues with foreign port authorities and complex currency conversion calculations are absent on a cruise around Greenland.*

When sailing, **don't** sit on the companionway. On smaller and medium sized yachts this ladder is often the busiest access point between the deck and interior of a boat. Although it is one of the most comfortable places to sit on any boat, you will be an obstruction to any crew movement and test the patience of those on board. It is valuable to remember the sailing adage: "Only admirals and ****holes sit on the companionway".

For many beginners, a yacht's plumbing can cause more fear than the prospect of storms and mountainous seas. **Don't** risk using the onboard lavatory (or 'heads' as they are often known) without instruction from an expert in this field. Marine plumbing on smaller boats is unreliable and has a notoriously high failure rate. Any embarrassment that may be felt through repeatedly asking for clear and precise instructions on the use of the heads is preferable to the drama and shame caused by improper or over enthusiastic use of the equipment.

Don't enter into an argument if the skipper shouts at you. He may be concerned for your safety or the safety of the yacht and yelling a command or warning may be the most effective method of communicating his concern. It is unwise to bear a grudge when you may be forced to spend the next six hours, six days or six weeks in close confinement. Once you are ashore, it is an **essential** sailing tradition that you buy the skipper drinks however abusive or unpleasant he has been while you were at sea.

The Brotherhood
of the Coast

There are hundreds of yacht cruising clubs and associations scattered around the globe, but none are as curious as The Brotherhood of the Coast (Hermandad de la Costa, Les Frères de la Côte, Brüder der Küste etc.): an international cruising fellowship founded by yachtsmen in Santiago, Chile during the early 1950s. From Angola, West Africa, to Orange Beach, Alabama, this fraternity of sailors exists to share the pleasures of cruising between like-minded yachtsmen.

When visiting yacht clubs in distant and hard-to-reach areas of the world it is often possible to spot a trophy left by visiting members of The Brotherhood nestling among the dusty collection of souvenirs in the club's bar. Should you wonder at the origin of the obscure flag showing an anchor with twin stars and crossed oars on a black background (reminiscent of the Jolly Roger flag of piracy), it is evidence that The Brotherhood has reached this yachting outpost before you. The author can confirm that the mysterious Brotherhood has left its mark in the world's southernmost yacht club, the Micalvi Club de Yates just 80 miles north of Cape Horn. Indeed, intrepid sailors from the Valparaiso chapter of the society have even left an inscription a few metres from the infamous cape's lighthouse.

Although The Brotherhood are quick to distance themselves from any association with quasi-secret societies or politically motivated groups, their hierarchy system reveals a familiar fondness for arcane orders of rank shared by Masonic organisations. A senior figure in The Brotherhood – 'Big Brother' – is supported by the 'Grand Scribe' and assisted by the 'Guard of The Treasury', who wields power over 'The Keeper of The Powder Keg'. Whether any members hold enough authority to order the execution of junior Brothers is unclear. Any yachtsmen who may fear encountering The Brotherhood on the high seas should be aware that all members must adhere to the fraternity's unbreakable Eight Commandments. The first commandment in this cruising credo demands that a Brother must "Obey with respect [his] Captain's orders". If this limit to lawlessness fails to inspire confidence, Commandment Five instructs acolytes: "Do not be envious of your brother's ship nor his sails or motors". The final Commandment confirms that The Brotherhood are a peaceful and benign group of yachtsmen who should not be feared or avoided and advises that "The love of the ocean should be the following cult of your days".

left: *Nerves of steel and precise crew co-ordination are required to negotiate the Antarctic Peninsular. Any damage sustained by a yacht cruising in remote areas must be rectified by the crew.*

The way we were

When yacht cruising experienced a renaissance in the 1950s after a period of post World War II austerity, it was necessary that newcomers to the sport received expert guidance. One of England's most experienced and eloquent sailors, Peter Heaton, achieved great success in this field and published the invaluable book, *Cruising*, in 1953. Although the language, style and presentation have changed since Heaton's era, reproducing some examples of his expert advice shows that little has changed in over half a century:

A warning to potential cruisers:
If you are accustomed to going to sea after lunch and returning in time for dinner, you will find that it may take a bit of time getting used to the more complicated routine of cruising.

The joy of navigation:
The ability to navigate a yacht far out of sight of land and to pilot her to the harbour of his choice increases man's self respect, his usefulness to his country in times of stress, and, perhaps most important of all, his own pleasure.

A different breed:
No one who has sailed a small yacht during a passage lasting more than 24 hours, taking day and night and weather in his stride, can fail to feel a sense of achievement and that feeling of participation in the freemasonry of the sea that sets seamen apart from the ordinary chap.

Essentials:
Unlike the racing sailor, who doesn't mind getting wet through, the cruising man, if he is to enjoy his cruise, must keep his inner garments dry.

Offshore dangers:
Beware of zip-fasteners at sea; they rapidly become utterly demoralized by the salt atmosphere, and refuse to function.

Motorized power:
There are many people who feel quite strongly about this 'mechanical topsail' business. There exists a kind of snobbery about it all – 'one just doesn't have an engine!' Be that as it may there are times when an engine can be very useful.

above *Yacht* Pelagic *in front of a 'drydock' iceberg in Fournier Bay on the Antarctic Peninsular. Icebergs are categorized in to five further types: tabular (medium freeboard, smooth topped), non-tabular (medium freeboard, irregular surface), blocky (sheer, tall sides), pinnacle (pyramid or mountain shaped) and wedge.*

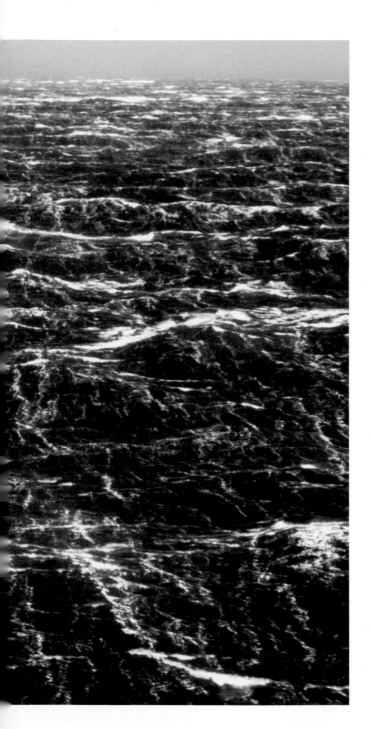

10

The
Southern
Ocean

- A TOURIST GUIDE

- SURVIVAL TIPS

- MAYDAY! MAYDAY! MAYDAY!

- CAPE HORN AND
  THE ALBATROSS

A tourist guide

Early in 2000, the International Hydrographic Organisation ratified the existence of a fifth ocean to join the watery realms of the Atlantic, Arctic, Pacific and Indian Oceans. Technically, the Southern Ocean comprises the sea area extending north from the coast of Antarctica to Latitude 60° South. For deep-water sailors, though, passing through the Roaring Forties (Latitude 40° South) into the Furious Fifties (Latitude 50° South) signifies entering this hostile environment. Those sailing further south, below the limit of the Antarctic Convergence – a defined, mid-ocean border where water temperatures differ by margins of 2–3°C north-south – and into the Screaming Sixties, penetrate the most remote ocean zone on the planet.

The Southern Ocean covers an area just over twice the size of North America with maximum depths ranging between 4,000–5,000 metres. The strongest average wind strengths on Earth blast across this area from the west, building tremendous seas from an eastward flowing current that rolls around the planet unchecked by any landmass until the treacherous funnel between South America and Antarctica at Cape Horn. In a region that is furthest from the reach of any rescue services, yachtsmen encounter gales, monstrous waves, persistent boat-breaking conditions and the threat of icebergs: the Southern Ocean is no place for the faint at heart.

previous page *The Southern Ocean contains the highest average wave sizes on Earth. 60-80 knot winds (Hurricane Force 12) and 12-15 metre waves are captured on film from the upper deck of a French training warship, Jeanne d'Arc, en-route to Cape Horn.*

below *A lone albatross patrols the Southern Ocean off the Sub-Antarctic island of South Georgia, 2,000 km east of Cape Horn at 54° South. Superstitious yachtsmen claim that each albatross carries the soul of a drowned sailor.*

opposite *Jean Pierre Dick and* Virbac *experienced one of the roughest Horn roundings during the 2004-05 Vendée Globe. Shortly after passing the world's southernmost cape, the French skipper made a brief satellite call to the race office: "It's extraordinary! I rounded with 45 knots established winds with 55 knots at times. It was raining and conditions were a little extreme. What satisfaction. It's a childhood dream come true."*

Survival tips

Shortly before the start of the 2004–05 Vendée Globe, single-handed, non-stop, round the world race, British skipper Mike Golding described sailing conditions in the Southern Ocean: "The South is just one long chain of being afraid, to being happy, to having just survived." A very experienced high latitude sailor, Golding knew the conditions he would have to endure for thirty days: "You're in a reefed down sail plan, the boat is barrelling along at top speed, she's on the boil… you just monitor it." During the race, French skipper Jean Le Cam on *Bonduelle* explained the dilemma facing skippers attempting to preserve their boats while continuing to sail at a competitive pace: "If you hoist too much sail you zoom off like a locomotive and risk slamming into waves and seeing your mast collapse. It's like walking a tightrope."

Does the sun exist? I haven't seen it for quite a while.

Patrice Carpentier enters the Southern Ocean on *VM Matériaux* during the 2004–05 Vendée Globe

left, top *A snow blizzard hits the Global Challenge fleet in the high latitudes of the Southern Ocean. Gale force winds, monstrous waves, thick fog and the threat of icebergs sustain the fearsome reputation of this remote area.*

left, bottom *Surfing Southern Ocean waves demands helming skill, nerves of steel and intense concentration from the helmsman of a Global Challenge yacht. On the early clipper ships, helmsmen were forbidden from looking over their shoulder in case the towering waves bearing down from astern should cause a distraction and endanger the boat.*

To combat the brutal physical conditions encountered sailing through the Southern Ocean, skippers endeavour to maintain a sleep routine and increase their calorie intake to counteract the effects of freezing conditions – a difficult and dull task when food is limited to a repetitive series of freeze-dried or irradiated (pre-cooked) meals. Safeguarding the boat and reducing the chances of sustaining personal injury or – in the worst case – being washed overboard, is paramount and the resulting mental stress can be acute. In the 2004–05 Vendée Globe, British yachtsman, Conrad Humphreys, pushed himself and his Open 60, *Hellomoto*, to the very limit of endurance. Humphreys overhauled eight of his competitors during a month in the Southern Ocean between the Cape of Good Hope and Cape Horn, but this extraordinary achievement extracted a heavy toll: "My body did not sense the extreme fatigue and shutdown. It allowed me to drift into a stage beyond exhaustion, where my world suddenly seemed to contain only obstacles and no solutions. For someone that does not see obstacles in life, this world was immeasurably depressing."

below *Vendée Globe skipper, Conrad Humphreys, checks his route to the finish line as he sails* Hellomoto *round Cape Horn in January 2005 after 74 days alone at sea. The British skipper was rewarded with a benign rounding after overhauling eight competing yachts between the Cape of Good Hope and Cape Horn during 40 days and 10,500 miles of tough Southern Ocean racing.*

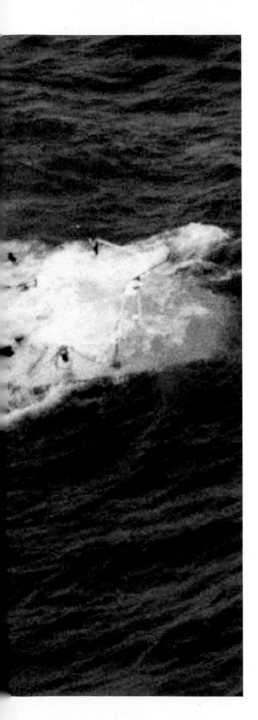

Mayday!
Mayday!
Mayday!

In 1996, yachtsman Raphaël Dinelli took part in the third edition of the Vendée Globe race as an unofficial entry. Dinelli's preparation for the race had overrun, leaving him unable to complete a qualifying ocean passage and enter the race officially; but this setback was not going to stop the French yachtsman fulfilling his dream of circumnavigating the world. The Southern Ocean, however, turned this dream into the blackest nightmare.

In 65-knot winds reaching gusts of 80 knots, Dinelli's yacht, *Algimouss*, capsized and refused to right herself. The mast soon shattered and – still connected to the rigging – began smashing holes into the upturned yacht as the boat was thrown around by violent wave action. Freezing water poured into the boat and mixed with diesel leaking from the fuel tanks. Vomiting from the effects of fumes, Dinelli was able to locate and activate the yacht's distress beacon. Finally, the violent motion of the sea wore through the rigging, the mast detached and *Algimouss* rolled upright. Battered by 50ft seas, Dinelli launched the liferaft, attaching it to his stricken yacht with a short line. This done, he strapped himself into the swamped cockpit and took stock of the situation. With all the electronic equipment on board flooded and useless, Dinelli had no way of knowing whether his distress signal had been successfully transmitted or received by the race organisation or rescue services. As *Algimouss* settled lower in the water as successive waves smashed across her semi-submerged decks, the yachtsman prepared for the longest and, possibly, the last night of his life. Then, shortly before nightfall as Dinelli spoke to his yacht encouraging and willing her to stay afloat, the line attaching his liferaft parted and the bright orange inflatable sanctuary tumbled across the waves, disappearing downwind….

Subjected to similar conditions experienced by Dinelli, British Vendée Globe skipper Pete Goss was close to exhaustion on 50ft *Aqua Quorum*, 160 miles downwind from *Algimouss*. A flashing light on the

141

left *Stranded 1,200 miles south west of Australia, Raphaël Dinelli stands on* Algimouss *as she sinks deeper into the abyss of the Southern Ocean during the 1996–97 Vendée Globe. Dinelli's liferaft had been lost overnight and a spare was dropped by the Royal Australian Air Force just minutes before the yacht sank entirely.*

satellite communications display mounted above the chart table alerted Goss of an incoming message from the race organisation and he quickly read through the details of Dinelli's catastrophe. It was clear that *Aqua Quorum* was the only yacht in the area and Dinelli's survival depended entirely upon Goss. Reaching Dinelli meant turning the boat around and heading directly into gale-force winds and mountainous seas, but the ex-Royal Marine commando was pragmatic about this monumental task and later commented: "It was simple; the decision had been made for me a long time ago by a tradition of the sea. When someone is in trouble, you help".

At daylight, a plane from the Royal Australian Air Force (RAAF) flew low over *Algimouss* and dropped a liferaft. Grabbing some supplies, Dinelli scrambled inside and found a written message telling him that Pete Goss was 10 hours away. Just five minutes after boarding the liferaft, the French yachtsman watched his boat sink to the bottom of the Southern Ocean. Meanwhile, *Aqua Quorum* was beating to windward, constantly knocked flat by winds, burying her spreaders in the sea every half an hour. With frequent updates from the race organisation in France and the Marine Rescue Control Centre (MRCC) in Australia, Goss carefully monitored his progress towards the position of Dinelli and his yacht. After one such check, it became clear that Goss had overshot and he turned the yacht around, dropped the mainsail and sailed under a storm jib, constantly zigzagging downwind at 3–4 knots searching for Dinelli in the huge waves, firing flares and sounding his fog horn. With impeccable timing the RAAF reappeared, dropping smoke canisters and flashing the aircraft's landing lights, guiding Goss through mountainous seas towards the liferaft. Having made visual contact with Dinelli, Goss threw two fenders attached to a line over the stern as an extra precaution should he fail to grab him on his first pass, and then released the jib halyard and cautiously approached.

Dinelli's extraordinary will to survive on a sinking yacht and his rescue by a fellow sailor ignited the public's interest in single-handed sailing and the story of endurance and courage is a fundamental cornerstone of solo sailing folklore. Goss delivered Dinelli to Hobart, Tasmania, before continuing the circumnavigation and later received the Legion d'Honneur from President Chirac of France for his outstanding bravery. Eight years after losing his yacht in the Southern Ocean – an experience that would deter many from re-entering the area afloat – Dinelli successfully completed the 2004–05 Vendée Globe.

right *British skipper Pete Goss turned his yacht around, then sailed 160 miles to windward through the Southern Ocean in hurricane conditions and rescued Dinelli. Later, in an Inmarsat message to his wife, Goss wrote: "I had a good Christmas because I saved a man's life and he is OK. I'm sailing home as fast as I can" (from* Close To The Wind *by Pete Goss).*

Cape Horn and the Albatross

Since its discovery in 1616, Cape Horn has been a craved destination and rite of passage for offshore sailors: a prime objective in sailing aspirations, part maritime bogeyman, part Holy Grail. The Horn marks the northern limit of Drake Passage, a fearsome stretch of water between South America and the Antarctic continent where the Southern Ocean is squeezed through a narrow and relatively shallow gap: a concentration of wind and waves that can produce monstrous seas. The cape's legendary status and fearsome reputation has filled the pages of many books, but the "*Long Drag Shanty*" conveys a true sense of dread that the area can inspire:

> *Round Cape Horn where the stiff wind blows,*
> *Round Cape Horn where there's sleet and snow.*
> *I wish to God I'd never been born*
> *To drag my carcass around Cape Horn*

Cape Horn has wrecked countless ships and claimed the lives of many sailors attempting to round this barren, rocky outcrop – the southernmost drowned peak of the Andes mountain chain. One survivor of a Horn gale was Charles Darwin during the voyage of exploration that formed his theories on evolution. This experience totally demoralized the brilliant naturalist: "The necessary discomforts of the ship heavily pitching and the miseries of constant wet and cold, I have scarcely for an hour been quite free from seasickness. How long the bad weather may last, I know not; but my spirits, temper, and stomach, I am well assured, will not hold out much longer."

Darwin's ship, the *Beagle*, came within minutes of foundering during the gale due to the captain's insistence that all the ports for deck drains should remain closed. Fortunately, the ship's carpenter chose to remain on standby with a handspike and saved the *Beagle*. Darwin's diary entry of Sunday 13 January, 1833 records this event, just 20 miles west of the cape:

> *"Our horizon was limited to a small compass by the spray carried by the wind; the sea looked ominous; there was so much foam, that it resembled a dreary plain covered by patches of drifted snow. At noon the storm was at its height; and we began to suffer; a great sea struck us and came onboard; the same sea filled our decks so deep, that if another had followed it is not difficult to guess the result. It is not easy to imagine what a state of confusion the decks were in from the great body of water. At last the ports were knocked open and she again rose buoyant to the sea."*

Although Darwin was clearly in a poor condition during the storm, he was still able make observations: "Whilst we were heavily labouring, it was curious to see how the albatross with its widely expanded wings, glided right up the wind". These solitary creatures symbolize the Southern Ocean. Their ability to harness the fierce winds raging at the bottom of the world coupled with a habit of following yachts and ships through remote sea areas has formed a mysterious bond between sailors and albatross: a connection that is highly evident at Cape Horn. There are only five manmade structures on treeless Horn Island. At the southern tip of the island sits an unmanned lighthouse marking Cape Horn and a second light is located above Point Espocon on the eastern end of the island. Behind the second light is a single-storey, 20m x 15m, six-room hut housing the Chilean lighthouse keeper and his family. Alongside the dwelling is a tiny chapel: a simple building constructed in timber, housing six pews and a plain, unfussy altar. Upon closing this building's double doors on the gale outside, the quiet within the chapel is entirely unnatural. This almost supernatural aspect increases with the final structure; a massive albatross statue dominating the plain above the island's southern cliffs. This diamond-shaped iron artwork features a cutout silhouette of an albatross in flight: aligned north-south, the prevailing westerly wind moans through the statue's void, producing a primal and highly disturbing sound. Carved on the concrete base of the statue is a sombre and melancholy poem in Spanish. It is very difficult **145** to turn one's back on the giant albatross:

> I am the Albatross Waiting for You
> At the End of the World
> I am the Forgotten Soul of Dead Sailors
> Those who Sailed Through Cape Horn
> From All Oceans in the World.
> But they have Not Died
> In The Furious Waves,
> In My Wings they Fly today
> To The Eternity
> In The Last Crevice
> Of Antarctic Winds

Sara Vial. December 1992

top *Albatross are often the only wildlife that deep ocean sailors will encounter. These magnificent birds represent the solitude and isolation of the Southern Ocean.*

left *Cape Horn's mystical status and cruel reputation becomes evident in gale force conditions. At 55° South, Horn Island is said to be the grave of 800 ships and 10,000 sailors lost at sea attempting to round the tip of South America.*

11

When It All Goes Horribly Wrong

Traditional safeguards

It is logical that a sport with so many inherent dangers should have a long and complicated tradition of taboo and superstition – a tradition that continues to flourish in our modern, secular society. Sailing superstitions differ between countries and cultures, though many are universal. Beginning a voyage on Friday is considered highly unlucky by sailors around the world, although few will realize that this stems from the Crucifixion being carried out just before the weekend. Other non-sailing days include the first Monday in April (Cain's birthday and the day on which Abel was killed), the second Monday in August (the day on which Sodom and Gomorrah were destroyed) and 31 December (the day on which Judas Iscariot hanged himself).

An auspicious launching is essential to limit any disasters befalling a new vessel. The seemingly harmless tradition of baptising a boat by smashing a bottle of champagne over her bow or – in the continental style – pouring wine over her decks, has its roots in the disturbing custom practised by Ancient Greeks of dragging a newly launched galley down a slipway covered in chained and bound slaves, washing the keel in blood from the crushed bodies. The Vikings continued this cruel theme by executing prisoners – or possibly any non-sailor loitering nearby – on a new longboat's deck. Today's innocuous ceremony is still fraught with superstition and should the champagne bottle fail to burst on the first swing, many sailors will wring their hands and crack their knuckles in agitation while muttering about cursed ships and doomed crews.

above *Heading for Padstow, Cornwall, under sail and motor in May 1995, disaster struck the 137 year-old tall ship,* Maria Assumpta. *Engine failure and a lee shore saw the boat smash into rocks and founder quickly: three crewmembers lost their lives in the wreck.*

left *Gusts of 50 knots, an open foredeck hatch, a forward compartment full of water and two waves over the bow send* Silk II *"down the mine" in Cowes Week 1996. One crewmember disappeared over the*

side and was swiftly recovered while
the bowman bravely held on as he was
plunged 4 meters underwater. The
44ft yacht sustained a few bent stanchions
and went on to win the Britannia Cup the
following day.

previous page *Worst case scenario:
Théodore Géricault's* Raft of the Medusa.
In 1816 the Medusa *left France sailing
to Senegal, West Africa. After running
aground on the Arguin Bank off Morocco,*

*a raft measuring 65 x 23 ft was built
from the ship's masts and timbers:
150 passengers and crew were cast adrift
while the captain and his 'friends' set off in
the ship's boats. Fighting and gang warfare
broke out on the raft and soon the
survivors began devouring flesh from
corpses. Only 15 men were rescued
after 13 days adrift when the raft was
discovered just 4 miles off the coast. The
artist studied corpses and body parts from
a hospital for added realism.*

What to pack, what to leave onshore and the problem with rabbits

above *Loïck Peyron's trimaran,* Fujifilm, *began to disintegrate in huge seas, snapping her starboard float between the crossbeams during the single-handed Route du Rhum of 2002. Determined to "bring the baby back home", Peyron sailed through 45 knot winds under bare poles: "The waves are 6–10 meters high, it's white everywhere, really beautiful. I now have to remember my boy scout years to make repairs." Unable to withstand the battering, the yacht later dismasted.*

opposite *Dismasted yacht,* Stand Aside, *tows a liferaft in the Tasman Sea during the 1998 Sydney-Hobart Race. Hurricane strength winds ripped through the 115 boats racing from Australia to Tasmania with tragic results: 66 yachts retired from racing, 5 boats sank, a total of 55 yachtsmen were rescued and 6 lives were lost.*

Before the introduction of buoyancy aids, emergency flares and the invention of the EPIRB (Emergency Position Indicating Radio Beacon), a highly prized item to prevent drowning was the caul from a newborn baby. This filmy membrane that often covers the head at birth was an essential talisman for sailors: newspaper advertisements offered large sums of money for remnants of the amniotic sac, and midwives could earn a considerable bonus.

Flowers on board are generally considered to bring bad luck and are destined to form a floating wreath as a vessel sinks into the abyss – a superstition that is still strongly held on many submarines. On Italian boats, any green-coloured clothing is forbidden and green boats in general are considered unlucky, as is carrying an umbrella, fitting a yacht with a new tiller and the eating of pears. On British boats, bananas are often discouraged. Italians realize that sailing on Friday is out of the question, but Thursday is also considered a bit of a gamble.

Many Spanish sailors will not allow books by the Argentine solo circumnavigator, Vito Dumas, to be kept or read on board. The Spanish also maintain that if a crewmember steps on deck having dressed carelessly with a shirt, jacket or trousers inside out or back-to-front, disaster will soon occur and the offending article of clothing is hastily thrown overboard, often while it is still worn by the negligent sailor. Bringing a black cat on to a boat heralds good fortune, but ensure that you step on deck right foot first.

The most rigorously obeyed superstition on French boats involves rabbits. The aversion to this animal can result in a farmhouse pâté that may contain traces of rabbit meat being tossed over the side followed by anything showing a picture of the detested creature or books on suspect, woodland topics. The mere mention of rabbits on, or near, a French boat can have dire consequences. If a crewmember becomes overpowered by an urge to discuss the despised beast, a number of pseudonyms may be used without invoking sinister phenomena: "Le gris-gris" (the grey one), "Le cousin du lièvre" (the hare's cousin) and "le mouton a cinq pattes" (the ram with five paws). This antagonism was taken to extremes in the Indian Ocean's high latitudes during a successful Jules Verne Trophy record attempt in 2002. A message was sent from the maxi-catamaran, *Orange*, stating that the only non-French crewmember on board had been dropped off on the barren Kerguelen Islands. Frantic questions flew through the ether from race control requesting further details whereupon it transpired that the hapless Australian crewmember, Nick Moloney, had committed a massive breach of protocol while the yacht sailed through iceberg infested waters. His crime was to observe that one of the bergs looked "a bit like a rabbit", causing the horrified helmsman to crash gybe the catamaran. This merited Moloney's instant marooning at latitude 50° South. The date of this draconian punishment was 1 April.

left *During the 2003 Mondial Assistance race from France to Spain via the Azores Islands in the Atlantic, ORMA 60 trimaran Foncia, collided with a mystery object. Her steering quickly became unmanageable and the multihull was flipped upside down. While most of the crew, including Ellen MacArthur, scrambled below as the yacht inverted, skipper Alain Gautier remained on deck and became temporarily trapped in the water under the yacht's trampoline netting. Two days later, the boat arrived in Lisbon under tow.*

above *An Ultra 30 at the Cardiff Grand Prix in 1994. These light, super fast boats were considered the ultimate gung-ho weapon afloat... until they fell over. Requiring lightning reactions and supreme crew co-ordination, keeping an Ultra 30 upright was a constant challenge.*

Whistling, women and priests: tricky issues

A woman and a ship ever want mending

Late 16th century, originally from 2nd century BC Latin

The trick with whistling at sea is knowing when to stop. It is widely agreed that whistling in calm weather can summon wind, while many sailors believe that whistling and simultaneously scratching the mast can guarantee the arrival of fresh breeze. However, whistling cheerfully in winds that are already blowing hard can court calamity and summon hurricane-force conditions. The ancient French warning to the "gabier", sitting as look-out in the crow's nest of a square rigged ship wisely advises: "Siffle, gabier, siffle pour appeler le vent, mais aussitôt le vent venu, gabier ne siffle plus" (Whistle, gabier, whistle to call the wind, but when it arrives, whistle no more).

There is an ancient belief that the sight of a woman angers the sea and men in many fishing communities would often refuse to leave shore should they meet a barefooted woman on the way to their boat. This superstition provided a convenient excuse for sailors to remain ashore in bad conditions, although – equally conveniently – should a naked woman appear before them during a storm, the immediate effect would be a calming of the wind. This tradition is the root cause of bare-breasted figureheads.

Priests are usually considered as bad omens and must be avoided immediately before setting sail. Should a mariner encounter a priest while walking to the quay before boarding a boat, it is prudent to cancel the voyage altogether. Furthermore, if the priest has red hair or is cross-eyed, a wise sailor will avoid boats for a considerable period. However, occasionally the clergy are extremely useful – especially when choosing to rename a boat. Normally, re-christening a vessel brings bad luck, but in France a system has evolved to limit this danger. On 15 August it is possible to carry out a name change if the correct rituals are adhered to. This ceremony involves sailing upwind performing a series of short tacks making a zigzag pattern, before turning the boat around and sailing downwind over the upwind route: an operation that signifies a snake eating its tail. Finally, arrange for a priest to bless the boat, but under no circumstances should he be allowed to step on board.

Wise words

Some international examples of man's relationship with the sea:

Weather lore...

Mackerel skies and mares' tails,
Make tall ships carry short sails

If woolly fleeces deck the heavenly way
Be sure no rain will mar a summer's day

When the sea-hog (porpoise) jumps,
Stand by your pumps

First rise after low (pressure)
Foretells a stronger blow

Seagull, seagull, sit on the sand,
It's never good weather when you're on the land

When the wind shifts against the sun,
Trust it not, for back it will run.
When the wind follows the sun,
*Fine weather will never be done**
[*This holds true for northern hemisphere, but reverse the wind
direction for southern hemisphere]

If wind is north-east three days without rain,
Eight days will pass before south again

When parrots whistle, expect rain

The wind...

The sea breeze blows the pelican where he wants to go (Corsica)

Fear blows wind into the sails (Japan)

Shipwreck and drowning...

Don't sail out farther than you can row back (Denmark)

It's too late to swim when the water is up to your lips (Denmark)

You cannot complain about the sea if you suffer shipwreck a
second time (Iceland)

Pray to God, but continue to row for shore (Russia)

The water in which one drowns is always an ocean (Armenia)

Why jump in the water before the ship turns over? (China)

Little leaks sink big ships (England)

Captain and crew...

If you are a friend of the captain, you can wipe your hands on
the sail (Arabic)

*God will help a seaman in a storm, but the pilot must remain
at the wheel (German)*

A ship with two captains sinks (Turkey)

*After a ship has sunk, everyone knows how she might have
been saved (Italy)*

When the sea is calm, every ship has a good captain (Sweden)

Nodding the head does not row the boat (Ireland)

What...?

If you want to drown yourself, don't torture yourself with shallow
water (Bulgaria)

If the seawater were hotter, we could catch boiled fish (France)

He who sees heaven in the water, sees fish in the trees (China)

*No matter how treacherous the sea, a woman will always be
more so (Brittany)*

The surface of the water is beautiful, but it is no good to sleep
on (Ghana)

left, top *Ignoring the vital role played by running backstays
had dire consequences for* Nippon *during the 1991 IACC World
Championships in San Diego.*

left, bottom *In 22 knots of breeze and choppy conditions,* Team New
Zealand *dismast off Auckland during the 2003 America's Cup as Swiss
challenger,* Alinghi, *disappears over the horizon. The Kiwis fitted a
spare mast for the final race, but the Cup was soon heading for Geneva.*

Index

157

Author's Acknowledgements and Sources

Further Reading:
A Narrative Of The Voyage Of HMS Beagle, edited by David Stanbury, The Folio Society
A Voyage For Madmen, Peter Nichols, Profile Books
Around The World Alone, Alain Colas, Barron's/Woodbury
Close To The Wind, Pete Goss, Headline
Cruising, Peter Heaton, Pelican Books
Gypsy Moth Circles The World, Sir Francis Chichester, World Books
In Quest Of The Sun, Alain Gerbault, Hodder and Stoughton
OSTAR: "Observer" Single-handed Transatlantic Race, GT Foulis & Co Ltd
Sailing Alone Around the World by Joshua Slocum, Penguin Classics
Sailing in a Nutshell, Patrick Boyle, Methuen & Co.
The Strange Voyage of Donald Crowhurst, Nicholas Tomalin and Ron Hall, Hodder and Stoughton
The Ultimate Challenge, Barry Pickthall, Orbis
Waters Of Wight, Douglas Phillips-Birt, Cassell
Winning In One-Designs, Dave Perry, Adlard Coles Nautical

Web sources:
www.teamellen.com
www.vendeeglobe.org
www.americascup.com
www.volvooceanrace.com
www.thedailysail.com
www.sailspeedrecords.com

Picture Acknowledgements

Anova Books Co. is committed to respecting the intellectual property rights of others. We have therefore taken all reasonable efforts to ensure that the reproduction of all content on these pages is done with the full consent of copyright owners. If you are aware of any unintentional omissions please contact the company directly so that any necessary corrections may be made for future editions.

Front Cover: Jon Nash Photography; **Back Cover:** © Jacques Vapillon; **1, 2&3** Yvan Zedda/ Bluegreen; **4** ©Ellen MacArthur/ Offshore Challenge Sailing Team; **7** ©Bettman/ CORBIS; **8** Bill Rowntree/ Knox-Johnston Archive/ PPL; **8&9** Jean-Marie Liot/ DPPI/ Offshore Challenges; **10&11** Yvan Zedda/ Bluegreen **12, 13** Photo Beken of Cowes; **14&15** Richard Langdon/ Bluegreen **16, 17** ©Jacques Vapillon; **18** Rick Tomlinson/ Bluegreen; **19** ©Jacques Vapillon; **20&21** Copyright ©1997. A. D. Blake/ Bluegreen. All Rights Reserved; **22** Photo Arnaud Février/ Bluegreen; **23**Carlo Borlenghi/ kospictures.com; **24&25** Francesco Ferri/ ACM/ SEA & See/ DPPI; **26** Christian Février/ Bluegreen; **26&27** Franck Socha/ Bluegreen; **28&29, 30** Christian Février/ Bluegreen; **32&33** Kaoru Soehata/ Bluegreen; **34,35, 36&37** Franck Socha/ Bluegreen; **39** Carlo Borlenghi/ kospictures.com; **40** Kaoru Soehata/ Bluegreen; **41** Francesco Ferri/ ACM/ SEA & See/ DPPI; **42&43, 44&45, 46, 48&49** Rick Tomlinson/ Bluegreen; **50&51** Bob Fisher/ PPL; **52** Rick Tomlinson/ Bluegreen; **53** Thomas Lundberg/ PPL; **54** Rick Tomlinson/ Bluegreen; **55** Richard Langdon/ Bluegreen, **56, 58&59** Rick Tomlinson/ Bluegreen; **61** ©Jean Guichard/ CORBIS; **62** Steven Pratt Rnas Culdrose/ Ajax News/ DPPI; **63** Gary Blake/ DPPI; **64&65** Carlo Borlenghi/ DPPI; **66,67** Daniel Forster/ DPPI; **68,70&71** marinepics.com; **72** Jacques Vapillon/ DPPI; **73T, 73B, 74&75** Carlo Borlenghi/ kospictures.com; **76&77** Bill Rowntree/ Knox-Johnston Archive/ PPL; **78** Chichester Archive/ PPL; **79** Collection Chevalier-Taglang/ DPPI; **80** Sunday Times/ Chichester Archive/ PPL; **81** Chichester Archive/ PPL; **82&83** Bill Rowntree/ Knox-Johnston Archive/ PPL; **85** PPL Archive; **86&87** ©Jacques Vapillon; **89** Chichester Archive/ PPL; **91** Photo Gilles Martin-Raget; **92&93, 94, 95** ©Jacques Vapillon; **96&97** Photo Gilles Martin-Raget; **98** Jon Nash/ DPPI; **99** Benoit Stichelbaut/ DPPI; **100B, 100&101** Yven Gladu/ DPPI; **102&103** Billy Black; **105** ©Jacques Vapillon; **106** Photo Gilles Martin-Raget; **107** ©Jacques Vapillon; **108** DPPI; **109** © Conrad Humphreys/ CHR; **110&111** Billy Black/ PPL; **112, 113** Billy Black; **114&115** Jean-Marie Liot/ DPPI; **116** ©Mark Lloyd Images; **117** Jacques Vapillon/ DPPI; **118, 119** Henri Thibault/ DPPI; **120&121** Benoit Stichelbaut/ DPPI; **124&125** Christian Février/ Bluegreen; **126** The Art Archive/ The British Library; **127T** Rick Tomlinson/ Bluegreen; **127B, 129** © Hamish Laird, 2005, www.expeditionsail.com; **130&131** Daniel Allisy/ Bluegreen; **132&133** Rick Tomlinson/ Bluegreen; **134&135** Christian Février/ Bluegreen; **136** ©Rex Features; **137** ©Jacques Vapillon; **138T** ©Kester Keighley **138B** marinepics.com; **139** © Conrad Humphreys/ CHR; **140&141** Sportshoot/ PPL; **142&143** Tony McDonough/ Sportshoot/ PPL; **144&145** ©Jacques Vapillon; **145T** Daniel Allisy/ Bluegreen; **146&147** The Art Archive/ Musée du Louvre Paris/ Dagli Orti; **148** Photo Beken of Cowes; **148&149** Nigel Bennetts/ PPL; **150** Yvan Zedda/ Bluegreen; **151** Ian Mainsbridge/ PPL; **152&153** Peter Bentley/ PPL; **152B** Yvan Zedda/ Bluegreen; **154&155T** Christian Février/ Bluegreen; **154&155B** Franck Socha/ Bluegreen.

First published in Great Britain in 2006
This edition published in Great Britain in 2009 by
PAVILION BOOKS
An imprint of Anova Books Company Ltd
10 Southcombe Street, London W14 0RA

© Anova Books Company Ltd, 2006
Text © Oliver Dewar, 2006
Photography © see Picture Acknowledgements

Senior Editor: Emily Preece-Morrison
Design: www.pinkstripedesign.com
Jacket Design: Lotte Oldfield
Production: Oliver Jeffreys

A CIP catalogue record for this book is available
from the British Library.

ISBN 978 1 86205 818 7

Printed and bound by 1010 Printing International Ltd., China.
Reproduction by Classicscan PTE Ltd, Singapore

10 9 8 7 6 5 4 3 2 1

www.anovabooks.com

CHARLEMAGNE
AND ROLAND

CHARLEMAGNE AND ROLAND

A Romance

Allan Massie

Weidenfeld & Nicolson
LONDON

First published in Great Britain in 2007
by Weidenfeld & Nicolson

1 3 5 7 9 10 8 6 4 2

A CIP catalogue record for this book
is available from the British Library.

ISBN 978 0 297 85069 4

Typeset by Input Data Services Ltd, Frome

Printed in Great Britain by Clays Ltd, St Ives plc

The Orion Publishing Group's policy is to use papers that
are natural, renewable and recyclable products and made
from wood grown in sustainable forests. The logging and
manufacturing processes are expected to conform to the
environmental regulations of the country of origin.

Weidenfeld & Nicolson

The Orion Publishing Group Ltd
Orion House
5 Upper Saint Martin's Lane
London, WC2H 9EA

www.orionbooks.co.uk

for Allison, as ever

Preface

This novel follows *The Evening of the World* and *Arthur the King*, but is complete in itself. The connecting thread is that all three books have the same narrator, Michael Scott, and the same audience, this being his pupil, the boy who was to be the Holy Roman Emperor, Frederick II.

Michael Scott was born in the Scottish Borders around 1175 and died there *circa* 1230. He was famous in his time as a scholar and astrologer, and re-introduced the works of the Greek philosopher Aristotle to western Europe by his translations of Arabic versions of the original Greek text. Reputed to be a wizard or sorcerer, he was put by Dante in the eighth circle of the Inferno. In Border folklore he is credited with having 'cleft the Eildon Hill in three and bridled the Tweed with a curb of stone', and his grave may be found in Melrose Abbey.

In this book he tells the story of the first Holy Roman Emperor Charlemagne and his nephew Roland, the hero of the greatest of French medieval Romances, the *Chanson de Roland*. He does so for the enlightenment and amusement of the young Frederick; no doubt the narrative was intended as relief from his more arduous studies. Scott is a lively but prejudiced narrator. His bias against the papacy is extreme, and may well have contributed to the quarrels with successive popes which marked Frederick's reign. On the other hand, he displays a sympathetic understanding of Islam, and what he has to say about the relation of that religion to Christianity is curiously relevant to the modern world. It cannot be claimed that he was an accurate historian, but he is, I would suggest, an agreeably lively one.

An account of the discovery – or supposed discovery – in the Bibliothèque Nationale in Paris of Scott's Latin manuscript (which I claim to have translated to the best of my ability) is given in the introduction to *The Evening of the World*, but it is not necessary to know the circumstances of its discovery to read and, I hope, enjoy this extraordinary Romance.

A.M.

I

Charlemagne, the Great King, the Emperor, was a mother's boy. The expression 'tied to a woman's apron strings' was not then current, but had it been, would have sprung to men's lips. His mother Berthrada dressed him in girls' clothing till he was six, and some say that it is for this reason his voice never broke but remained high and piping like the treble of a boy chorister. But to my mind this is ridiculous, and the shrill voice that accorded so ill with his fine, manly figure was more likely to be the result of a childhood illness that is sometimes termed 'mumps'. On the other hand, it is well known that in the case of boys stricken with that illness misfortune ensues and their testicles never descend as they should; so they are called often 'eunuchs by nature'. Yet it is equally well attested that Charlemagne was no eunuch. On the contrary, he fathered many children, at least a dozen born in wedlock and more than that number born to his many concubines. So he may not have suffered from the mumps, though some accounts of his childhood insist he did; or it may be that the illness was not sufficiently severe to have prevented his testicles from descending. We must therefore conclude that any explanation offered for the shrillness of his voice is mere conjecture, and that the truth is veiled in the mist of ages.

What is certain is that Berthrada adored him and disliked his elder brother Carloman, almost as intensely as she loathed Pepin, her husband and the boys' father. That loathing was such that she never admitted him to her bed after the night – or, as may be, afternoon – on which the younger of the princes was conceived. But precisely because she evinced such distaste for the act of congress – never, as is well attested, taking a lover in the remaining fifty-three years of her life, not even a youth at that age when women in their maturity are often enraptured by soft skins and strong legs – no one ever questioned the future Emperor's paternity.

Berthrada was a pious woman, on her knees, praying, for several hours a day, and, sometimes in the season of Lent, for three days and three nights without intermission. Being of conspicuous virtue, she let it be known that she prayed for all the poor of the world, and this had some influence on Charles, for he was always forward in succouring the poor, and when in his old age he discovered that there were Christians living in poverty in Syria, Egypt and Africa, at Jerusalem, Alexandria and Carthage, he had compassion on their wants and would send money over the seas to them. So says his biographer, the holy Einhard. Being myself, as you know, my Prince, inclined to scepticism, I would guess that little of this money reached those for whom it was intended, but was intercepted by courtiers or applied to their own purposes by the abbots and priests by way of whom it was transmitted. In Scotland where, as you know, I was born and reared, we have an expression: 'tarry-handed', which is to say, sticky-fingered; and I have observed that charitable donations often suffer this fate. They are so attractive that those charged with the duty of dispensation are loath to fulfil it, but discover a more urgent use for the money; and it is for this reason that I have made it my habit or custom to give alms freely into a beggar's hand, but to refuse money to all who beseech it on behalf of some brotherhood of charity.

But I digress. Which is not, as some say, reprehensible, for it is often from digressions that wisdom may be plucked, and in this instance the advice I have given you is good. Beware of institutions.

As I was saying, Berthrada detested her husband, not without reason; for this Pepin, short and squat, ill-proportioned, his arms being as long as those of the apes in the menagerie collected by your royal grandfather, was possessed of a vile temper. Once, for example, when Charles grew pale at the sight of a corpse much eaten by maggots, Pepin picked the youth up by his collar and the tail of his tunic, and rubbed his face in the carcass, shouting that this would cure him of his namby-pamby, ladylike airs and graces. Then he laughed when the young man spewed,

2

and threw him on to a midden. Pepin was not only choleric, but violent and uncouth, much given to rape. It was no wonder Berthrada loathed him.

Nevertheless, he was not without qualities, and may indeed be reckoned a remarkable man. He was the first of his family to assume the crown. It happened like this.

You must know that for many centuries the kings of the Franks had been taken from the family of the Merovings, which race was of a nigh-impossible antiquity. According to pagan legend, they sprang first from the coupling of the god Wotan with a water-sprite, but this is improbable. Others – Christian heretics – report what I scarce dare write, so impious is the claim: that they were descendants of a marriage, or perhaps liaison, between Our Saviour, the Lord Jesus Christ, and the harlot Mary Magdalene.

However, it is true that the ancestral line of the Merovings was of unfathomable antiquity, and that before your ancestors the Franks saw the light of the True Faith, and heard the Gospel of Christ, they held their kings to be gods, or at least supposed that they sat on footstools by the throne of the gods.

Be that as it may, by the time of which I now write, they were sorely fallen from this high estate, and the former divinities had dwindled into being no better than drivelling idiots. They still received reverence, but wielded no power. That was now exercised by their chief minister, who was given the title mayor of the palace.

He ordered all things and there was nothing left for the King to do but be content with the name of King, his flowing hair (which it was deemed impious to cut) and his long beard. He sat on his throne and pretended to rule. He received ambassadors and gave ear to them, but offered no answer till he was supplied with one by the mayor of the palace. He had nothing that he could call his own and no money save the pittance that the mayor granted him. His palace would not be recognised as such by any monarch in Christendom today; it was a long hut made of wood. Once a year he was driven thence to an Assembly of the People, and his mode of transport was a farm cart pulled by

3

oxen and guided by a servant who on other days of the year performed the duties of a ploughman.

Nevertheless, for a long time not even the boldest mayor of the palace dared to usurp his place, for an odour of sanctity hung about this idle and useless King.

Even Charlemagne's grandfather, the mighty Charles the Hammer, who, in two great battles, had routed the Saracens, or Moors, and driven them from the fair land of France (which they had thought to make their own, as they had Spain) did not choose, or did not dare, to dethrone these royal idiots. It was enough for him to enjoy the reality of power as mayor of the palace; he cared nothing for its semblance.

His son Pepin thought otherwise, perhaps because he was so much a lesser man. It irked him to be obliged to approach the last of the Merovings, whose name was Childeric, as one doing homage to his master.

There had been a time when the Merovings were formidable, in the days of the wars between Chilperic, who ruled northern and western France, and his sister-in-law, the terrible Brunnhilda, daughter of a prince of the Visigoths, who, as Regent for her sons, governed the south and east of the realm. Chilperic, compared by the monkish chronicler, Gregory of Tours, to Herod and Nero, on account of his impiety, heresy and cruelty, denied the reality of the Holy Trinity. Brunnhilda, ruthless as Jezebel (wife of Ahab, King of Israel), burned the castles of the nobility and had the Bishop of Verdun murdered, stoned somewhat in the manner of the first Christian martyr St Stephen. Brunnhilda, hated as deeply as she was feared, was at last seized by her enemies on the shore of Lake Neufchâtel. She was subjected to three days of torture, and then tied to the tail of a vicious horse, which was whipped to the gallop. This was rough treatment for a woman then in the seventh decade of her life.

Pepin listened to palace bards sing of these monsters, and blenched, yet could not withhold admiration. This in itself deepened or intensified the contempt in which he held his current master, the amiable, blond and vacant-minded Meroving Childeric. Yet for some time he hesitated, biting his nails to the quick in his perplexity. Despicable as the King was, he yet

4

retained something of the mysterious sanctity of the now-distant pagan times. No one might now worship Wotan, nor credit his liaison with a sea-nymph. Nevertheless ...

There must be an answer, and Pepin found it in the Pope. Having first won the approval and loyalty of the Frankish bishops and abbots by generous donations, Pepin led an embassy to the Holy Father, himself sore beset in Italy by the Lombard kings, who were ambitious to seize what was already known as the Patrimony of St Peter. He proposed a deal: if His Holiness would sanction the deposition of the wretched Childeric, then he, Pepin, would constitute himself the arm of Holy Church and True Religion.

'As my father, Charles the Hammer, expelled the infidel from the fair land of France,' he said, 'so also will I serve as the sword and shield of St Peter.'

What could be more agreeable to the Pope, Stephen II? It cost him nothing to dispose of the Meroving. Accordingly, the miserable Childeric was seized and his long hair was cut – an act that would formerly have been regarded as sacrilege, and the remaining loyalists may have condemned it as such. He was compelled to submit to the tonsure. His eyes were put out (though Pepin let it be known that the guards who had done this had exceeded their orders), and he was confined in a monastery where – it is to be hoped – he devoted the remaining years of his wretched existence to prayer, fasting and submission to the will of God.

Yet, even in his hour of triumph, Pepin remained uneasy. Men observed that he sat silent at feasts, drinking deep and biting his long moustaches. 'Uneasy,' some said, 'lies the head that wears an ill-gotten crown.' The Pope remarked his ally's perturbation, and understood its cause. Pepin had been accepted as King by the Assembly of the People, which in truth had had no choice but to do so. But something was lacking, and this the Pope was now ready to supply.

He came to Paris. He spoke, long and secretly, to Pepin, in a manner which both flattered the new King and disturbed him.

His Holiness said, 'There are those who regard you as a usurper; at the first check you receive they will rise in rebellion and seek to

5

depose you. Do not delude yourself that this may never happen. No man is blessed with good fortune from the cradle to the grave. It is related in the Holy Scriptures that even the mighty King David, though the favourite of the Lord, was driven from his royal palace and the city in Jerusalem when his son Absalom rose up against him. I cannot guarantee your fortune. Such power is denied even to the successor of St Peter. Moreover, the Evil One, even Satan, conspires against the most virtuous of men. But, though I cannot secure you utterly against his wiles, it is within the power vested in me by the Almighty, and confirmed by the Donation the great Emperor Constantine made to the throne of St Peter, to supply you with the legitimacy which you now fear you lack.'

Accordingly, having persuaded Pepin, the Pope celebrated a Mass at the basilica of Saint-Denis and anointed the King with holy oil, then formally crowned him. This was a novel rite for the Franks. Whereupon the Pope took Pepin by the hand, embraced him, hailed him as the eldest son of Rome and declared him to be 'His Christian Majesty'.

Then, a few months later, Pepin at the head of his army descended into Italy, and in two or, as some have it, three battles smote the Lombards hip and thigh. 'Truly,' said the Pope, 'the Almighty has sent me a sword wherewith to destroy the Amalekites.'

Doubtless this was so. Nevertheless, matters, and especially the relationship between the Holy Father and the Frankish monarchs, were more complicated than this easy formulation suggests. It is therefore necessary, my Prince, that I explain them to you, if you are to understand firstly the mystery and majesty of Charlemagne, and secondly, more urgently, the problems that will confront you as his heir when you assume the government of the Empire yourself.

My exposition may be a little dry. But do not for that reason close your ears and eyes to what I have to say. Do not skip the next chapter, in order to hasten to the more alluring delights of the wars of Charlemagne and the Romance of Roland and his peers. There will, I promise you, be delights enough, chivalrous adventures and lovely maidens to be rescued.

But meanwhile you must possess your soul in patience.

6

II

You must know that in the time of which I write the Roman Empire in the West had long ceased to exist, even in name. No Emperor since Arthur had been recognised by his colleague who ruled in Byzantium, the city of Constantine. The Germanic tribes had swept over the Empire; Goths, Vandals, Lombards and Franks. The cities were decayed. Learning survived only in a few monasteries. The Latin tongue itself was forgotten in many parts, corrupted in others, so that the language we now call French was already in formation, and even in Italy the tongue of the Empire no longer held sway, but, like a river which, as it approaches the sea, divides into the numerous streams we call a delta, ran not in a single course but had separated itself into dialects.

For a time it had seemed that Christendom itself would not survive in the West, for the Arabs had carried the name of Mohammed into Spain, and established kingdoms and emirates there. They had crossed the Pyrenees and been checked only, as I have already told you, by the valour of Charles the Hammer, grandfather of Charlemagne. But they had also conquered and occupied even this fair island of Sicily, and Arab corsairs ravaged and plundered all the coastal districts of Italy. There, it is true, the Roman Emperor still claimed to rule the exarchate of Ravenna from his palace in Byzantium; but how feeble was his hold, how little regarded his authority!

Yet the city of Rome itself still stood, though sadly fallen from its high estate. The pagan temples had long since been torn down or converted to Christian use; and many of these churches were also dilapidated. The great aqueducts of Augustus and Agrippa still marched across the *Campagna*, but they did so as mighty ruins, broken in places, and no longer carried water from the mountains to the city. There the Forum, where the heroes of

7

antiquity had in the days of the Republic competed for office and solicited the votes of free citizens, was now a grazing-ground for cattle; and the Palatine, the hill where the emperors had lived in splendour, was deserted by all but goats. Owls nested in the broken masonry, and foxes littered in the ruins of the Colosseum.

But Rome was more than a name, more than a memory to make the world grow pale. It was still lent a radiance by the presence there of its bishop, the Pope. He was its sovereign and he claimed the land around it as the Patrimony of St Peter. More than that, however. There was that document of which I spoke in telling you the story of Arthur, the so-called Donation of Constantine. You have, I fear, forgotten it, or its significance.

Briefly – for I set no store by the tale – the popes asserted that when the Emperor Constantine was miraculously cured of leprosy, by the intervention of the saints, or perhaps by happy chance, he turned to the True Faith. He decreed that henceforth Christianity should be the official religion of the Empire, and that all the old pagan gods were false, impostors or devils. Then, on removing to the city that bears his name, he bestowed on His Holiness, who at that time was named Sylvester, the Imperial Government of the Western Empire. He resigned to him the Lateran Palace, long the seat of emperors, and offered him the diadem and the imperial purple, while his clergy, who were henceforth to replace the ancient Senate of Rome, were granted the privilege of adorning themselves with the senatorial boots, and garbing their horses in the white trappings that denoted senatorial rank. Thus His Holiness in Rome was the equal and colleague of the Emperor in Byzantium, though I must add that in all the history I have studied, no emperor there viewed the Pope in that light; nor did the Patriarch of Constantinople, who held himself to be of equal rank to the Bishop of Rome in all ecclesiastical matters.

And rightly so, for this document, this purported Donation of Constantine, was fraudulent, a forgery concocted in the papal chancery. It was no more authentic than the legend that had the Merovings descended from the union of Wotan and a sea-nymph. The most I shall concede is that by the time of Charlemagne, the popes and the Roman *Curia* may have persuaded themselves

8

of its authenticity. Men find little difficulty in believing whatever seems of benefit to them.

Meanwhile, as if to mock the lofty claims and transcendent aspirations of the Bishop of Rome, Stephen II and his successors on the throne of St Peter, Hadrian I and Leo III, were sore-pressed by the Lombards, for it was the ambition of the Lombard kings to rule over the whole of Italy, and to suppress even the memory of the Empire. More than once they came close to success. Long before the events of which I write, one Lombard king, Authari, rode into the sea at the southern extremity of Calabria, and touched with his spear a solitary column that rose up from the waves, crying as he did so, 'And this shall be the boundary of the Lombard realm.'

No wonder the Popes were alarmed. No wonder they feared and hated the Lombards. No wonder they looked to the noble Franks for succour.

III

Pepin died, to the great delight of his widow Berthrada. She not only expelled his concubines from the palace, but ordered that all but one whom she cherished should be branded with the mark of a whore, that men might know them for what they were. In truth, such was the hatred and contempt she felt for them that they were fortunate to escape with their lives.

As was the custom among the Franks, the kingdom was then divided between Pepin's two sons born in wedlock, Carloman and Charles. Carloman, the elder, had been his father's favourite as Charles was his mother's. Yet Berthrada did not dare try to prevent the division of the kingdom. Charles inherited the north and west of what is now France, so that his kingdom stretched from beyond the Rhine to the River Garonne, while Carloman took the south and east.

The brothers had no love for each other. Carloman thought Charles a mollycoddle, on account of his high voice and because his mother had dressed him as a girl until he was six. Charles hated Carloman because he resembled their father, and resolved to destroy him. He said, 'There can never be peace between us, and therefore it is better to make an end of my brother as soon as possible.' To accomplish this he even made an alliance with Didier, then King of the Lombards, and married his daughter Desiderata. So Carloman found himself surrounded by enemies. His nerve failed him, he fell into a decline and died. This was very convenient for Charles, so convenient that it is probable the death was not natural but hastened by poison. Charles always denied this, and once ordered a man who had repeated the story to be blinded and have his tongue torn out. In fact, there is reason to believe Charles innocent of the murder, and that the guilty party was Berthrada. Poison is said to be a woman's weapon, though I have known many men employ it also.

Charles was resolved to be a mighty warrior, and not only because he was ashamed of his high-pitched voice. As a child he had loved to hear the stories of Alexander and Julius Caesar, and longed to emulate them. So, as Alexander had conquered the Persians and Caesar the Gauls, Charles made war on the Saxons, seeking to expand his empire beyond the River Elbe.

These Saxon wars went on for more than forty years until the Saxons were utterly subdued and incorporated in the Empire. I shall not relate them in detail because the story is wearisome and repetitive. I would ask you to remember only that they continued while the more glorious and interesting adventures that are my proper subject were going on. They were a refrain running through the whole life of Charles. In finally achieving the suppression of the Saxons, and in compelling them to accept the True Religion, he certainly showed himself the equal of Alexander and Caesar, pushing far beyond the limits of the Roman Empire.

In old age he liked to hear the story of Aeneas, the father of the Roman people, and when his reader told him how the gods had promised Aeneas 'empire without limits', he would smile complacently and say, 'That's me, that's what I've done.'

In truth, it was hard, grim work, unworthy of a tale of Romance. Charles imposed a reign of terror on the conquered people.

Empire-building is no work for the squeamish or tender-hearted. How could it be, since it takes the form of the subjection of one people by another, and the suppression of long-established cultures? So, after the defeat of a rebellion led by a Saxon chieftain named Widukind, Charles embarked on a policy of coercion. Its agents were to be the ecclesiastics. In that remarkable document, the *Saxon Capitulary*, Charles commanded the priests to 'see to it that these my orders are not disobeyed.' Paganism, which had made the Saxons believe themselves a free people, was to be exterminated, and the whole manner of Saxon life, from birth to death, from cradle to the grave, was to be utterly transformed according to the word of the Great King. Should any Saxon refuse to accept baptism into the True Faith, he should suffer the penalty of execution. The eating of flesh during

Lent was also punishable by death. Parents who omitted to have their child baptised before it was a year old were subject to heavy fines, and the cremation of a corpse – long the practice of the Saxons – was also to be a capital offence. Anyone found sacrificing to the pagan gods was to be disembowelled and then hanged. Priests were enjoined to employ the confessional in such a way as to secure submission to the will of Charles, and loyalty to the King and Christian people – that is, the Franks. Meanwhile, tithes were levied on every Saxon commune to support the Church, which they regarded as alien and tyrannical.

There were some who questioned the wisdom of these measures. The English scholar Alcuin, more understanding than his royal master, told Charles, boldly, to his face, 'Faith comes from free will, not compulsion. How can a man be compelled to believe what he does not believe? You may, sire, force a man to the font, but not to the Faith.' But Charles, who had a tender affection for Alcuin, merely smiled, and said, 'Believe you me, my friend, I shall hammer these pagans into observance of the True Religion as a farrier hammers a shoe to fit the most mettlesome steed.'

Or so it is related.

And, I think, accurately, for, as I have said, Charles was inspired by the example of Julius Caesar and his conquest of Gaul. As Caesar had forced Romanitas on the Gallic tribes, so that in time Gaul became one of the gardens of the Empire, so likewise he would force Christianity on the Saxons. 'It is not fitting,' he said, 'that a Christian king should tolerate the worship of devils and idols, or permit the practice of human sacrifice.' Accordingly, his armies laid waste, slaughtering thousands, that the True Faith might prevail; and he pushed his armies even beyond the River Elbe, across also the Danube, to crush the kingdom of the Avars, cousins of the terrible Huns.

Thus a mighty empire was created, and the deep piety of the German people today testifies to the wisdom of the policy.

IV

It is on account of these Saxon wars, my Prince, that Charles became known to all as Charlemagne, or Charles the Great. For it was he who restored the Empire, extending its bounds beyond the limits set by Augustus, and therefore he may truly be said to have made Christendom what it is. And yet, if Charles had been only a mighty conqueror it is probable that his fame would be confined to chronicles and the inscriptions on monuments. So it is meet that I recount now these tales which have ensured that his memory lives in our hearts and quickens the imagination of generous youth.

Charles built for himself a magnificent palace on the banks of the Rhine. It was decorated with the treasures of his Avar wars, treasures that had themselves been taken by the barbarians from the monasteries, churches and palaces of the Eastern Empire.

One night, as he slept there, he felt the light touch of an angel's hand pressing on his temple. He awoke, and the dazzling radiance of the angelic presence lit up the winter darkness, so that he recognised his visitor for what he was. Secure in his faith, he knew no fear and asked the angel why he had come to him.

'I have a mission for you,' was the reply.

'Why, that is good,' the King said, believing that he was to be summoned to some noble enterprise that would do honour to his high estate and to the Holy Church, for he could not suppose that an angel would be sent to him from the Lord for some other purpose. Judge therefore his surprise when the angel commanded him to rise from his couch and go forth to steal.

'To steal?' said the King. 'Surely I cannot have heard you right, for it is well known that stealing is forbidden by law and according to the commandments delivered by the Lord God to Moses.'

'Nevertheless,' the angel said, 'that is what is now required of you. Do not question the reason, but obey, for that too is a commandment, and obedience without argument is of the essence of the Faith. Therefore, I bid you again: go forth and steal.'

Yet the King still hesitated. How do I know, he thought, that this is indeed an angel, a messenger from the Almighty, and not a devil in disguise? I have often heard that evil spirits may assume even a heavenly shape in order to lead man astray.

He kept this thought to himself. Yet the angel read it, and replied to the unspoken words.

'Belief is trust,' the angel said, 'not knowledge. And so I put you to the test: go forth and steal.'

With these words the angel vanished, slowly fading from Charles's sight, and with his departure went also the warmth he had engendered, and the King was left shivering in the darkness.

For a long time – how long he could never tell – he lay there, perplexed and fearful. He thought of summoning his confessor, or perhaps Alcuin, in whose wisdom and discretion he trusted. And yet he dared not, for two reasons. In the first place he feared to seem foolish and to be told he should not be alarmed by what was only a disturbing dream; and in the second place he was afraid lest his visitor was indeed an angel whom it would be accounted sin to question and whose command must be obeyed. The words 'belief is trust, not knowledge' echoed in his mind.

At last he rose and dressed himself in breeches and a jacket made of bearskins, and, having drunk a cup of wine from the pitcher that stood by his bedside, slipped quietly from his chamber. The guards beyond its door were both asleep, though required to be wakeful, and did not stir as the King approached. They were breathing heavily as if they had drunk deeply. So he passed them by, having first noted who they were, that he might reprimand and punish them if his adventure turned out badly, and he descended the great staircase to the hall. There was no sound or movement; it was like a palace of the dead. He crossed the courtyard to the stable where he found his favourite horse, a dark-bay stallion that went by the name Galcador, ready saddled and bridled. But there was no groom in the stable, and the only sounds were the shuffling of hooves in the deep straw,

14

the munching of hay, and the clinking of chains. The King armed himself with sword at his belt, and mounted Galcador. Then, taking a spear, he rode out in to the night.

He had ridden a league, without direction, but letting his horse pick its way, till he found himself in a deep forest. An owl cried and far away he heard the shriek of a vixen, but otherwise the night was still, and the King, brave as he was, felt his heart gripped by a chilling fear, as once again it came to him that the angel was perhaps no angel but a demon who had led him astray in order to destroy him. Then the moon slipped out from behind a cloud and lit up the clearing, and he saw a stream before him. A voice called out, abruptly, and Galcador shied, so suddenly that the King was unseated and fell to the ground. His helmet was dislodged and rolled away, and for a moment he lay there, as if stunned.

'A pretty horseman,' said the voice, 'and a bold knight to lie there as if he had met the force of my lance.'

Charles blushed for shame and struggled to his feet. He took hold of Galcador, remounted and looked around, but the speaker was nowhere to be seen.

'Over here,' said the voice, full of mockery, 'across the stream. I await your challenge, sir knight.'

So Charles put his horse at the water, which was deep to its withers, and advanced on to level ground on the farther bank. A knight sat on his horse there, serenely, lance at rest. He said again, 'A pretty horseman you are and a bold knight to be unseated by my challenge.'

'Be that as it may,' the King replied, 'we shall soon see which of us is the better man.'

And with these words, he made to lower his visor, forgetting for the moment that he had lost his helmet. This caused him to hesitate, but pride drove him on and he charged his challenger with such force and fury that he dislodged him from the saddle and sent him crashing to the ground. Charles dismounted and stood over his fallen foe, with the point of his sword at his throat.

'Tell me your name, sir knight,' he said, 'that I may know who so insolently bars the way of an honest traveller.'

As he spoke these words he remembered that he was in truth engaged on a dishonest mission, and felt himself blush. But the moon was behind him and his rival did not remark his embarrassment.

'My name is Elgebast, but some call me Alberich,' was the reply, and, though the sword pricked the skin of his throat, there was mockery in the man's voice and in the smile he boldly summoned up.

'Elgebast?' the King said. 'That name is strangely familiar.'

The man smiled more broadly and did not attempt to move his neck away from the sword, but lay there as if on a couch taking his ease.

'Elgebast ...' the King said again. 'Are you not that notorious brigand and highway robber excommunicated by the Holy Church?'

'I have that honour, and may fairly claim that my name is known in every tavern between Rhine and Loire.'

Charles withdrew his sword and, extending his hand, drew his late enemy to his feet, for it seemed to him that this encounter was no matter of chance but had been arranged by his heavenly visitor.

'Come,' he said, 'you are the very man for me, and since I have spared your life it is now properly mine to command till daybreak.'

Elgebast said, 'I have never heard that such is the custom among you Franks. Nevertheless, you have indeed spared my life, for I was quite at your mercy, if only because my horse slipped as you charged, and therefore I am happy to be yours to command till the dawn breaks. Moreover, if you are engaged on some daring adventure, I may assure you that you could not look to find a fitter companion than myself.'

Even so, Charles hesitated to tell him the nature of the adventure on which he had embarked; for, despite the angelic command, he was ashamed. So for some time they rode in silence through the forest until, with the moon now high, they came in sight of a castle standing on a rock.

A happy idea now came to the King. He explained that he had been commanded by a lady to enter this castle and take a

16

token from its lord who had, he said, betrayed the lady so that she wished now to embarrass him.

'A pretty ploy,' Elgebast said.

'But to enter the castle unseen and accomplish the deed without being apprehended . . .'

'Why, that is no great moment,' was the reply.

Elgebast then led the king to the little village that nestled under the castle walls, and hammered on the door of a tavern with the pommel of his sword. It was opened by a man in a nightshirt. He held a lantern in his hand and raised it to examine these untimely visitors.

'Yes, old friend, it is indeed me,' Elgebast said, 'and we require a flask of Rhenish wine, and that chamber which I am accustomed to occupy. If it is already taken, you must eject your guest.'

'No need of that,' said the innkeeper, a villainous-looking fellow with a scar on his cheek and a cast in his left eye. 'Your Honour has paid me good silver to keep it for you, and I have been as good as my word.'

So he led them to the chamber, which was but a mean room, and fetched them the flask of wine, then said he would leave them to their business, 'which is no business of mine,' he added, 'and I have no wish that it should be or to meddle in your Honour's affairs.' So he left them and they each drank a cup of wine, which was strong and sweet and of a quality that surprised the King.

'This is welcome,' Charles said, 'but we are still without the castle.'

Elgebast smiled and stepped into the chimney. Then calling the King to him, he revealed a door let into the wall. He unbolted it and, lifting the lantern which the innkeeper had left him, disclosed a staircase climbing up through the rock.

'This leads to the lord of the castle's antechamber,' he said. 'It is a secret passage constructed, I believe, by the Druids of old, who were priests of the Gauls and skilled in all the arts and crafts of necromancy. But others affirm that it was carved from the rock by the command of the famous knight Sir Lancelot, who was enamoured of the lady of the castle and sought by means of this staircase to gain entry to her bedchamber that he might seduce her. Who knows? For this explanation too is plausible, since men will go to any lengths to seduce a woman they desire. Why I myself, though accounted virtuous—'

'Enough,' said the King, who disliked the lewd look that had spread across his companion's face. 'Some other time, for I must complete my mission before the cock first hails the morning.'

'Very well,' Elgebast said. 'I am, as we agreed, yours to command. But are you not fortunate, my friend, to have happened upon me?'

'As God wills it, I am,' the King said, 'for I should have been at a loss to find some means of entry for myself.'

They mounted the stair, which was steep, narrow and twisting, so that they had to press their bodies against the rock at each turning. At the top there was an iron ring hammered into the stone. Elgebast pulled on the ring and twisted it, and the stone moved, allowing them entry to the castle.

As Elgebast had promised, the stair led them to the lord's antechamber, which was separated from his bedchamber by only a curtain of crimson velvet. Voices came to them from beyond, and the King pressed his ear to a gap in the curtain that he might hear what was being said. The first voice was a woman's.

'I did not think,' she said, 'that I had joined myself to a coward.'

'You dare not call me that.'

'Since you, my lord, no longer dare to pursue the plan which you unfolded to me, it requires no daring on my part to call you coward.'

'It is not cowardice that holds me from that purpose,' was the reply, 'but honour and obligation. The King has been as a brother to me.'

'A brother to whom you must bow the knee! A brother by whose side you are diminished! A brother you have sworn to remove from the throne that should be yours by rights as the eldest natural son of his father Pepin!'

Hearing these words, Charles felt a surge of rage, for he knew the voices to be those of his bastard half-brother Dietrich and Fassolda, the Lombard princess whom he had received as a hostage and given Dietrich for wife, because he had conceived

18

so great a passion for her. And that passion, I may say, was mysterious to others, for, though Fassolda had skin as white as swan's down and was graceful of figure, being long-legged and high-breasted, nevertheless, her face was pock-marked, her chin so prominent that her jaws could not meet, and she had one blue eye and one brown. Therefore, some said that she had bewitched him, which was not indeed improbable, for her grand-mother, whose name I forget, was a notorious sorceress by whose magic the citizens of Bologna were stricken by plague, having, but for what reason I know not, incurred her wrath. Bishop Turpin, however, who had been the bosom-friend of Dietrich since boyhood and had lain with him often, and was now Charles's most trusted confidant and adviser, merely sniffed and said that talk of sorcery was nonsense. He happened to know, he said, that Fassolda was better acquainted with mere carnal arts, and a mistress of practices which had rendered Dietrich her devoted slave. 'But don't,' he added, 'ask me to describe them, for since I took the cloth and became a servant of the Holy Church, to speak of such things is for me abomination. I shall say only that as Jezebel enslaved Ahab, and Cleopatra that puissant general Mark Antony and, as it may be, Queen Guin-evere the noble knight Sir Lancelot, so also it is with Fassolda and my poor dear Dietrich.'

Charles remembered these wise words of Turpin's and now shivered as he heard Fassolda murmur, 'Now put your tongue here, my lord – is that not sweet?' and heard Dietrich moan and cry out with pleasure.

Then she said: 'But it is so simple, my dear. Tomorrow is the king's birthday, and I have prepared for him a little basket of sugared plums, of which he is, as I know, inordinately fond. You will offer them to him as a token of our regard. Among the plums will be one which I have filled with a deadly but slow poison, according to a recipe given to me by my grandmother. The King will fall into a fever and die two days later. Poison will not be suspected and there will be nothing to connect you or me with his death. Then, as the eldest surviving son of your father, you, my loved one, will be elected King and I shall sit beside you on the throne. Together we shall do great things and fulfil the ambition of my forefathers, the Lombard kings, ruling all Italy and confining the Pope to his proper office. Think of it, my love, dream of your glory ... and all you must do is offer Charles a basket of sugared plums.'

There was a silence, during which the King required all the self-control he could muster not to break in on the wicked pair and smite them with his mighty sword as they so richly deserved. Who could blame him had he done so? Surely never before or since has a monarch been suffered to hear such talk of treason and so restrained himself!

Dietrich said, and there was a timid questioning note in his voice, 'You say there is only one plum poisoned among so many. Might not Charles offer that to his queen or one of her ladies, or perhaps to Bishop Turpin who sits always by his right hand, and so escape death himself?'

Fassolda laughed. 'The King is as greedy as a little boy and especially for sugared plums. He could no more offer to share our gift with others than he can fly.'

Hearing this, Charles's blood seemed (as he later reflected) to boil, for it appeared that Fassolda, to whom he had ever been kind, not only hated him, but despised him too. No king can be happy to hear himself described as a little boy who stuffs his face with sweetmeats which he refuses to share with his fellows. So once again his hand closed on his sword-hilt, but once again he held back. For the thought now came to him that perhaps the angel had foreseen all that he was now compelled to endure, and he remembered the command the angel had given him: that he go forth and steal. Steal, not kill, he said to himself, biting his lower lip to prevent himself from calling out in anger.

Then there was silence, and then the sound of lovemaking and Fassolda's sighs and yelps; and it infuriated him still more that, having agreed to compass his death – to murder me, were the words he formed in his mind – the wicked pair should so take delight in each other's bodies.

At last the sounds ceased, but not before he became aware that his companion Elgebast was breathing heavily, as if himself infected by the sounds of lust, so that he had to dig him in the ribs to enjoin silence on him. In a little he heard Dietrich snore, and soon the even breathing of Fassolda told him that they were both asleep.

The King then crept into the bedchamber, lit only by shafts of moonlight. Dietrich and Fassolda lay in each other's arms, and their faces glowed with satiated pleasure in the pale-yellow light. Charles stood over them like David in the camp of King Saul, and, like David, spared them. He slid his sword into its sheath and took from the chest that stood by the bed a ring with a ruby the size of a sparrow's egg. He took also Dietrich's sword, which he had laid at the foot of the bed, and slipped back through the curtain.

Charles and Elgebast descended the stair, and when they were free of the tavern and had mounted their horses, dawn was breaking and they heard the first cocks crow in the village.

Elgebast said, 'I have done that which you required of me and may now take my leave.'

The King smiled. 'Are you not curious,' he said, 'as to the reason for our adventure?'

'It was your business, not mine,' was the reply, 'and I make it a rule to hold my peace in such circumstances. I would have been a dead man often if I had meddled in what concerns others alone. Besides, there is an old adage: ask no questions and you'll be told no lies.'

'And what makes you think I would lie to you?' Charles said.

'All men lie when it suits them, which is more often than not. That is something I have learned in my life on the road.'

'Nevertheless,' the King said, 'I should wish to reward you for what you have done tonight.'

'I have had reward enough, for while you stole a sword and a small jewel, I took advantage of the opportunity to abstract a fine necklace belonging to the lady.'

And with these words he wheeled his horse around and galloped off in the direction of the forest.

The winter sun had just passed its zenith when the trumpets sounded and the King entered the great hall of the palace and took his seat at the high table. Charles smiled on the company, and all men warmed in the sun of his regard. Then he leaned across to his bosom-friend, Bishop Turpin, and said, loud enough for all the company to hear, 'I am so happy that so many of my peers and paladins have come together to greet me on my birthday, for the power of a king depends on the love and loyalty he inspires in his followers, and so it is that the kingdom remains in good health.'

Then, after his familiar manner, he tweaked the Bishop's ear and, lowering his voice (which was, however, still audible to all those assembled), said, 'But I do not see my dear brother Dietrich. It is not like him to be tardy on such a day. I trust he is not ill or that no accident has befallen him?'

Turpin said, 'It may be he has been detained by his wife.'

'And who would not be enchained by the lovely Fassolda?' the King said, so serenely and, as it were, innocently that none dared to laugh, interpreting his words as irony.

'Indeed,' Turpin said, 'Fassolda's charms are well known,' and this time the King observed two of the younger knights biting their lips to restrain their laughter.

'She is a princess,' he said, 'of rare and infinite resource.'

Then, with a crook of his finger, he summoned these same two knights, Yves and Ivor, to mount the dais that he might speak with them. But, because he wished his words to remain secret, he withdrew with them behind the arras, and they followed, the colour fleeing from their faces, for they feared they had offended the King by their levity. And indeed his first words seemed ominous to them.

'It is not fitting,' he said, 'for young knights to mock a lady.'

They dared not look at each other or at the King, but kept their gazes lowered.

'Young knights, moreover,' he said, 'who have scarce proved themselves by any deed of daring.'

At these words each felt the sweat start to his face and run down the back of his legs. They are not to be condemned for this, my Prince, for in truth, the wrath of Charlemagne was terrible, all the more so because of his high-pitched voice that was so at odds with the magnificence and dignity of his appearance.

Then he chuckled. 'And if the lady is ill-favoured, so much the more reprehensible is it for young sparks like yourselves to make mock of her. What punishment, I wonder, is suitable . . . ?'

He stretched out his hand and stroked first Yves then Ivor on the cheek.

'Beardless boys,' he said, 'and pretty ones . . . It is not enough to deprive you of today's feast, though that is certainly my will. I must devise a mission for you, that you may prove yourselves not mere effeminate scoffers, but men worthy of respect.'

He paused, as if deep in thought, though in truth he had no need of that, for his mind was already made up.

'There is a robber-knight,' he said, 'who dwells in the forest beyond the river, hard by Saint Antony's chapel. A fierce warrior who goes by several names, among them Elgebast and Alberich. I see from your manner that you have heard of him.'

'Indeed, yes,' said Yves.

'Many tales are told of him,' Ivor said. 'Did he not waylay the Abbot of St Pandulf's monastery and steal his plate, then send him scampering home naked as the day he was born?'

'And did he not throw the Mayor of Limoges down a well and keep him there till the citizens paid a ransom?' Yves said. 'Which seems to me strange, that they should wish to ransom their Mayor.'

'Be that as it may,' the King said, smiling to see how the young men were alarmed, 'it is my pleasure that you seek him out and bring him to the palace before nightfall.'

Yves looked at Ivor, Ivor looked at his friend, and each saw fear in the other's eyes.

'And if he will not come willingly . . .' Yves said, unable to disguise a tremor in his voice.

'Why then, you must bring him to me unwillingly,' the King said, 'and since there are two of you and the knight is a solitary, you would be unworthy to be numbered among my paladins if he should overcome you. Nevertheless, I shall tell you how to avoid battle. You must say to the knight that his companion of the hours of darkness would fain speak with him, and, should he still hesitate to accompany you, then you may say it is a matter of a necklace and a ruby ring. Now be gone.'

So the two young knights rode forth in puzzlement and apprehension, while the King returned to the banqueting hall.

He drank a cup of the red wine of Burgundy, and said to Turpin, 'Is there no word yet come from my brother Dietrich?'

The servitors, at a signal from the major-domo, now brought in the feast: wild boar slain by the King's verderers in his forest of Champagne, barons of beef from cattle raised in the lush pastures of the Marne, mutton from the salt-pastures of Brittany, carp from the monastic fish-ponds, salmon from the Loire and pike from the lakes of the Auvergne. There were great raised pies, stuffed with liver, kidneys, sweetbreads and mushrooms, and the open tarts which are the pride of Strasbourg and Nancy. For the King's table alone there was foie gras from the geese of Perigord, and lobsters and crayfish and great platters of oysters. Jellies and syllabubs were provided in abundance, and fruit tarts and cheeses – the straw-coloured rounds of Cantal, and the creamy Brie and Camembert in which Charlemagne was known to delight.

And yet the King, whose appetite was famous, sat fingering his goblet of wine and ate nothing.

'Is there no word from my brother Dietrich?' he said again.

Light was fading and candles flickered on the tables when at last the great double doors were thrown open, and Dietrich stood there, tall and handsome as the King his half-brother, but his face white as a bishop's surplice.

All fell silent as he advanced up the hall towards the King's table, for there was that in his countenance which made men wonder whether he had come to announce some disaster. But when he greeted the King, and wished him God's grace and prosperity on this auspicious day, his voice, which was used to be gentle and pleasant, was firm and hard as the Harz rock.

'You are late, brother,' the King said, 'so late that I feared that some accident had befallen you or that you were sick.'

Dietrich bent his knee and kissed the King's hand in token of allegiance and friendship. Then he gestured to the squire who accompanied him, and, blushing, the youth, whose name was Denis, held out the basket which he had concealed under his cloak.

'There is no gift fitting for so great a king as you, my half-brother,' Dietrich said, 'but as a mark of the love we bear you, my wife Fassolda has prepared this little basket of sugared plums stuffed with a sauce of almonds, which is, she tells me, a dish of which you are inordinately fond above all others. Or so she says, and one must trust a woman's judgement in such matters.'

'Sugared plums stuffed with the essence of almond,' the King said, 'and prepared by our dear Fassolda's own fair hands – nothing could please me more. So, as a mark of my gratitude, brother, I entreat you to share your gift with me, and indeed to be the first to eat one of the plums.'

Dietrich hesitated. He scarce dared refuse, yet feared to obey.

The King smiled. 'Come, brother, eat,' he said, 'it is my pleasure. I can happily spare you one plum from Fassolda's generous gift.'

So saying, he slipped the ruby ring on to his finger and, extending his hand, picked a plum from the basket and offered it to his brother. At the sight of the ring, the colour fled from Dietrich's face. His lips quivered. He recoiled in horror, fear and dismay. He made to speak and could not.

Charles looked him in the face and continued to smile. 'So you will not eat, brother? Then you shall come sit by me.'

This time Dietrich, trembling, obeyed. He took his place by the King, who now commanded that all should resume the feast.

'Perhaps you are wise,' he said to Dietrich. 'These plums, which have so delicious an appearance, will be better eaten after the meat. Pleasures postponed are all the more to be enjoyed.'

Meanwhile, the two young knights, Ivor and Yves, rode through the forest in the gathering gloom of the winter afternoon, until they came within sight of St Antony's chapel which stood in an oak grove above a stream.

The young men looked at each other and, even in the twilight, each read fear in his companion's eyes. Strange to relate, this emboldened both, for the discovery bound them still more closely together. They drew their horses side by side and embraced. Their lips met and each was conscious of the other's heart beating behind the breastplate of their armour.

'We are two and yet we act as one,' Ivor murmured.

Then they heard the sound of cantering hooves and, in a moment, the knight Elgebast was before them. He held his lance upright, stood high in his stirrups and laughed to see them disengage.

'We come in peace,' Yves said, his voice faltering, for the knight's aspect was truly terrifying.

'In peace? Or for a lovers' tryst?' Elgebast laughed again. 'Are you outlaws like myself? Have you fled the justice of the Church that claims to speak in the name of the Almighty and would punish you for your unnatural affections?'

The mockery in his voice gave Ivor the courage to speak.

'We are comrades, not lovers,' he said, 'and our affections are natural, for we have sworn an oath to live and die together as brave knights should. And we have come hither in search of the knight who goes by the name sometimes of Elgebast and sometimes Alberich, whom some call a notorious brigand and others an honourable man driven to this solitude by the malice of his enemies. If you are he, we have a message for you.'

'And if you are not the man we seek,' Yves said, made resolute by his friend's bold words, 'perhaps you would have the kindness to tell us where we may find him, for, I assure you, we intend no harm to you or to the knight himself; our purpose is peaceful.'

'Harm?' Elgebast said. 'Harm? What harm could two youths of your stamp do me? Yes, I am Elgebast, otherwise known as Alberich, and I eat beardless boys like you for breakfast.'

'Nevertheless,' Ivor said, 'we are glad to have come upon you, for we bear a message for you.'

'It comes from—' Yves began.

'Your companion of the hours of darkness,' Ivor broke in. 'He bade us say to you that he would fain speak with you again, and so he has sent us to invite you to accompany us to the meeting-place he has appointed.'

Elgebast did not immediately answer. He chewed the corner of his moustache, which he wore long in the manner of the ancient Gauls.

'My companion of the hours of darkness,' he said, in a musing tone. 'A fine fellow certainly ... Nevertheless, if this should be a trick ...

'It is no trick,' Ivor said.

'We may be young and, as you say, beardless,' Yves said,

26

'but we are honourable men who would not be party to any deception.'

'That's as may be,' was the reply, 'and I have no wish to insult you, but my experience has taught me to be wary of men when they speak of their honour, for I have found that many do so the more fervently when they are about to lie or practise deception. However, I shall come with you, but I warn you that if you play me false I shall split the pair of you from gizzard to guts.'

So they rode through the black forest in a silence broken only by the beat of their horses' hooves, the jangle of harness and the distant howling of wolves, until they came to the brow of a hill and saw the lights of the royal palace below.

Elgebast drew rein. 'Where are you leading me?' he said, and his voice was harsh.

'We were told to say,' Ivor said, 'that it is a matter of a necklace and a ruby ring.'

'A necklace and a ruby ring,' the knight said, and put his hand to his throat. 'I mislike the sound of that. Yet no man shall say that Elgebast turned back from a venture.'

So they descended the slope and came to the palace. They gave their horses to the grooms, then entered the hall. Elgebast now strode ahead of his companions and the eyes of all were turned upon him. When he saw the King seated at the high table, he paused a moment, looked disdainfully about him, and then marched towards Charles. The King rose and extended to him the hand which wore the ruby ring. Their eyes met. Then, keeping his gaze fixed on the King, Elgebast bowed his knee, took his hand and kissed the ring.

Charles said, 'I am pleased to welcome you, my friend.' Then, turning, 'And I believe my brother Dietrich is no stranger to you either. See, he has brought me a basket of sugared plums prepared by the fair hand of his Lady Fassolda. Will you eat one, friend.'

'I think not.'

'You hear that, Dietrich? Like me, like you yourself, my friend here declines to eat of your wife's gift. Now why would that be, would you say?'

Dietrich looked now this way, now that. The sweat stood out

27

on his temples and coursed down his cheeks. To give himself courage, he stretched out for his cup of wine, but his hand shook and he could not raise the cup to his lips. He felt the eyes of all fixed upon him in wonder, and it seemed to the wretched man that his guilt was known.

The King picked a plum from the basket and held it out to him. 'Eat,' he said.

But Dietrich, though a brave warrior in battle, shrank away from the sugared fruit.

Then Charles called on Elgebast to speak and to relate their adventure of the night before, and what they had overheard in the castle. When he had done so, there was a silence as profound as on a morning when the earth is buried in deep snow. Then some called out for Dietrich to suffer the penalty prescribed for traitors, for murderers and for those who would compass the King's death. But Charles stilled the tumult by raising his hand.

'It was an angel,' he said, 'sent by the Lord who came upon me last night and bade me go forth and steal, and the angel guided me to my encounter with my friend Sir Elgebast here, who led me to my brother's castle. And he has told you what we learned there. So, my friends, you see that I am in the care of the Lord Almighty and that Dietrich and Fassolda could no more harm me than they could have slain the angel who watched over me. So is Evil powerless against those who walk in the way of the Lord, and thus is Satan once more defeated.'

When he heard these words Dietrich flung himself to the ground, and lay there, his fat thighs quivering in his terror, prostrate before the King.

But Charles lifted him up and said, 'My poor brother. You have been led astray even as our first father Adam was led astray, because your lady has listened, as did our mother Eve, to the promptings of the Serpent that is Satan, the enemy of mankind.'

Then he said to Elgebast, 'Give me the necklace.'

And Elgebast obeyed, though unwillingly.

'Fear not,' the King said, 'I shall recompense you with more than jewels.'

So he took the necklace and handed it to Dietrich, saying, 'Take this and bind your lady with it.'

Then all marvelled at the king's magnanimity.

He said, 'From this day on, this my palace shall be known as Engelheim, the dwelling of the Angel.' Then he ordered them to resume the feast, and Elgebast sat with the young knights Ivor and Yves and made merry with them.

But the basket of sugared plums remained untouched on the table before the King, who poured wine for his brother Dietrich and commanded him to drink.

This, my Prince, is the story as related by the poets. It is charming, but you have no reason to think it literal truth. It would certainly be agreeable if it was that. True history is grimmer, however. It relates that Dietrich, prompted by his wife Fassolda, raised up a rebellion against the King, was defeated in battle and deserted by his men. Dietrich and Fassolda were taken prisoner. She was thrown into prison where she starved to death. Dietrich was hanged and then dismembered, his limbs being hung one on each gate of his city, which is now known as Clermont-Ferrand. For many years the legend 'thus perish all traitors' was attached to them.

Some say that this happened after Charles had spared him once, that he rebelled despite the King's magnanimous act. But others assert that the story I have related was invented to obscure the reality of the injustice which drove an honourable man to rebellion, rightly called treason.

V

Charles had three heroes to whom he looked for inspiration.

The first was Our Lord Jesus Christ. The King's devotion to Our Saviour was conspicuous. Not only at Easter but on the first Friday of every month, he had himself scourged by his confessor, Bishop Turpin; and he submitted to this not only in imitation of Christ's Passion, but, as I believe, to satisfy some inner need of which he was himself unconscious. For there existed in uneasy harness within that remarkable man the lust to dominate and the contrary desire to be subjected to humiliation.

His favourite text was Christ's assurance that he came to bring not peace, but a sword. It was ever on his lips, and he used it to justify all his wars. Each, he insisted, was fought in the name of Christ Jesus and to further his purposes. He really believed that the kingdom of the Franks was the kingdom of Christ here on earth. Bishop Turpin encouraged him in this conviction, for he too loved war and was never happier than when in camp and on campaign. Indeed, his love of war was such that he invented a weapon for his own use. This was the mace, which enabled him to lay about himself in battle without breaching the injunction that prohibits those in Holy Orders from shedding blood. Of course, a blow from a mace may sometimes result in wounds that bleed, but this may be considered fortuitous, not of design. At any rate, many bishops, following the good Turpin's example, have since employed the mace in battle, and done great execution with it, happy all the while in the knowledge that they are not committing an offence against canon law.

The King's second hero was Julius Caesar, and such was his admiration for the Roman dictator or emperor that it did not distress him that Caesar had been a pagan who worshipped the false gods of Rome and even served as the high priest of Jupiter. Nothing impressed Charles more than Caesar's conquest of Gaul, and I have no doubt that his wars against the Saxons were undertaken in imitation of Caesar. For he often said: 'As Caesar brought our ancestors the Gauls within the body of the Roman Empire, so likewise I shall compel the Saxons to acknowledge my supremacy. Caesar made Romans of the Gauls, and I shall make Christians of the Saxons.'

Such was his devotion to Caesar that he was often heard to say that, to his mind, not even the infamy of Judas Iscariot exceeded that of Brutus, Cassius and the other conspirators who murdered Caesar in the theatre of Pompey. He would say this with such ferocity that not even Bishop Turpin dared to contradict him.

His third hero was Arthur, the emperor who defied the barbarians and sought to keep the light of Christ burning in a Dark Age. His hatred of the Saxons was undoubtedly fuelled by his knowledge that they had been Arthur's enemies, too. Charles loved to trace his descent from Arthur, and the genealogical table he had drawn up to establish this was every bit as honest and accurate as that by which St Matthew traces Christ's descent from David, King of Israel.

Nothing pleased the King more than to listen to minstrels and troubadours singing of Arthur and recounting the stories of his knights. It was in imitation of Arthur's Order of Chivalry, the Knights of the Round Table, that he gathered his paladins about him, and he was determined that they should emulate the feats ascribed to those whom he held to be their predecessors; and indeed, as I shall relate, the glory of the paladins was to be equal to that of Arthur's knights.

But, before I do so, I must say something of the King's prejudices and temper, for Charles, though a great hero, was not in all respects admirable. I write this with reluctance but a historian is bound to speak truth and is therefore obliged to paint the portrait of even a mighty king, warts and all. Moreover, inasmuch as I would have you, my Prince, model yourself on Charles in his virtues, so also I would have you recognise his vices and eschew them.

First, then, Charles had a great horror of deformity. He could not bear to have cripples near him, and when one of his daughters

31

was born with a hare-lip would have had her set aside to die if the infant's mother, a Saxon slave-girl, had not succeeded in persuading Bishop Turpin to carry the child off to a convent to be reared as a bride of Christ. Likewise, Charles refused to allow dwarves into his presence, for he believed their influence was malign. He had a horror of lepers, too, and on one occasion ordered a colony of these unfortunate beings who had been found sheltering in the forest of Soissons, where the wretched creatures subsisted as best they could, to be put to the sword; and this, to his great shame, was done.

Then he loathed Jews whom he held to be worse infidels than Muslims, for, he said, while the Muslims honoured Jesus as a prophet, even if, heretically, they refused to acknowledge him as the Saviour of Mankind, the Jews had been responsible for his death. Therefore, he held the Jews guilty of the most grievous sin in the history of mankind, and, though he could not drive them out of his Empire, subjected them to constant persecution. 'For,' he said, 'they were offered the Light and chose to live in darkness. They were the Chosen People who rejected God. Therefore, they in their turn are rejected.' In this, as you will understand, my Prince, he showed himself but a poor theologian, for it was necessary that Christ should die on the Cross that mankind should be redeemed by his blood. I write as one well versed in Jewish philosophy, and I tell you, my Prince, that hatred of the Jews is the mark of an inferior mind and a narrow spirit.

VI

I must now speak of the paladins.

There is some dispute as to whether Bishop Turpin should be numbered among them, being an ecclesiastic and not a knight. Nevertheless, since no man was closer to Charles than the Bishop, it is right that I should say something of him.

He was born at Sens in Burgundy, the son of a merchant. He was not a Frank, but a Gaul, and his mother was of Roman descent; she claimed consuls among her ancestors, and the Bishop's first language was Latin. He adored his mother and disliked his father, in this resembling Charles, which resemblance was the first bond between them. From childhood he was intended for the Church, and early showed a talent for scholarship, writing a commentary on the Gospel according to St John when he was only twelve. All his life he had a particular devotion to that saint, a devotion that some thought sat ill with his own warlike character.

Turpin was not handsome. He had blubbery lips, a crooked nose, and even before he was twenty had become grossly fat. He was also afflicted by a skin disease which made him smell of the privy. Or so it is attested.

His devotion to Charles was absolute, his loyalty never in doubt; and this was the best feature of his character. At the same time he was jealous of anyone who might have influence over the King, and the difficulties that Charles had with his wives have been attributed to the Bishop's mischief-making. For he could not bear that any man or woman should stand closer to the King than he did.

Wise in council, brave in battle, resolute in adversity, and devout in worship, Turpin commanded the respect, if not the affection, of all. He was cold to his inferiors and insolent to those who thought themselves his superiors by birth. Denied the

33

love of women, for unlike many bishops he abstained from fornication and fathered no bastards, he was accused of an unseemly tenderness towards the choristers of his cathedral and the clerks and squires of his retinue. Some who saw him stroke the downy cheek of a youth, or address his young men as 'angels', accused him of that vice which is deemed 'unnatural', though what else but nature, however perverted, inspires its expression? In any case, the charge was false, for Turpin spoke out frequently against the sin of sodomy.

In truth, Turpin, like many remarkable men, was composed of contradictions. He preached a gospel of love and was yet also mighty and even pitiless in battle. No one did more in that time to teach the Franks to honour the monastic life and to encourage them to endow monasteries; yet, on campaign, he was heard to speak disparagingly of a life devoted to prayer, and to extol the military virtues. Then he was a zealous churchman who nevertheless resisted the attempt of successive bishops of Rome to extend their power.

One of the noblest of the paladins was Ogier the Dane. He was the son of Geoffroy, King of Denmark, and when he was born, his father summoned six wise women to the chamber where the child lay by his mother, that they might foretell his future and bestow gifts upon him. One of these, Morgana, was a descendant of King Arthur's half-sister Morgan le Fay, and she said, 'Beautiful infant, I claim you as my own; and I shall watch over you and shield you till at last I call you to keep me company in the Lake Isle of Avalon, among my heroic lovers, where rests also the wounded body of Arthur the King.'

Later Geoffroy made war on Charlemagne in alliance with the rebellious Saxons. But his army was brought to battle on the north German plain. Outflanked and outnumbered, they fought bravely, but before the winter sun set, half the Danish army lay dead. Geoffroy, rejecting flight, offered his naked breast to Charlemagne's sword, but the Frankish King, displaying that magnanimity of which he boasted, spared his life on condition that he accepted Christian baptism. Then, as surety for his future conduct, Charles demanded that he surrender hostages, chief among whom was the young Prince Ogier. So it came about that he was first held at the Frankish court, then given into the care of Duke Namo of Bavaria, a loyal ally of Charles. When later the Franks made war in Italy against the Saracens, young Ogier served as Duke Namo's squire.

That battle was fought north of Rome, so far had the Saracens' advance taken them. The Pope, expelled from his capital, or having taken to flight in terror, urged Charlemagne to descend from the position he had taken up on the flank of a hill, and destroy the Saracen army arranged on the plain below. At first the King demurred, and in doing so was supported by Elgebast, the former brigand who was now among the most trusted of his lieutenants.

'It would be the sheerest folly,' Elgebast said. 'The Saracen army is much larger than ours. Indeed, it is to ours as Rome is to the village where I was born. To descend upon it and launch an attack in open field is to invite disaster. Far better to hold our ground, and wait for them to attack us, for I tell you, as sure as eggs is eggs, the advantage of the ground is the only advantage we have. Yield it, and we are dead men, I fear.'

'You fear,' said the Pope, and his voice was as cold as the north wind and as scornful as a whip is cutting.

But Elgebast held his ground. 'Indeed yes,' he said, 'I fear to act on such a proposal as yours as any man not devoid of his wits or altogether ignorant of the rudiments of the art of war would fear to do so. I yield to no man in courage and would split any who dared call me a coward from gizzard to guts, and yet what you urge on the King lays the chill finger of fear upon me. Go you and pray, Your Holiness, and leave war to those who know it.'

The Pope grew pale. Never had he been so insulted, not since he was a novice in the monastery of Monte Cassino. Then two angry spots red as a cardinal's hat stood out, one on each cheek. He turned to the King and said, 'When Samuel the High Priest commanded Saul, King of Israel, to smite the Amalekites and destroy them utterly, sparing neither man nor woman, not child nor ox, and Saul did not keep this commandment, the Lord God Almighty, through the voice of Samuel, his humble servant as I am, however unworthy, removed Saul from the office of king

35

and his sons after him. Now, as the instrument of the Lord God of Hosts, I command you to pay no heed to this impious fellow, but to do as I say, and lead your army against the infidel to drive them in flight, terror and disorder from the land. Are you afraid that you hesitate, or so stiff-necked and stubborn that you disobey the word of the Lord?'

When Charles heard these words he was sore afraid. Reason told him that Elgebast's advice was good. Experience told him it was foolish to abandon a strong position and engage the enemy on the plain. But what are reason and experience to set against the word of the Lord?

The Pope saw him hesitate. 'Fear not,' he said. 'The heavenly hosts of angels fight by your side.'

'Words, words, words,' muttered Elgebast, 'and words that make no sense.'

'The angels are with me?' Charles said, wonderingly, remembering how the angel had come to him as he lay asleep and ordered him to go forth and steal, and how well, despite his doubts, that enterprise had turned out. So now he ordered the trumpets to sound and commanded Elgebast to lead the attack. The old brigand frowned and ordered his squire to dress him in black armour, for black is the colour of death, which he expected.

Many of the Franks were of Elgebast's mind, for to abandon their strong position seemed to men who had been in so many battles to be the sheerest folly. Not a few of them cursed the Pope for a meddling idiot. Even the young and ardent, men of the highest spirit, could not look on the mighty host of the Saracens without trepidation.

As they prepared for battle, Ivor took his dear companion Yves in his arms and said, 'Should I fall today, remember how I have loved you.'

Yves said, 'My sentiments with regard to you, dearer to me than any brother.'

Then they embraced and shed tears, thinking of what might befall them, before setting their faces to the foe.

Let no one condemn them for their apprehension, or accuse them of weakness. To look open-eyed at the imminence of death, and yet ride into battle is the mark of a man. And indeed that day, as the sun rose in the sky, the courage of the Franks, outnumbered and committed to a fight against fearful odds, was wonderful to behold.

So banners flying, trumpets sounding, they formed in line, and advanced down the hill, the horses at first picking their way cautiously over the rough ground. Then the trumpets were silent, and the only sound was the jangling of harness and the iron of the horses' hooves striking stone. The Saracen army stood silent also, but in amazement, as if they could not credit what they saw; for they had been preparing to mount an assault on the Franks' strong defensive position.

'What manner of men are these?' one asked.

'Fools,' was the reply. 'Whom Allah wishes to destroy, he first deprives of their wits.'

Meanwhile Charlemagne, commanding the rearguard, watched the advance, and was torn between pride and fear. He turned to the Pope and said, 'Pray, Your Holiness, that your counsel is good, and that you have not misinterpreted the will of the Almighty.'

The Pope flushed and replied, 'It is through the successor to St Peter that the Lord speaks to mankind.'

'So be it,' Charlemagne said, and turned his attention to the narrowing gap between the two armies; it could not escape his notice that the Saracens were now advancing on either flank and would soon be in a position to draw the horns of their army together, encircling the Franks, as the historian Livy tells us Hannibal's Carthaginians encircled the Romans at Cannae.

Then he saw Elgebast stand high in his stirrups, his lance aloft, and hold up his left hand to halt the advance, that his troops might form themselves in line. He saw him lower his lance and lead the charge at a sharp trot against the main body of the Saracen army. The earth itself seemed to shake as the Frankish cavalry struck the enemy, who gave way before the first shock, so that a cry of victory rose from the Franks. But then the wings of the Saracen force closed on their prey, and the battle became a mêlée of desperate hand-to-hand fighting; and the screams of the wounded and dying rose to the watchers on the hillside. But still Charlemagne held the rearguard in reserve, though Bishop Turpin, his face red as an apple and sweating on account of the excitement which the prospect of battle always awoke in him, urged that the moment was ripe for him to launch himself on what was now the rear of the Saracens' left wing, which had now so nearly completed the encirclement of Elgebast's force. But Charlemagne still ordered him to stay his hand.

Some say this was a mark of his sagacity, his feel for the decisive moment. But others say that the King feared to launch his reserve, for, if its charge failed, then all was lost.

Now it so happened that the royal standard, the Oriflamme, had been carried that day into the battle by a knight called Alory, a particular favourite of the king, for he had been reared in the court and had served when a child as Charlemagne's cup-bearer, and then, when a youth, as a page of the bedchamber. He was an ardent young man with a lively imagination and an ease of manner that charmed all. This was his first experience of combat and he had besought Charlemagne that he might have the honour of carrying the Oriflamme. Other young men were jealous, as was proper, for every young man of spirit thinks naturally that such honours should come his way, and foremost among them was Ogier the Dane, who accompanied Duke Namo as his squire and who had not yet received the order of knighthood. Furthermore, he resented Alory whose lively wit had been exercised at his expense on account of Ogier's accent, which Alory mocked as uncouth.

Alory did not lack courage, but who can tell when courage will fail? And such was Alory's fate now. A Saracen scimitar swung at his head, knocking his helmet askew and drawing blood from his beardless cheek. This was not battle as he had dreamed it. His blood turned to water (as the saying goes). Fear took possession of him. He turned his horse's head and fled from the field, the Oriflamme lowered, and others followed him, terror being ever infectious.

Ogier, on the hillside, observed all this, and looked on the fleeing Alory with anger and contempt. He pointed him out to the other squires who stood about, and then, putting his horse at the gallop, rode hard towards the terrified standard-bearer. With one blow of his club he struck him from his horse, dismounted himself and, giving the reins to a companion, immediately stripped the unworthy Alory of his armour as he lay stunned on the ground, and swiftly dressed himself in it. Then, remounting, he led the other squires, with the wild cry of his berserker ancestors, into the fray, once more bearing the Oriflamme aloft. The sight of the royal standard resuming the battle gave heart to the Franks, who now once more held their ground, so that the fighting became still more intense.

Now Charlemagne himself, judging the moment right, led his reserve against the enemy. But his timing was, for once, at fault. The Saracens, recovering from the shock of Ogier's charge, rallied. The King was soon surrounded. Wielding his mighty sword, Joyeuse, he cut down Constable, one of the Saracen commanders, and was about to dispatch him, when he was himself set upon by two Saracen knights. His horse reared and he was thrown to the ground. Perceiving by the eagle on his helmet's crest that this was the King, they both dismounted to deliver the death-blow. Never in his long life was Charlemagne in such danger. But Ogier now flew to the rescue. He thrust the standard, the Oriflamme, in the face of one of the Saracens, as it had been a lance, and then drove his brave horse at the other, so that he fell to the earth and was trampled under its hooves. Then he helped Charlemagne to rise, and enabled him to mount one of the horses belonging to the fallen enemy.

'Brave and noble Alory,' cried Charlemagne, recognising the armour and the Oriflamme, 'I owe you my honour and my life.'

Ogier disdained to correct the King's mistake. Instead he plunged back into the fight and, followed by the young warriors inspired by his example, carried the Oriflamme forward till the standard of Mohammed was seen to waver, and the Saracens drew back. So disciplined and experienced was their hitherto victorious army that they were able to effect this manoeuvre in orderly fashion, even though the Christian knights continued to press hard upon them. Then Elgebast gave orders that the recall be sounded, for he well knew the wiles of the Saracens and how, in many battles, they were accustomed to feign flight in order to lure their enemy into a trap.

So darkness began to draw in with the issue still not settled, and both armies, as it seemed, ready to renew the contest the next day. Notwithstanding which prospect, Bishop Turpin laid aside his helmet and his mace, took his mitre and crozier, and intoned a *Te Deum*. He did so forgetting the presence of the Pope, and indeed, when one reminded him of this, His Holiness was nowhere to be seen.

Meanwhile, on the field of battle, the noble Elgebast moved among the slain, the dying and the wounded, and tears mingled with the blood from his gashed cheek, as he wept to see so many brave warriors whose day was done. Then he heard a man howling, a wild cry of pain and sorrow rising from where the battle had been fiercest. He pushed forward, stumbling often, for he had been wounded also by an arrow that struck his thigh, and there he came upon young Ivor cradling the head of his beloved comrade Yves. Elgebast knelt by him, and looked on the face already overtaken by the pallor of death. Ivor leaned over his friend and kissed him on the lips, and hung there a moment as if there might be some response. But there was none. So Elgebast hugged Ivor to him, burying his own face in the young man's hair, and said, softly, 'He died as a true warrior. See, all the wounds are in the front. That is no comfort now, but in winter nights the memory of how he lived and how he died will warm you.' But, silently, in his heart, he cursed the Pope, whose counsel had forced this battle on them. His tears flowed anew and he clasped Ivor to him, for he had come to love these young men as if they had been his sons or nephews. There is nothing sadder, he thought, than this moment of stillness after the battle, whether it be won or lost. And as for this one, I do not know if it should be called victory or defeat. Certainly we have driven the Saracens back, but, in doing so, we have lost more noble knights than I can number, and this poor Yves among the finest of them.

Then he called on a sergeant to fetch a long shield, and they laid the body that had been Yves upon it, and carried him up the hill to the camp.

There they found the King seated on a chair which served as his throne. He looked dazed, and a page pressed a wet cloth to his head while another held a cup of wine to his lips. Elgebast approached, and, for a moment, it seemed as if Charlemagne did not know him, so bemused was he on account of the blow to the head he had received.

Elgebast declined to kneel before him and said, 'Where is that villain of a Pope who forced this battle on us and has cost us the lives of so many brave knights?'

For a little there was no answer, and the King still looked as if his wits had deserted him. Then a grizzled sergeant stepped forward and, tugging his forelock, said to Elgebast, 'I have enquired among the camp followers, the cooks, ostlers and women who march with the army, and at first none could tell me, till at last one woman, a girl from my own village, an honest lass as I can attest, came forward and said that she had observed him steal away mounted on a mule and surrounded by his papal guard. But where he has gone she could not say, save that it was far from the battle.'

'God damn him for a cowardly Italian,' Elgebast said, and some trembled to hear him speak of His Holiness in such a manner. But the King neither moved nor spoke, and it seemed again as if he did not understand. The page once more raised the cup to his lips and this time the King drank and swallowed, and the colour that had fled slowly returned to his face.

At this moment the noble Dane Ogier, bedewed with blood and his armour covered with dust, came to lay the Oriflamme at the king's feet. He was accompanied by the youths he had led into the battle, and they walked slowly, being weary on account of the weight of their armour, the exertions of the day, and the wounds they had suffered. Ogier knelt at the King's feet, and, seeing him, Charlemagne revived, recovered his wits and recalled that the young man had rescued him from ignominy and saved his life. But he did not yet recognise him and, when he embraced him, again addressed him as Alory.

Bishop Turpin, who had a tenderness for that young man, sang out his praises, and said, 'Surely those who mocked this young man, calling him a carpet-knight and scoffing at his gentle manners, must now hail him as the bravest of the brave.'

Whereupon young Roland, the King's nephew, of whom I shall have much to say subsequently, unable to endure this misapprehension, unlaced Ogier's helmet that all might see his face, and called out, 'But look, it is not Alory, who fled from the battle and now skulks wherever he may hide his shame, but Ogier, the noble Dane, your hostage, who saved your life, uncle, and is worthy of the accolade that Bishop Turpin bestows on another.'

Charlemagne shook his head, stroked his long white beard and, concealing his shame (if kings can feel shame, Charlemagne must have felt it now), said, 'Noble youth. I owe you my life. My sword leaps to touch your shoulder, and the shoulders of your brave young companions.'

So he drew Joyeuse, and knighted Ogier and the other young men, there on the field of battle. And there is no nobler way for a man to receive the honour of knighthood.

VII

Spare a thought now for the wretched Alory. His head ached from the mighty blow Ogier had delivered, but this pain was as nothing to the misery into which he was cast. He withdrew to his tent, threw himself on the ground and lay there sobbing, overwhelmed by shame. All his life he had dreamed of the heroic deeds he would perform in battle, of how he would win such renown as to inspire minstrels to sing of his fame; and now he had failed at the first test of his manhood. I am dishonoured, he thought, I knew fear and surrendered to it, and am become an object of contempt. So, for a long time, he continued to weep and his boyish legs quivered. Truly his state was pitiable.

Then he heard himself being addressed. He struggled to his feet, ashamed again to be discovered in this womanish condition, and saw two sergeants standing at the doorway of the tent, grizzled veterans, their faces streaked with mud and blood, and heard that they had come to bring him before the King. They spoke harshly and he heard scorn in their tone.

He fell to his knees before the king and could not raise his head to look him in the eyes.

Charlemagne said: 'I raised you in my household, and made you a page of my bedchamber. Before we left Engelheim I bestowed upon you the honour of knighthood. Then, deceived by your pleasant manner and on account of the love I bore you, I entrusted you with the Oriflamme. You have betrayed my trust and shown yourself to be a coward and a poltroon, unworthy of my confidence, unworthy of the estate of knighthood.'

Each word the King spoke drew a sob from the young man, and he buried his face in the dust.

'Had it not been for the valour of the noble Ogier, you would by your cowardice have brought ruin on the army, and even as it is you have cost me the lives of many brave men and noble knights.'

Then he signalled to the sergeants and they hauled the boy to his feet and stripped him of the insignia of knighthood. They led, or rather dragged him to where a bar had been set across two posts and threw him over it, strapping his wrists to the posts. The King was seen to smile and one of the sergeants took a birch rod and lashed Alory till the blood stained his tunic and he pissed himself. The blows fell and he screamed with pain, then he lapsed into a faint and hung there.

Silence descended like a dark cloud over all who watched. Then the King spoke, in his high, piping voice, 'There is no place for cowards in the army.'

He called Ogier to him and, placing his arm round the Dane's shoulders, led him to his pavilion where dinner awaited.

It was dark when Elgebast came with Ivor and cut Alory free. They carried him to the old brigand's tent where they bathed his wounds.

'Was this necessary?' Ivor said.

'It was the King's pleasure,' Elgebast said. 'Truly his wrath is terrible.'

'But was it necessary? I had thought that nothing could make me forget even for a moment the grief I felt because Yves is dead, but watching that ... it is not good to humiliate anyone in such a manner.'

'No, it is not good.'

Then the moon rose and all was still in the camp, and Elgebast and Ivor gazed on the bonfires which the Saracens had lit on the distant plain. But in the morning they found that the Saracen army had slipped away and was nowhere to be seen.

'So we have won a famous victory?' Ivor said.

'And besmirched it.'

When Alory was sufficiently recovered from his beating to be able to walk, he took rope and hanged himself from a tree.

Self-slaughter is reputed a sin against the creator. But no man, Ivor thought, can live with dishonour. And from that day his heart was turned against the King.

VIII

You say, my Prince, that you are disturbed by what I have just related. Good. So you should be. The story is horrible. You ask why Charles acted as he did.

The explanation is complicated.

He had taken pleasure in the young Alory's careless charm and impudence. To have the page of his chamber call him 'nuncle', tease him and pout prettily when reproved, was pleasing. It let him escape, if only for a little, the loneliness of his station. You will come to know that solitude yourself, that removal from the common run of humanity. You will learn that few ever speak to you without calculation. So it was with Charles. Even in bed with wife or mistress, even when engaged in that most natural of acts, that carnality which testifies to our animal nature, Charles knew the woman was not free from calculation, that she was wondering if she was doing enough to please him; putting this question not as a lover may put it, but out of apprehension, fearing dismissal, rejection, replacement by another. He himself drove hard into his women, seeking to escape his royalty, which set him apart from men. Certainly, most of the time he relished that apartness. He was the King, not as other men are; God spoke through him. And yet, there were times when he was oppressed by the knowledge of his loneliness. He was like one marooned on a rock while the ocean surged round him. So, when the boy Alory with his squashed cat's face addressed him impudently with a ready smile and laughter in his eyes, Charles knew an unaccustomed warmth; it was like having a talking dog.

But now the puppy he had cherished, and on whom he had bestowed the privilege of bearing the Oriflamme into battle, had disgraced himself. And the King shared in that disgrace, for all saw that he had let his judgement be corrupted by affection. He read reproach in the faces around him; and his love for Alory

45

soured, then turned to disgust and anger. He had been betrayed by this boy who now trembled before him, ugly in shame and misery, his face stained by tears.

The day had gone badly for the King. He had been persuaded by the Pope to act against his better judgement. He had hesitated when Elgebast spoke out against the Pope, and then he had yielded; weakly, men would say. In the battle itself Charles had been unhorsed and owed his life to the Danish prince. His favourite had disgraced himself. Therefore the boy's humiliation should be made complete, that all might see how terrible was the wrath of the King. There would be scarce a man in the camp who did not feel fear as the whip bit into Alory's flesh.

You ask me, my Prince, how I know all this, and the question does credit to your intelligence. I have often told you that I am no Romancer, but relate and write down only that which I have good reason to think the truth. My first authority for all that I write about the chivalry of the Franks is the memoir written by, or at any rate ascribed to, the good Bishop Turpin, who, whatever his faults – very real, I assure you, for his Latin is barbarous and corrupt – nevertheless strove to tell the truth as he understood it, even though he tells some tales which appear so incredible that sensible men put him down as a liar or fantasist. Notwithstanding which, it is possible for one as well versed as myself in the ways of both the world and of literature to separate the wheat from the chaff, and preserve from the Bishop's work whatever is authentic.

Incidentally, in this context, you are not to believe that Italian tale beloved of indifferent versifiers, in which the hero tells of how he was carried by a witch riding on the back of a ram to a high cavern in the Alps where Bishop Turpin's true chronicles were preserved. This is mere flummery and fantasy, as you will acknowledge when I tell you that I have not only studied the Bishop's writings in the monastery attached to the basilica of Saint-Denis in Paris, but also transcribed them. So, when I quote Turpin, you will appreciate that I speak truth; and this is the case even when I do not cite him as my authority, because he is merely the framework of what I write.

As it happens, Bishop Turpin tells us nothing of what the

King thought and felt on the occasion of Alory's disgrace and punishment which I have just related. Indeed, the whole episode escapes him, either because he had a tenderness for the young man and found it too distressing to recount what I have told you, or because he could not bring himself to do so without speaking harshly of the King, his hero. Therefore, pusillanimity prevailed and he kept silent.

This being so, I therefore confess that I have no textual authority for my analysis of the King's state of mind. But does this signify that I have invented it? Not at all; for knowledge is not only of one sort.

There is the knowledge which is preserved in books and handed down from one generation to another; and this knowledge I revere, even while recognising that in books there are as many errors as in common speech. Books may utter calumnies, too, and you must beware of this.

Then there is a second kind of knowledge, which I call the knowledge of experience and observation. I have myself a great store of such knowledge, for I have travelled far, being driven, now by curiosity and now by the malice of my enemies, from one end of the world to the other; and all the while I have kept my mind open, and made mankind my study.

Finally, there is what I call the knowledge of penetration, which some prefer to call the knowledge of imagination. If I do not use this term it is because the imagination is too commonly thought to be an idle faculty, in no way superior to fancy or even day-dreams. But the knowledge of penetration is that which is revealed by the imagination in active operation, employed as a tool to unlock the secrets of our inner nature.

So it is out of the exercise of this faculty which can penetrate the veil of flesh and enter into the innermost part of another's being that I am able to reveal to you the thinking of the King in his relation to Alory.

IX

The Saracen army withdrew to its ships and thence to Africa or Spain. The Pope placed a laurel wreath on the King's brow and hailed him as 'the Shield of St Peter', 'the defender of the Faith' and 'the favourite son of the Church'. Charles received these honours as his due, and ordered a medal to be struck commemorating his great victory. Then, to His Holiness's relief, the Franks retired beyond the Alps. Italy was at peace, the harvest was good, wine and oil flowed. The Emperor in Byzantium, who still pretended to be master of what had been the whole empire of Rome, sent to Charles commending him on his victory over the Saracens and for having reduced the Lombard kings to pale shadows of what their fathers had been, and nominated him Exarch of Italy, that is, governor and imperial deputy.

At first Charles was flattered by the praise, and proud of the appointment. Bishop Turpin also approved it, for he had conceived a dislike of the Pope who claimed, as you will remember, to exercise the imperial authority in the West conferred on him by that Donation of the Emperor Constantine. 'That's one in his eye,' he said. 'That will make that greasy Italian shit himself' – for there were times when Turpin forgot to speak with the decorum proper to a bishop.

Only Elgebast grumbled. 'We didn't fight the infidel on behalf of that purple-clad nincompoop in Byzantium, who has never ventured to set foot in this Italy he claims as part of his empire, and who is in any case a mere boy dominated by his wicked mother, herself, men say, the puppet of the palace eunuchs.'

Yet even Elgebast, bold as he was, did not dare to speak in this fashion except to the young knight Ivor, in whom he had come to place an absolute trust.

The truth is that the old brigand was bored by the placid time that had succeeded the war, and was therefore cantankerous. Moreover, he was suffering from rheumatism.

Ivor, wise beyond his years, said, 'But surely it means nothing, and, if it pleases the King, well, we are all the more at ease on that account.'

'It demeans him to be pleased by such a letter,' Elgebast said. 'And it is an insult to the memory of our dear Yves.'

At the mention of his friend, Ivor shed a tear, then said, 'Nevertheless, there's no remedy. That being so, let us open another bottle. Wine, you have often told me, is the consolation that never fails. What's more, it will ease the pain of your rheumatism.'

So they drank deep and then slept. But Elgebast woke before the cock crow and looked at the moonlight falling pale on the young man's cheek, and sighed for new adventure, for to one of his temper, peace was irksome.

There were many who felt or thought like that, and among them was the King's nephew Roland, whom the Italians call Orlando, and of whom I must now speak.

X

Roland was the son of the King's favourite sister whose name was Bertha. Charles loved her dearly. She was the youngest of his siblings and, as a small child, delighted to follow him everywhere, to sit on his knee and be petted. When he was absent on campaign, she would mope and even seem to fall into a decline, so much so that on one occasion, when she had refused food for a fortnight, it was thought she was like to die. News of her condition was sent to the King and, abandoning his army, even though he was hard-pressed by the Saxons, he sped back to France to care for her.

Bertha grew up to be very beautiful. Her hair was the colour of ripe corn, her eyes were blue as a sunlit sea, her skin smooth as silk, and her carriage incomparably graceful. She was athletic and could draw a bow as well as any but the best archers of the royal guard. And, with all these perfections, she was modest, gentle and loving. Poets made verses in her praise, and one said that she was breasted like a swan. Naturally she had many admirers and suitors, but to the King's mind, none was worthy of her. Even when foreign kings, who had heard of her beauty, sent ambassadors seeking her hand in marriage for the kings themselves or their eldest sons, Charles would have none of it.

This was, as you may imagine, a great grief for her. Like any young woman she was eager to fall in love and make a suitable marriage. 'What else is there,' she was heard to say, 'for princesses?'

The brother she had adored now came to seem like a gaoler. She would sit in a high tower looking out over the meadows bright with spring flowers, across the river to the forests and the hills, and sigh for the love she did not have. All her songs were sad.

She rode out one day with only a single attendant, and that a woman. She had refused other company, for she wished to indulge her melancholy. They went as far as the chapel of St Agnes where she prayed and gave the nuns who served the chapel an offering for the poor. Then she drew out her purse again and gave the priest gold, telling him that he was to apply it to the needs of a band of lepers who dwelled in a refuge deep in the forest. 'They are outcasts,' she said, 'deprived on account of their condition of the ordinary pleasures open to others more fortunate, and I feel deeply for them.' The priest said he would do as she asked, but whether he kept that promise I cannot tell. I suppose he may have done so.

The sun had sunk below the top of the tall pines and a mist was rising from the river long before Bertha and her attendant came within sight of the castle. Indeed, the road seemed longer than that which they had followed on their outward journey, and both feared that they had mistaken their route and were lost. Bertha looked around her in perplexity while her companion began to whimper fearfully. They had come into a clearing where there stood a fountain, which, from its appearance – had they had leisure or inclination to examine it – seemed to be Roman.

'Certainly,' Bertha said, 'we did not come by this way, for I should have remarked such a fountain.'

'Oh, my lady,' the attendant, Gretchen, said, 'I know it well, and I know the place is uncanny. There was a great lord rode here one evening, just at dusk, as it is now, and he discovered a beautiful maiden sitting among the broken masonry and moss-covered stones. She was combing her hair, which was long and yellow, and when she saw the great warrior approaching she sang to the accompaniment of instruments he could not see. Her music was wistful and other-worldly, and the great lord was captivated. Then she slipped away, as the sun sank and darkness fell, but not before commanding him to be at the same place at the same hour in seven nights' time. And he obeyed her summons, and this time they kissed, and her kisses were sweeter to him than honey. And so it continued and each meeting ended in the same fashion, with her disappearance in a manner he could never remember. So he came to wonder if she was a spirit, or perchance one of these wood or water nymphs who were so frequently met with in the time of the old gods. And this thought perturbed him, so much so that he spoke of it to his confessor.

'When the priest, whose name was Father Zachery, heard the tale, he questioned the great lord more narrowly, and so learned that the girl or nymph, who had caught his master in her web, so to speak, ma'am, vanished as soon as she heard Vespers toll from a nearby chapel. Whereupon he knew, with that certainty which is given or granted to priests, that this nymph was a limb of Satan, the Enemy of Mankind and Lord of Darkness. At first the lord would have none of it. She was as pure as the lily in the dell, he declared. But his confessor supported his opinion with citations from Holy Writ and the works of the Fathers of the Church, and at last persuaded the great lord to put the matter to the test. He arranged that the vesper bell should be rung an hour later than was the custom, for, he said, the Evil One, deceived in this manner and remaining beyond her accustomed hour, would be compelled to assume her true shape and show herself devil indeed. The lord consented, being certain it was not so.

'So he and the maiden met, embraced, spoke loving words and kissed. Darkness closed in but the vesper bell was silent. The nymph remained lovely as ever, but, when the shadows lengthened, she seemed to grow uneasy. Her voice failed her. She looked rapidly from side to side. It seemed to the lord that the sweet scent of her person turned sour and rank, till, suddenly, with a loud shriek, she tore herself from his embraces and plunged headfirst into the fountain and vanished from his sight. The water bubbled and turned crimson, and when he dipped his hand in it, he tasted blood ...'

The Princess shuddered, as you might expect, to hear the conclusion of this tale, and would have questioned Gretchen further, but at the very moment the girl finished speaking, both were alarmed to see a grey wolf emerge from the forest and approach the fountain as if to drink. Seeing the young ladies, the beast snarled and blood dripped from its fangs. Straight away Gretchen fell in a swoon and Bertha was seized with terror and unable to move. The wolf approached, snarling most horribly. The princess screamed. It was fortunate that she did so, for her cry alerted a young man who was wandering in the forest. Running towards the sound, he saw the wolf, the terrified princess and her companion lying motionless. Just as the wolf was about to spring, the youth snatched an arrow from the quiver, fitted it to the bow and drew back the string. The arrow flew to its mark and the great grey wolf crumpled lifeless to the ground, at the very feet of the Princess, who now raised her eyes and sought out her deliverer.*

She saw a young man of middle height and slim build, with red hair and a pale freckled skin. He wore a shirt of some coarse cloth; it was torn at the side and was indescribably filthy. Below it, covering his lower body, was a skirt or kilt, as was the regular habit of the ancient Gauls and is now worn by the mountaineers of my native Scotland. His feet were bare and scratched and bleeding.

The young man stood before the Princess and, for a moment, seemed about to upbraid her on account of the rashness which had exposed her to such danger. But when, before he could speak, she thanked him for her deliverance in accents so sweet and yet regal, he was both touched and amazed. He bit back the harsh words he had been framing, dropped to one knee and kissed the pale hand she extended to him. Then she raised him up and, taking hold of his hand, examined him closely.

'I had thought you a forester,' she said, 'or one of the royal verderers perhaps; and yet there is, despite your wild appearance, a gentleness in your manner that speaks of higher birth. What is your name?'

* Readers familiar with the Waverley novels will doubtless have remarked the resemblance between this scene and that in *The Bride of Lammermoor* in which the heroine Lucy Ashton first encounters the Byronic hero, the Master of Ravenswood. There are only two differences. In Scott's novel the heroine is threatened by a bull, not a wolf, and is in the company of her father; while the Master employs a gun, not an arrow, to dispatch the beast. It is not to be supposed that the author of the Waverley novels had access to Michael Scott's manuscript, and the similarity of the stories is probably merely coincidental. Nevertheless, since this episode is found in none of the *Chansons de Geste* from which our author has drawn so much of his material, it may be that there is a common origin for the two stories to be discovered in some folk-tale handed down over the generations in the Scottish Borders where both Scotts, Michael and Sir Walter, were reared – A.M.

The young man sighed and said, 'I had once a name that I might lay claim to, and it may be one honoured in story, but alas, it has been taken from me. I am an outlaw, fair lady. Among my comrades in the wild forest, I go by the name of Milan, which is of no significance.'

'But who was your father?' Bertha asked, for she was already determined to learn all she could of the young man who had saved her life and who, moreover, seemed more attractive the more she looked upon him. In any case, like any well-born Frankish lady, she had a passion for genealogy and often composed herself for sleep by reciting silently the names of her ancestors as far back as the seventeenth generation.

The young man shook his head. 'My sainted mother,' he said, 'ever declined to name him to me, and would give no reason for her silence even when I pressed her.'

'So,' Bertha said, breaking into an enchanting smile, which seemed to light up the clearing already obscured by the deepening twilight, 'you are that most romantic of beings, the mysterious stranger ...'

'As your ladyship pleases,' he said, 'but the night is closing in. If I am to escort you to wherever you lodge, it would be as well for us to revive your friend, or perhaps maidservant, and make haste, before darkness is complete and we are lost in the forest.'

And so they made Gretchen stir, and the two ladies mounted their horses and set off, with the red-haired Milan holding the bridle of the Princess's palfrey, and the more she looked on him, the more she admired what she saw, and the more curious she became. It was evident that the young man, who had come so timely to her rescue, nursed a secret sorrow, and was indeed what she had on one occasion heard Bishop Turpin call an enigma. (He had been speaking of an abbot who alternated between long periods of conspicuous piety and spells of drunkenness in which time neither choirboy nor nun was safe from his roving hands. She had been struck by the word and later enquired as to its meaning.) Yes, there could be no doubt that this Milan presented an enigmatic figure; so, for example, when they came within sight of the castle and she desired him to accompany her within that she might present him as her rescuer to her brother the King, he started like a frightened colt, said, 'Your brother the King? If I had known of that relationship ...' and declined on the lame excuse of urgent business from which he had been interrupted when he happened on the scene in the clearing. It was all she could do to arrange a meeting-place for the following afternoon. After some hesitation, he agreed, and even in the gloaming she was sure that he blushed.

Gretchen said, 'Though it's by no means my place to say so, your ladyship, and you may bite my head off if you choose, I would think it well that you say nothing of your little adventure to the King. Something tells me he would not approve of that young man.'

'Stuff and nonsense,' Bertha replied. Nevertheless, having considered the matter, she took her maidservant's advice.

The following afternoon they rode out again and came to the appointed place. There was no sign of the young man. Perhaps we are early, Bertha thought, and settled herself to wait, more patiently than was her custom. No sooner had she done so than Milan dropped to the ground from the upper branches of a leafy oak tree where he had been concealed. At first she was overjoyed to see him, particularly since he seemed even more handsome than she had remembered. Then she felt that his hiding in the tree showed a lack of trust in her, before she recalled that he had said he was an outlaw, and that lack of trust must be as natural to him as the habit of trust was to her; and this she found a delicious thought. So she dispatched Gretchen to 'keep *cave*' (as they had said in their schoolgirl games) and invited Milan to sit by her on the flowery bank where she had settled.

At first they said little, but gazed into each other's eyes. Then she stretched out her forefinger and traced the line of his lips.

'I was afraid you would not come,' she said. 'Being an outlaw, you understand.'

'I scarce dared to believe that you would,' he said, and took hold of her hand and kissed it. 'Being a princess, you understand.'

'What do you know of princesses,' she said, 'to judge us so harshly?'

'Why, little directly,' he replied with a smile in which she read a secret sorrow, 'for, living in the forest, I have met princesses

55

but rarely. Indeed,' he blushed, 'you are the first I have ever spoken to since my mother died and I perforce took to this life. But she, poor lady, told me much of the inconstancy of royals ...'

'Did she indeed? She had a wide experience of them, I suppose?'

'Why, yes, of course. My poor dear mother had no talent for inventing stories, and no need of one, for her own life would have furnished material for any troubadour. And so, having, as she often said, no imagination, she spoke only of what she had known and experienced.'

Bertha's irritation subsided. The young man, scarcely more than a boy, had had no intention of insulting or criticising her. He was an innocent and had spoken from the heart. Even now, as he explained himself, there was something so open, unguarded and frank in his manner; so trusting, she thought, so different from the hypocrisy of the court. And she liked the way his mouth hung a little open when he fell silent. She leaned forward and kissed it.

So they lay together on that bank scented by wild thyme, camomile and the overhanging rose-bush – its flowers pale-pink like the princess's cheek. They lay throughout the sultry afternoon, saying little, for both knew that the time for words, explanations and planning was not yet, but content to be lazily together, forcing nothing, exploring each other with eyes, hands, lips, tongue; both learning new delights, both conscious, for the first time in either's life, of being more vibrantly, self-consciously, individually alive than ever before, and yet at the same time absorbed in the other, the two becoming as one. And how this could be puzzled the Princess as, that night, she lay in her bed in the castle tower, touching herself where he had been, hearing in the solitude of the dark the music of his murmurings. Being untrained in philosophy, she was of course unable to unravel the mystery of the simultaneity of singularity and conjunction; she had no words to explain to herself how the otherness of the other might be subsumed in the intensity of the consciousness of self, how, as one of my masters in natural philosophy so precisely puts it, 'Thatness may be transformed into thisness, while never-theless remaining obstinately and distinctly thatness.' Which is a matter I have explored, studiously and with zeal, in library and chamber.

What's that you say, my Prince? You are weary of this analysis? I promised you the story of Roland and we have not even got him born yet? Well, I forgive you your impatience – and your impertinence. But you in turn must excuse me for lingering by the way. The truth is that I hate to take the direct route, that I love to explore by-ways. The traveller who holds to the well-beaten path and hastens with downcast look to his destination, refusing to let his eyes rove or his thoughts wander, lest he be diverted, is ever to my mind a dull dog, unworthy of the freedom, which is to say the free will, granted him by Our Father in Heaven.

What's that? How, my Prince, are we to advance to my galloping narrative if you keep interrupting with questions? So, what is it? Ah, you say that at other times I have denied the concept of free will, and told you we are all prisoners of destiny, bound to follow the course that is pre-ordained or, as we say in Scotland, condemned to dree our weird.* I daresay I have; look, dear boy, to find consistency only among fools. The mind of a wise man is like a river, a flowing stream ever in motion, apparently unchanging and yet, you will observe, never the same. A wise Greek, Heraclitus, affirmed that we cannot bathe in the same river twice. Sometimes I wonder if one can do so even a single time, for the water is past you and the river carrying all away even as the cold stream strikes your flanks. Therefore, as to the weighty question that you raise, I have but this to say: that often we are conscious of being free to think, speak and act as we choose; and at other moments, it may be for years at a time, we know we are constrained; it seems that our path has been lit for us and we may not, cannot, depart from it. Now, inasmuch as I have ever maintained to you that existence is prior to essence, man is inescapably responsible for what he is. He is his own reality, and therefore if he feels himself now free in the exercise of his will and now – what did you call it? – a prisoner

* In Scots in the original – A.M.

57

of destiny, why then, that is what he is. Both these things. We live in a duality, dear boy. You, for example, are already a mighty sovereign and an impudent pupil, a man of power and a pretty youth.

Now, I trust I have made myself clear. Where was I? What do you say? Bertha — yes, I agree it's a frightful name, but I didn't choose it, you know, I take what history gives me — Bertha was in bed touching herself up? That's a coarse way of putting it. Say, rather, she was reliving in imagination the delights of the afternoon, and they seemed all the sweeter than they had been in actuality. Which is often how it is. We live more fully in the imagination, which is to say the mind, than in the flesh.

Be that as it may, her delight was soon succeeded by perturbation and anxiety. The moonlight conspired with memory and mental activity to drive sleep away, and the more she thought the more wakeful she was.

It was clear, she reflected, that Milan's secret sorrow certainly made him even more attractive, because it was mysterious and what the troubadours call romantic, but it was disturbing also, for she could not hide from herself the suspicion that this sorrow, and indeed the dear boy's miserable condition, was in some manner connected with her brother, Charles. Why else had Milan started, the colour fleeing his face, when she had suggested bringing him before the King? Why indeed had he on both occasions taken his leave of her as soon as the castle came in sight?

It was not long before the King, who loved his sister dearly, became suspicious of her daily journeyings in the forest. He prized her chastity, not only because chastity in an unmarried woman is approved by Holy Church, but because an unchaste princess is what traders call 'damaged goods', unmarketable; and it is natural that princes seek advantage from the marriages of their sisters and daughters. Such is the way of the world. So he set spies to watch her, and, when one, an unfrocked priest whom the King had often found useful, reported that she met every afternoon a red-haired youth and ... At which point the former priest paused, licked his lower lip with his sharp-pointed tongue, and ran his sweaty hands over his belly.

'And what?' the King said.

'They toy with each other. I do not think it has gone further,' the priest mumbled, 'not while I was watching and, knowing that Your Majesty would wish to know all, I was watching intently. The youth slipped his hand under her ... her nether garments, but only his hand, so far as I could see ...'

'Enough,' the King said, and, his wrath rising, boxed the man on the ear, on account, as he doubtless explained to his confessor, of the indecent pleasure he read in the priest's face and heard in his voice.

'What manner of youth is he,' the King said, 'apart from the red hair?'

'Why,' the priest said, picking himself off the floor where he had fallen and rubbing his ear, 'no manner of youth at all. Comely enough, I suppose, well-formed, athletic, pleasing doubtless to a maid's eye, and to many a man's too. A peasant? I should say not. But not noble. No manner of youth really, a boy of the forest. He is by no means a yokel, and yet, it goes without saying, he is unworthy of the gracious lady, your sister.'

'And is the Princess truly ...' Here Charles paused and swallowed twice before continuing, being (to my mind) ashamed to discuss his sister with this unsavoury and disreputable fellow, yet unable to restrain his curiosity, his need to know. 'Is the Princess,' he said again, 'truly enamoured of the young man?'

He spoke the word 'enamoured' with distaste, and chose it rather than some more earthy term to put a distance between him and his spy.

Who, however, carried on the buoyant wind of his narrative and either momentarily forgetting that it was the King he was addressing, or perhaps taking a mean pleasure in embarrassing him, sniggered and replied, 'As the hen is of the cock.'

Charles flushed and was tempted to have the former priest, whose name by the by was Ambrose, whipped for impertinence. But then he thought how this would lead to the story becoming public knowledge, for it could not be expected that the man would not avenge himself for the pain and humiliation of a flogging by spreading the tale of the Princess's affair, unless, that is, he ordered the man's tongue to be torn out, which also he briefly considered. But then he reflected how Ambrose had been useful to him in the past, and might be again, for, sadly, it is often necessary for kings to make use of mean and contemptible agents. So, instead, he gave Ambrose gold, and told him to keep these matters to himself till he, the King, had reflected on them.

'It may be,' he said, 'that I shall have further tasks for you to perform.'

He then retired to consider what best might be done, and found himself sore perplexed. He hesitated to confront his sister, for the truth is that, though brave in battle and resolute in public policy, Charles was also a moral coward. His sister might weep, which would unman him. She might wax indignant because he had set spies on her; and this alarmed him. 'Women,' he muttered, chewing the end of his long moustaches. He might order her to be confined and forbidden to leave the castle, but she would undoubtedly demand an interview and it would be hard to deny her. Moreover, scandalous rumours would be spread, and this probability dismayed him. Eventually he concluded that on the one hand he should say nothing to Bertha but treat her with the utmost affection, and on the other hand should order some trusty knights to lay hands on the young man and dispose of him. And why not? he said to himself. It would seem that he is after all an outlaw.

XI

While Charles turned these matters over in his mind, a solution was presented to him, unexpectedly; for which reason he grasped at it without reflection. I say this advisedly, having often observed in the course of my wide-travelled life how men who in placid times will turn a matter over in their minds, examining it in detail from every angle before arriving at a decision, will rush to judgement when anxious or otherwise disturbed.

There was a certain nobleman called Ganelon, a duke whose estates stretched for many miles either side of the Upper Rhine. This Ganelon had been a childhood companion of the King's, and they had then formed a close friendship. Restless by nature and being avid for experience, eager too for the acquisition of wisdom, Ganelon had spent the years of his early manhood in wandering. He had sojourned in Byzantium, and had fought in the wars of the Empire against the Bulgars and the Saracens, and won great honour, for, though but rarely to be found in the forefront of the battle, he was mighty in council, and the Emperor, a poor thing himself, valued him on account of his prudence and wisdom. Moreover, Ganelon had sat at the feet of philosophers and sages, and had also, it was rumoured, been admitted to the brotherhood of those who still clandestinely celebrated the pagan mysteries at Eleusis. He was reputed to be learned in sorcery, but this is a charge often levelled by dullards at those who have sought enlightenment.

Be that as it may, Ganelon had now returned from the East, presented himself at court, embraced Charles in the manner of their youth, and proposed himself as a husband for his sister Bertha. Had Charles enquired of his old friend's activities in the East, he might have hesitated, for he would have learned that Ganelon had been accused of the rape of a young virgin in Aleppo, and had kept a troupe of dancing-boys while serving as imperial procurator in Antioch. This certainly was not remarkable, for at that date every notable in Antioch kept a boy as well as a wife, and was accustomed to lavish more affection on the former than the latter, certainly in public.

But the King saw in his old friend's proposal merely a solution to the problem of his sister. Moreover, there were political advantages to the match, for Ganelon's mother had been a Saxon princess, and, on her account, he had great influence with that troublesome and unruly people. So Charles sent to inform Bertha that he had secured her a husband worthy of her high estate and that the marriage would be celebrated (by Bishop Turpin) seven days hence.

Bertha was furious. She might have been furious even if she hadn't met Milan and fallen in love with him, for she remembered that Ganelon squinted and smelled of rotten apples. Besides, she disliked the idea that her brother was ready to dispose of her 'just like that, without consulting me,' as she said to Gretchen, even though she acknowledged that this was the usual practice of kings. So she sent Gretchen to the stables to order that their horses be prepared for their afternoon ride.

Gretchen returned in a little to say that their horses were lame, 'or rather, that's what they told me, but I could tell from their manner that they were speaking as they had been instructed to speak. If you ask me, they've found out about you and the young man, and the King intends to keep you prisoner till you're safely married to that Ganelon, the nasty piece of work. You remember I told you I saw Father Ambrose snooping, horrid little sneak that he is.'

Bertha grew pale at her words – naturally enough. Who wouldn't? For a moment she could not think what to do. She felt herself to be a bird trapped in the hunter's snare. She began to weep.

'Tears will mend nothing,' Gretchen said. 'You have a choice: submission or action. Which is it to be?'

'I love Milan,' the princess sobbed, 'more than life,' she added, speaking the language of the troubadours.

'Leave it to me, then,' Gretchen said.

*

62

Now it so happened that there were in the castle a cousin of Gretchen's who was a sergeant of the guard, and also a boy from her home village in Brittany who worked as a scullion in the kitchens. Both the sergeant, whose name was Boris, and the boy, Benoni, were deeply attached to her. Indeed, each was in his different way in love with her.

First she approached Boris. He was a big flaxen-haired fellow, loyal as a sheepdog but slower of wit, and he did not immediately understand what she asked of him. But when he did so, he blushed deeply and nodded his head. She had often told herself that Boris would do anything for her, and it was pleasant to be proved right.

Then she sought out Benoni, stroked his cheek and told him what he must do. So he slipped out of the castle and into the forest.

That night, when all was silent save the cry of the owl, Boris came to the Princess's apartments and led the two women by a concealed staircase to where a gate in the northern wall of the castle gave on to a flight of steps leading down to the moat. The sentry who guarded the gate lay drunk before it, for Boris had laced his wine with a distillation of poppies that Gretchen had long since purchased from an apothecary – prudently, as she remarked, in foresight of trouble to come. The sergeant then unlocked the gate and the three descended, slowly and silently, moving with infinite care, the worn and slippery steps that gave access to the moat. There Benoni waited for them in a punt, and, as soon as they were aboard, poled them across the water. Fortunately there was no moon and the night was black as a villain's heart. Reaching the other bank, the boy handed the ladies out of the punt and then withdrew a stopper from it, so that it filled with water and sank. The four made haste to gain the forest, and, following the path that was now familiar, came to the clearing by the Roman temple, where they found Milan waiting with horses in hand.

Milan embraced the Princess but found no words to express his feelings. He was overwhelmed by a mixture of desire, happiness, apprehension and relief. When the lad Benoni had come to him as he waited for the princess, he had feared some trap, feared it even while the boy expounded the plan Gretchen had devised. He kept hold of the handle of his knife all the while they talked, and, even when the boy departed, still evidently alone, Milan could not relax. Might not the trap be sprung in the night hours, and, instead of his love, might he not be confronted by armed men, ready to seize him and hurl him into a dungeon whence he would never emerge alive? Such had been his thoughts while he waited there, in the silence broken only by the owl calling and the distant barking of dogs guarding some farm on the edge of the forest.

But now she was here, and there was no time for rapture. The sergeant, pulling at his sleeve, said, 'If we are not a day's march from here by cock-crow, then we are dead men, and the Princess married to the Duke Ganelon, believe you me.'

They rode south, travelling by night and lying up in the woods or in the *maquis* by day. Once, as they took their rest, with Benoni keeping guard, a troop of cavalry passed below them on the old Roman road, and the boy trembled to see that the King himself rode at its head. So that night they turned off the high road and journeyed by rough paths that skirted the hillside.

On the fourth day Gretchen fell ill. She coughed and blood spurted from her mouth. Her legs felt heavy yet weak, as if turned to water. They would not support her. The sergeant Boris lifted her on to the horse and rode beside her with his arm around her waist to prevent her from falling. 'It's impossible,' he said at last. 'She can go no further, she's as weak as a newborn kitten.'

They came to an inn and the princess gave silver to the stout woman who kept it so that Gretchen might have a chamber with a bed. Her fever was high and she was scarce able to speak; nevertheless, she urged the princess to leave her there and continue her journey. She would follow when she was stronger. But all, except Milan perhaps, knew that day would never arrive. The sergeant added his pleas to those of the dying woman. All she had risked for the princess would be in vain if she would remain there. He himself would bide and tend to Gretchen. She was all he had ever wanted in life, he said, lying nobly.

So the other three continued on their journey, having lost a

64

day and a half. They travelled still south and the sun rose higher in the heavens.

The next morning the searchers arrived. They seized the sergeant and pinioned him, then broke into the chamber where Gretchen lay. She opened her eyes and cursed them, in a faltering voice, then closed them again for the last time. Boris too was silent. When they tore the nails from his fingers he screamed but still would say nothing. In a fury, Ganelon, who commanded the troop, ordered that he be hanged from the inn-sign.

Impatient, Ganelon urged his men onward. 'They cannot be far ahead,' he cried, hope and lust warping his judgement. In his haste he departed before Boris was quite dead. The woman who kept the inn cut him down and revived him. Later she would marry him and their inn would be called 'At the Sign of the Half-hanged Man'.

Milan, the Princess and the boy Benoni lay up in a cave on the hillside above the Roman road, and watched Ganelon and his troop jangle past below them. Then, when night had fallen, Benoni retrieved their horses from the high wood where he had tethered them, and they turned off the road, following sheeptracks up into the mountains. So they journeyed for seven nights, sleeping by day, till they came to a hill village where the inhabitants spoke a tongue which none of them could understand. They rested there, paying for shelter and sustenance with one of the Princess's jewels. For a little they believed themselves safe, and Milan and the Princess were joined together in the fullness of their love. But Benoni kept his eyes open, being one whom experience had taught to be niggardly in trust. He observed the men of the village talking together in a manner that seemed to him suspicious. They are plotting against us, he said to himself. They reason that if the princess has paid with one jewel, she must have others. Therefore they will kill us. So he roused Milan and the Princess and said they must slip away in the darkness. Ever afterwards, when anyone complained to her of Benoni and spoke against him she would say, 'But he saved our lives in that mountain village, and not for the first time.'

So they made their escape and, after many wanderings and much hardship, came to the summit of a pass and, looking down, saw Italy spread before them. They descended into the plain and came to a city which was held by the Lombards. They presented themselves to the count and explained, at Benoni's urging, that they were seeking refuge from the wrath of the Frankish King. But they did not disclose that Bertha was the King's sister, for they thought it wise to keep him in ignorance of this, lest he see advantage in returning her to Charles. Benoni said, 'I am only a boy, but I have learned that there are occasions when it is wise to be economical with the truth. Bishop Turpin used to say that the truth is a forked adder. Who knows whom it will strike, or when?'

The Lombard King, whose name was Arnauf and who was the nephew of that Didier whose daughter Desiderata had been Charles's first wife, now long deceased, welcomed them therefore as allies, and, seeing that Milan was a young man of quality, gave him command of a fort guarding the frontier, for, he said, 'This is one man who will not betray me to the Franks.' And it was there that Roland was born, which is why the Italians claim him as their own and call him Orlando.

XII

I have been long in arriving at the birth of my hero, but you must not complain. Much, otherwise obscure in the story of his remarkable life, is made apparent by the circumstances of that birth and his childhood. His tenderness towards women and his search for constancy in love derive from his matchless mother, while Milan was to be for him ever the pattern of daring and the chivalrous spirit. Moreover, the ambivalence of his feeling for his uncle the King, and the mixture of love and hatred with which they came to regard each other, reflected the King's passionate, even incestuous, feeling for his sister, the jealousy she sparked in him, and his mingled admiration and resentment of Milan, who had won her despite his royal will. The ferocity with which he pursued Milan, seeking to destroy him, was something Roland could neither forget nor forgive.

When Charles learned that the guilty pair – for so he regarded them – had found refuge with the King of the Lombards, his fury knew no bounds. He sent emissaries demanding that Milan be surrendered to him as a notorious felon, outlaw, ravisher of women and traitor.

Arnauf heard the ambassador read this charge, pulled at his moustaches and said, 'You must tell your master, with my compliments, that I know nothing of any individual who answers to so monstrous a description. Were there such a one it is inconceivable that I should wish to harbour him.'

At first Arnauf was pleased with this reply, and took pride in the defiant words which had sprung as naturally to his lips as water surges from a mountain spring. But then, after the embassy had departed to carry his message to Charlemagne, he doubted its wisdom. In the first place, it seemed to him, the Frankish King might be so angered by his response that he would lead his army over the Alps; and Arnauf had no wish to engage Charles in battle, for he feared him greatly. Secondly, he now asked himself whether Milan might indeed by the villain described to him, and whether he had himself been deceived by the young man's fair face and ingenuous bearing. 'Truly,' he said to himself, and to several of his courtiers as the days passed and his perturbation became more intense, 'I have been too trusting.' He therefore resolved to seize Milan and deliver him in chains to the Franks. But he still did not know that Bertha was a princess, for Charles had been too proud to confess to his sister's shameful elopement.

Chance, which in the affairs of men plays a part that historians ignore at their peril, now came to the rescue of the fugitive lovers. It so happened that during their sojourn at the Lombard court, the boy Benoni had caught the eye of a Saxon knight, an adventurer by name of Astolf, who had taken service with Arnauf. This Astolf had spent many years in the East, where he had indulged tastes and practised vices which the Holy Church condemns as sinful. Delighted by Benoni's ready smile, strong limbs and grace of manner, he plied him with wine in order to seduce him. Benoni, still mourning his beloved Gretchen, resisted his attentions, but did so with such charm as rather to quicken Astolf's desire than dampen it. Now Astolf approached the Lombard King and asked to be given command of the troop sent to arrest Milan, and Arnauf, suspecting nothing, consented.

Milan, also without suspicion, made Astolf welcome and ordered a great feast to be prepared in honour of so distinguished a guest. He gave Astolf a tour of the fortress and showed him proudly the repairs he had effected. Astolf smiled and approved. They came to table and ate well of trout from the mountain streams, wild boar and hill mutton, and drank the green wine of upland vineyards. Minstrels sang, Astolf delighted the company with his stories of campaigns against the Saracens, his travels in the frozen Caucasus, and the wonders of Byzantium where (though he made no mention of this, being a gentleman) he had been the lover of the Empress Eudoxia; and often he gazed on Benoni, who seemed to him more beautiful than ever, to see how his tales of adventure and strange places entranced the boy.

Indeed, Benoni sat open-mouthed and, as it seemed to Astolf, drinking in every word.

So, when Milan and Bertha retired to their chamber, Astolf laid his hand on Benoni's shoulder to detain him, and said, 'A word with you, boy, if I may.'

Benoni said, 'As many as you please, so they be but words.'

Astolf sighed as one might sigh who wishes others to remark his deep sorrow, regret or dismay. Then, apparently recovering himself, he smiled and said, 'But it must be in private, for what I have to tell you would put us both in danger if overheard.'

He tightened his grip on the boy's shoulder.

Benoni therefore led him up a stair that gave on to the battlements and guided him to a secluded corner.

'Only the jackdaws can overhear us now,' he said.

'I speak to you as a friend and one who would be more than friend,' Astolf said. 'And yet it is not in friendship that I have come here, or rather have been commanded hither. Your master Milan is in peril of his life.'

Benoni, having nothing immediate to say, remained silent.

'You do not ask from whom?'

'He has been in such danger from the day I met him, and yet here he is.'

'But not for much longer, unless … Let me be open with you, dear boy. I say I have not come in friendship, and yet it is friendship that I feel.' He laid his hand on the boy's leg just below the fringe of his tunic. 'Warm friendship,' he said. 'And yet, again, the command I bear is cruel. Do you understand me? I see I must be open; therefore, listen. Ambassadors came from the King of the Franks demanding that King Arnauf surrender Milan to them, as a notorious criminal and outlaw. The King, though at first refusing, considered the matter in his chamber, summoned me to him – and here I am. You understand me now?'

Benoni scratched his curly head, then gently removed the knight's wandering hand from his thigh.

'I understand you,' he said. 'That is, I understand why you have come to this castle and even why you have played at friendship with Milan. But I do not understand why you have told me your purpose when you have come here as a thief in the night. It makes no sense.'

But Benoni's smile persuaded Astolf that in truth the boy understood him well enough. He took hold of his hand and said, 'If indeed I am here as a thief in the night, what is it you suppose I wish to steal and take possession of?'

Benoni said, 'If I was to do as you wish and then slip away and warn Milan, he could seize you and throw you chained into the castle dungeons, which, I must tell you, are deep, dark, damp and infested with rats of a quite unusual size and voracity.'

'Indeed, yes,' Astolf replied. 'I am at your mercy as, had I not spoken as I have, Milan was at mine.'

So, for a little, they sparred in words, each enjoying the encounter which may properly be termed a game, while Astolf's hand crept, now unrestrained, along the boy's yielding thigh.

Then Astolf said, 'If I return to the King without Milan in chains, I am a dead man.'

Benoni leaned forward to kiss him on the lips.

'So,' he said, 'it were best not to return.'

'Others will be sent in my stead,' Astolf murmured, tracing the line of the boy's cheek and jaw with his forefinger.

'So ...' Benoni said.

'So ...'

In the dark hour before dawn, Benoni left Astolf and went to rouse Milan. When he had explained the position, Milan said, 'Either we hold the castle against the Lombard King, or we make our escape. Will Astolf stand by us whichever course we follow?'

'Let me bring him to you to speak for himself.'

Milan woke Bertha, who held the infant Roland in her arms as she listened to what he had to say.

'This is my brother's work,' she said. 'He is determined to destroy you and hand me over to Ganelon.'

Then she paused and dried her tears. The first cock of the morning crowed.

'We cannot run for ever,' she said.

'But we can fight.'

'Can we?'

'Let us hear what Astolf has to say.'

'Have you reason to trust him?'

'Benoni thinks so, and, after all, why else would he have revealed the purpose of his coming here, if he is not ready to join himself to us? As Benoni said, by doing so, he has put himself at our mercy.'

XIII

When Arnauf discovered that his plot had failed and that Astolf had betrayed him, his fury was wonderful to behold. He flung himself to the floor and chewed the rushes that covered it, and cursed Astolf for a treacherous sodomite, an ingrate and dissembler. To do the King justice, his rage was sharpened by terror, for he could not doubt but that a Frankish army would descend into Italy if he did not soon either surrender Milan to Charles or give proof that the young man was dead. 'Why,' he cried in his anguish, 'has Fate so loaded the dice against me?'

For two days he drowned himself in wine, as if the oblivion it offered could avert what he feared.

But then his wife, a stout, black-haired woman, stern-featured and strong-minded, came to him as he lay whimpering in his bed. She looked down on him with contempt, and, when he turned away, took a bucket of water and threw it over him, so that he rose up spluttering and indignant. He was about to protest when he met her eye, and, wisely, held his tongue.

'Why rail against Fate,' she said, 'when it is your own folly that has brought us to this strait? I warned you against that Milan and his conniving woman – no better than she should be, I'll be bound. I warned you against Astolf also. I told you they were not to be trusted. But, as ever, you allowed yourself to be seduced by their pretty ways and easy manner, and so set your judgement above mine.'

The King could not deny that she spoke truth, and therefore resented her words the more. It is ever thus: we hate those who show us our foolishness, and see us when we are weak.

Nevertheless, Arnauf roused himself. He collected his army, swore mighty oaths to demonstrate his strength of will, and marched north to lay siege to the castle which Milan held. He told his wife: 'If I bring not the villains back dead on my shield, count me no true knight.'

'If you do that,' she muttered, 'you will do more than I think you capable of.' So she resolved to take advantage of his absence to usurp his throne and replace him with their oldest son, Ebana. But that is another story which is not germane to my matter.

The siege was long and terrible. It lasted throughout the winter, and both armies endured many privations. Three times at least the defenders essayed to break out, and three times were driven back into the fortress with much loss of life. The besieging army was ravaged by sickness; yet the condition of those within the castle was still more grievous. Stocks of food ran low, and, by the end of January, Milan, as commander, was compelled to reduce rations to one cup of polenta a day. Scarce a night passed without a death. Once, when a child of three years perished, two men-at-arms took the body from its cot and roasted it on a spit before dawn. Milan ordered them to be hanged but the sight of their bodies dangling from the battlements encouraged the besiegers. Yet the attack they launched the next day was repulsed, though with many fallen in both armies. 'Better to die in harness than starve to death,' said Milan, preparing to lead another attempt to break out from the trap in which they were held. But this too failed and they were driven back again.

That night he summoned Astolf and Benoni to join him and Bertha in their chamber high up in the tower. For a long time they sat silently, none daring to speak the words which all knew must be spoken. Milan's head was bandaged from a sword-gash he had received in that day's fighting, and, even as he considered how best to open the discussion, his tongue roving in his mouth dislodged a tooth loosed by a blow from the flat of a sword, or perhaps a swinging mace. He looked on his companions with love and pity, and it seemed to him that all were as corpses, their beauty and vigour alike fled. I am no better myself, he thought.

Then he said, 'Our plight is extreme. I do not think we can hold out longer.'

Astolf said, 'It is worse than you think, my friend. Tell him, Benoni.'

Benoni blushed, or would have blushed if there had still been vigour enough in his blood to send it coursing through his cheeks.

He said, 'At dusk, after the battle, I slipped out of the castle by a passage which leads through the rock and emerges on a ridge above the camp of the Lombards. I was seeking a means by which we might escape. But all is well guarded. However, as I lay in a gully, near the enemy outposts, I chanced to overhear the conversation of two sentries. I do not think they were ordinary men-at-arms, for they spoke as if with authority; and this is the gist of what they said. The Lombard King, despairing perhaps of reducing the castle, sent some time ago to your brother Charles, ma'am, to say that he had us caught in a trap which, however, he could find no means of springing. Or something like that. The conversation was not altogether clear. But what followed was unmistakable. They said that Charles himself, at the head of a Frankish army, has crossed over into Italy, and will be here within days to reinforce the besiegers. At first, I confess, I could not believe my ears, for we all know what enmity there is between the Franks and the Lombards ...'

'Indeed yes,' Bertha said, 'it is why we thought ourselves safe in coming into Lombardy.'

'You are certain?' Milan said.

'As certain as I am that my name is Benoni, and that I hunger for a beefsteak and a bottle of wine, be it ever so rough.'

'As certain,' Milan said, 'as the hate Charles bears me?'

'So certain.'

Milan drummed his fingers on the table. 'Then there is only one thing to be done. When King Charles arrives in the camp, I shall send a herald to offer my surrender, on condition that you three and the rest of our gallant defenders are spared.'

Milan's words were greeted with dismay. Bertha wept. Benoni lowered his eyes and shook his head. Astolf leapt to his feet, swore a mighty oath, and declared that on his honour as a knight − and a Saxon Englishman of good family, cousin (he added) to the King of Wessex, even though twice removed in that cousinship − he could not permit his dear friend Milan, for whom he had formed so deep an affection, such high regard, to sacrifice himself in this manner, while he ...

At this point he broke off, having lost his thought in the confused syntax of his sentence. He swallowed twice, then pulled at his moustaches and said, quietly but with determination, 'To owe my life to another offends my sense of what is fitting. It is a gift no Englishman can accept. It would besmirch my honour.'

'My dear friend,' Milan said, 'this is no time to speak of honour.'

'And there,' Astolf said, recovering for the moment his spirits and speaking in that audacious manner which had won him renown throughout Christendom, 'and there, my dear friend, you are mistaken, for there is no better time to speak of honour than when hope has slipped away, and we look in the face of death and feel his icy fingers pull at our limbs.'

'That is all very well,' Benoni said, 'but I am a poor boy from Brittany, and I value life more highly than this abstraction called honour. I know what life is: it is to feel the wind of the morning in your face, to hear the surge of the sea, to smell the wild thyme, to fill your belly with good meat and bannocks, to drink wine, beer and cider, to taste good company, to feel the flesh' – and here he looked Astolf full in the face – 'responding to a lover's urging. Keep the windy abstraction you call honour, and . . .'

But here, he too broke off, and bit his lip before resuming, though now unable to look the others in the eye.

'Of course,' he said, 'I am only a peasant boy reared in a cabin at the edge of the salt-marshes, and it is perhaps for this reason that I do not respond as you who are gently born to this word honour. But there it is, I prize my life and have no wish to die . . . honourably . . . And yet I cannot agree – for here I am at one with my dear Astolf – that you, Milan, should lose your life that I may keep mine.'

For a little there was silence, till Benoni added, 'It may be that I speak nonsense.'

'No,' Bertha said, 'you speak perfect sense, Benoni, as you have done ever since that night you led us out of my brother's castle of Engelheim, and we made our escape through the forest. But there is another life to be considered and it is one that cannot speak for itself. I mean of course, my darling child Roland –

your darling child also, Milan. What will become of him if you sacrifice yourself as you propose?'

Again there was silence. It was a still night of hard frost, and the pale flame of their solitary candle rose between them, burning steady without a flicker. All four were now brought up hard against reality. For weeks they had put it from them, assuring themselves and each other that the worst could yet be kept at bay. Nothing, my Prince, is more remarkable than man's ability to hope when reason for hope has withered and died. Even now Astolf said, 'We can still fight,' but there was no conviction in his voice.

'We are too few,' Milan said.

'The fewer men, the greater share of honour. I apologise, my dear Benoni, I know you dislike the word, but it means something to me. I speak as an Englishman, you understand. For us, honour means playing the game to the bitter end. Ours not to reason why, as one of the bards of Camelot used to say.'

Bertha said, 'A sacrifice need not to be of blood.'

'What do you mean?' Milan and Astolf spoke as one.

Benoni said, 'I think I understand. There is more than one way to skin a cat, as my grandmother was wont to say.'

Bertha said, 'My brother is swift to anger, although his anger burns slowly and, like the bush which Moses saw in the wilderness, is not consumed. But he is not vengeful by nature. Indeed, his impulses when not perverted by anger are generous and noble. We, Milan, in loving each other, have offended him, and so he has pursued us here, to this extremity. Yet he loved me dearly when I was a child, and I am persuaded he loves me still. I cannot believe he would not love our little Orlando, our Roland-baby.'

'But I am the obstacle,' Milan said. 'That is why I must surrender myself to him and submit to Fate.'

'It is I who must surrender,' Bertha said, 'and then bargain for your life, for all your lives . . .'

Milan sprang to his feet, more vigorously than might have been expected of one in his wretched condition.

'Shall I owe my life to a woman's tears?' he cried out.

'Would you rather I shed tears of bitter grief because your

pride condemned you to a cruel death?' Bertha replied.

And in this way the argument continued through the black night till the candle guttered and the first grey of dawn crept into the tower, continued till that dawn was streaked with pink and the winter sun rose over the mountains. Round and round they went, more tears were shed, oaths crashed out, and only Benoni's quiet voice restored calm.

In the end Bertha prevailed, as women usually do. 'We must think of our son,' she said, 'our little Roland, who is worth more than all the honour that may be found in this sad world.'

XIV

So it was that some days later, when the Frankish army had joined the Lombards, that Bertha, with the child Roland in her arms, stepped across the lowered drawbridge that now spanned the deep moat where ice had formed on the surface of the water. She was preceded by a herald, who served as trumpeter, and was accompanied by Benoni and by a priest, Father Joseph, who acted as chaplain to the garrison and who trembled with fear, though, in a whisper to Benoni, he blamed it on the cold. As they approached the Frankish outposts, Bertha hesitated for a moment, and looked back over her shoulder to see if Milan was watching her progress from the battlements. But there was no one there: shame had driven Milan to his chamber. Astolf too was absent. He had suggested himself as her companion in place of Benoni, but Bertha had refused, though finding no words to placate him or soothe his injured pride. The truth was she could not trust him to restrain his tongue.

They passed through the outposts, a sentry leading them to the royal pavilion. Bertha kept her chin high, her gaze fixed, looking neither to right nor to left, but Benoni could not fail to observe the interest the little party aroused.

Charles did not look up when they approached, but continued his conversation with the Lombard King. Conversation, Benoni realised, wasn't the right word. This was an argument, and a fierce one. It was a pity they were too far away to hear what was being said. Charles was thrusting his face at Arnauf, who backed away from him. A bad time to come calling, Benoni thought. It looked as if Charles was going to hit him. He lifted his stick high above his head, then paused and turned. Perhaps he had seen Bertha out of the corner of his eye. He looked straight at her now, then, collecting himself, moved to the ornately carved chair in front of his pavilion, and settled himself.

He picked up a chicken leg and began to gnaw. But his eyes didn't leave his sister.

'This is your nephew Roland,' she said. 'You've come close to killing him. He should be twice the weight he is now.'

Charles took the chicken leg from his mouth, and licked the exposed bone.

'Why are you here?'

'To submit. I should have thought that was obvious.'

'To submit? You've taken your time about it. Why?'

'Again, I should have thought that was obvious. I hoped I wouldn't have to.'

'But now you do?'

'That's why I'm here. To submit, but on conditions.'

'Conditions?'

The sparring went on for some time. Benoni felt himself relax. It was going to be all right. He hadn't thought it possible that it would be, yet it was. They understand each other, he said to himself.

Charles took Bertha's arm and led her into the tent. The Lombard King was left outside. He looked at Benoni and scowled. Benoni, modestly, lowered his own gaze. He stood there conscious that so many fierce eyes were directed at him. Meanwhile Father Joseph told his beads and muttered a prayer, which Benoni, ignorant of Latin, could not understand, yet found strangely comforting. An eagle flew overhead, in the direction of the mountains. A soldier's cry attracted his attention to the bird's flight and he dared to lift his head so that he could watch it. Perhaps it is a good omen, he thought. Perhaps the eagle represents Milan or Astolf, or both of them.

The Lombard King now approached, took Benoni's chin between his thumb and forefinger, forcing it upwards, then spat in the boy's face, and said, 'If the Frankish King is fool enough to be persuaded by his sister's wiles, that is his business. But you will in that event carry this message to that false-heart Milan and the traitor Astolf: that I, Arnauf, ever-mighty King of the Lombards, will never forget the treachery they have practised on me, and will pursue them with my vengeance even to the end of the world.'

He stepped back, hesitated, swayed as if intoxicated, and then raised his fist and struck the boy hard on the side of his head, just by the temple, so hard indeed that Benoni staggered and fell to the ground. The King turned on his heel and stalked away, while Benoni, dazed, heard the mocking laughter of the Lombard soldiers who stood around. He picked himself up, and turned away to hide the evidence of the tears that sprang to his eyes.

Meanwhile, in the royal pavilion, Charles and Bertha looked on each other a long while without speaking. This much at least is known. Charles saw a sister who was no longer the slim girl he had adored, no longer the nymph he had called sometimes dryad, sometimes naiad; but a woman whose face was already lined by care and as a result of the privations she had endured. And, to her surprise and gratification, Bertha read pain in her brother's eyes. I say 'gratification', not because she was one to take a cruel pleasure in another's misery, but because what she saw there testified to the justice of her surmise. Charles still loved her. His anger and pursuit of vengeance were indeed the measure of that love. The fire was not dead, but might be rekindled.

Yet, when he did speak, his voice was harsh, his manner chilly.

'Why should I bargain with you, woman?' he said.

'Bargain?' she said. 'I am here at your mercy. And nothing becomes a great king like the exercise of mercy.'

Again he lapsed into silence, pulling at his moustaches and chewing his nether lip.

'Our father Pepin,' he said, 'would have known how to deal with you, how to punish your defiance of the royal will.'

Bertha, seeing him discomfited by the thought and a victim of doubt, permitted herself a smile.

'I have no doubt of that,' she said. 'He would have had me tied to the tail of a horse and dragged through the streets. Or perhaps he would have been content to order that I be disembowelled. But you are not Pepin, brother. Indeed, you have always detested him. Why, then, should you seek to imitate him now? Your mother called him a monster. I know that because when Pepin cast her aside and took my mother, then a shepherd-girl in Lorraine, as first his concubine and then his wife – even

80

if the marriage was of dubious legality – your saintly mother took pity on the girl, befriended her and comforted her when Pepin beat her and otherwise made her wretched. You and I are Pepin's children, for our sins, but our virtues derive from our mothers, and I know that there was never a better, more dutiful, or more loving son to his mother than you, Charles. Then I recall also how you in turn guarded me from our father's brutality and came to my rescue when he attempted to rape me. So let us not speak of Pepin, but of what is now to be done. I am ready, as my very presence here indicates, to confess that I have sinned against you, and to submit now to your will. To submit without any conditions other than that which I now lay before you.'

'An unconditional submission flanked by conditions,' Charles sighed. 'That was ever your way when you sought to twist me round your little finger.'

'Hear me then,' she said, and laid out the terms of her submission as she had already agreed them with Milan and Astolf, terms to which they had perforce given reluctant and ashamed agreement.

Again, Charles made no immediate reply. Wounded pride, desire for revenge, fear of appearing weak, and the innate generosity of his nature struggled for mastery in the breast of this most remarkable of men. The issue was still unresolved – and who knows how it might have been decided? – when the infant Roland slipped from his mother's lap, took uncertain wobbly steps towards his uncle, and slipped his tiny hand into the King's great paw. All at once the stern visage of the King relaxed. He smiled and took the child on to his knee.

'I have been conquered', he said, speaking with the magnificent majesty he could so effortlessly assume, 'by your eloquence and by the trust this little child has placed in me. It shall be as you ask. But with this one proviso, sister. You shall marry Ganelon to whom I promised you before you defied me, for I gave him my word that you should be his wife, and my word is a seal that I have never broken.'

'Marry Ganelon?' Bertha said. 'Marry Ganelon? If that is your price, brother, so be it.'

Thus it was that Milan and Astolf were spared, to ride

eastwards in search of new adventures, hoping to win yet greater fame in the ranks of the Roman Emperor defending Constantinople and the Faith in never-ending wars against the paynim. Benoni took leave of Astolf, and many tears were shed by both, for, though Astolf desired to keep him at his side, Benoni had pledged his first loyalty to Bertha. And thus it was that Roland achieved his first victory, softening the heart of the Great King and saving the life of his father Milan.

XV

Ganelon was overjoyed to have won Bertha as his bride and so to have become the King's brother-in-law. He had admired Bertha from the day he first cast eyes on her, and had even then set his heart on the match. Therefore his pride, which was extreme, was sorely wounded when she eloped with Milan. He could not believe that any princess could of her own will prefer a penniless outlaw to a prince such as himself, with his vast estates and reputation for prowess in battle. So for a time he persuaded himself that she had been bewitched. At least, that was what he wanted to believe. Wounded pride must ever seek solace in such deceptive medicine. Now that she was his, only one thing disturbed his perfect happiness: that the King had weakly consented to let Milan escape without punishment. But it was some time before this thought soured his temper.

At first all seemed well. Though Bertha still sighed for Milan, she did so secretly; his loss was the price she had paid. Besides, as she told Benoni, her only confidant, 'I have known true love, and that is more than most women can claim. To be wed to a man one does not love is the common experience of my sex, and I am resolved to make the best of it. Nothing can deprive me of the memories I possess. And if I had not submitted to the King my brother, what would have become of my darling Roland?'

'What indeed?' Benoni would reply. 'It doesn't bear thinking on.'

So Bertha yielded as a wife should to her husband's will, and did not deny him her bed, though, to tell the truth, where she had known joy with Milan, she found now only pain and disgust. Ganelon pressed himself on her and she did not resist.

'Perhaps we all have to do penance for happiness,' she said to Benoni.

Ganelon's joy in possession did not long endure. He felt her reluctance, that she consented only in form. And, within a year, he found himself the victim of both jealousy and boredom. It was not what he had looked for. So he left the court and carried Bertha and the rest of the household off to his castle at the little town of Sigmaringen on the Danube. It was perched on a high, scarce accessible rock, and to Bertha it soon seemed to be a prison. She lost all joy in life, refused even to go riding, spoke to Benoni of the past as if she had been an old woman, and was often found weeping over her sleeping child. Then she grew pale, lost appetite and fell into a decline. As the days shortened and the winter set in she was daily weaker. She heard Mass on Christmas Day, but three days later, on the feast of the Holy Innocents, she died, with Milan's name on her lips. Benoni suspected poison, and this suspicion hardened when, only a few days after the Princess's death, Ganelon married again. His new bride was a Hungarian countess, a thin, black-eyed woman, reputed to be a witch. Her name was Irma, and she was already carrying Ganelon's child, born only a month after the wedding, and given the name Rodolfo.

Irma was jealous of Roland and urged Ganelon to rid himself of the boy. But though Ganelon was obedient to her in most things, and might indeed be said to have been in thrall, he did not dare to do as she bid. For, if he feared his new wife, he feared Charles even more, despite the fact that Irma was to hand, forever inciting him against Roland, and the King hundreds of leagues distant. Yet, because in every dispatch Charles sent to Ganelon in his capacity as Count of the Eastern March of the Frankish Empire, he never failed to enquire as to the health and education of his 'dearest nephew Roland', Ganelon did not dare yield to Irma's importunities.

Meanwhile, Benoni prudently sought to ingratiate himself with Irma, not because he had either liking or respect for her – and indeed he often said in later years that she terrified him – but because he saw this as the best means of continuing to be able to protect Roland, for whom he had an absolute devotion.

So the years passed, and Roland, watched over by Benoni, grew in strength and beauty. Yet, conscious of the resentment, even hatred, with which both Ganelon and Irma regarded him – the

84

former because he could not look at the boy without being reminded of Milan, the latter because he so outshone her Rodolfo – he learned to act with circumspection. Naturally blithe and open of nature, he perforce cultivated hypocrisy. He schooled himself to conceal thoughts and feelings, and to speak only in empty platitudes. He learned to pretend to sentiments he did not possess, and his manner to Irma especially was guarded and deferential. Indeed he played the part he had assigned himself so skilfully that she came to speak of him to Ganelon as a milksop. Yet, even as she pretended to despise him for the softness of his manner, she could not avoid comparing his outward appearance with Rodolfo's, and seeing that, as Roland grew more beautiful, Rodolfo remained small of stature, sharp-featured, timid and insignificant.

It is not to be supposed that Roland was content. His movements were restricted and his education neglected. He would have liked to write to his uncle the King asking if he might come to the royal court at Engelheim, but he could not trust any of the priests to whom he would have to dictate the letter not to betray its contents to his stepfather. Benoni could of course be trusted to carry a message, but this too was impossible. In the first place Benoni was loath to leave him, for he feared what might befall in his absence: Roland might succumb to some convenient illness which would carry him off. Secondly, his own comings and goings were carefully watched and he could not doubt that if he set off for Engelheim, he would be pursued and brought back a prisoner, or killed. Often as they talked the matter over, which was indeed whenever they could meet without fear of being spied upon, they could arrive at no solution. And yet, with every year that passed, it seemed to Benoni that Roland's position was more perilous.

One day he found the boy in tears, which had never happened before, for Roland had schooled himself to display a Spartan reserve and fortitude. What was the cause? It was a little time before an answer was forthcoming. Then words tumbled forth, expressing the boy's long-pent-up rage, resentment and disappointment. Greatly daring, he had yielded to the frustration that had so long consumed him, and enquired of Ganelon when he might begin the training that would fit him for knightly duty.

85

'He laughed in my face,' Roland said, 'and told me that my uncle the King had decreed that I was to take Holy Orders. When I protested, he said, "If you won't be a priest despite the King's command, then you are to be shut in a monastery, and, should you resist further, you are to be blinded and castrated first." Is this possible?' the boy cried, tears starting from his eyes. 'Can my uncle the King really be so cruel? Cannot he understand that my dearest wish is to serve him in the field of battle, and to be ranked among his paladins? Surely he cannot suppose that I shall be content to spend my life mumbling prayers?'

'There are priests who fight in battle, bishops, too,' Benoni said. 'The noble Turpin especially. Yet things may not be as they seem.'

'What do you mean?'

Benoni hesitated, then led Roland a little further away from the castle walls towards an orchard of apple and cherry trees that stood by the bank of the Danube.

'I mean,' he said, 'that how things are depends on how they are viewed. So, in this instance, Ganelon tells you that the King has decreed that you should take Holy Orders, and you, with some reason, think this improbable. But turn it on its head, dear boy, and how does it look?'

'Well, how?' Roland said. 'I do not understand this game of turning things upside-down.' His brow was furrowed. Charming, brave and delightful though he was, he found thinking difficult.

'Your uncle the King has not seen you in years.'

'Through no fault of mine,' Roland said.

'No, indeed. My point is that he does not know you, does not know what manner of boy or young man you have become. Suppose therefore that Ganelon plays on the royal ignorance – which is to my mind what courtiers do, for kings must ever pretend to a knowledge they do not possess, at least that's how it seems to me, even if I speak as the son of a poor Breton farmer ...'

'Benoni,' Roland said, 'would you please speak clearly and come to the point? I know perfectly well that you are the son of a poor Breton farmer. How could I forget it, seeing that scarce a week goes by but you remind me of it. Go on, please.'

'Suppose your stepfather has told your uncle the King that you have expressed a desire to take Holy Orders—'

'Which I haven't—'

'Which indeed you haven't. What might the King reply? Perhaps something like this. If that's the boy's ambition, it may be the will of God and who am I to set myself up against the Almighty? Whereupon the King's approval, however reluctantly given, is translated by your stepfather into a royal command.'

'You may be right,' Roland said. 'You sometimes are. But one thing is certain: I am not going to become a priest.'

'Then again,' Benoni said, 'it may be that the King himself knows nothing of this business, and that the plot has been concocted by one of your enemies at court.'

'But why should I have enemies at court? I have never been there.'

Benoni was caught between a smile and sigh. The candid innocence of youth was delightful; yet he feared for Roland while the boy remained ignorant of the wickedness of men.

'Be assured you have enemies there,' he said, 'for that is the nature of courts. One among them, I greatly fear, is the King's eldest son, your cousin Charlot. He is mean, jealous and depraved; Ganelon and he are old confederates.'

'How can you know all this, Benoni, when you have not left this accursed castle of Sigmaringen in all the years of my childhood and youth?'

'I keep my ear close to the ground. I let everyone speak to me as they please, and I listen to the conversations of others, and say little myself, no more than is necessary to jog a dialogue along. Men are ever quick to spill confidences if you affect to be indifferent. So now I know what I know and what you have told me confirms what I have long suspected. You are not safe here. It's time you and I were on the move ...'

How this was contrived I shall tell you tomorrow, my Prince.

No, it is not a case of my memory failing and requiring to be refreshed; nor – this is impertinent on your part – have I exhausted my power of invention, for may I remind you that I set down nothing but what is well attested. It's simply, if you must know, that I have an appointment with a very charming young person. No, I shan't say any more. You must permit me a life of my own.

XVI

Where then were we?

Ah, yes, Benoni was contriving, or seeking to contrive, the means by which he and Roland might make their escape.

What's that? My evening? What evening? Oh, since you insist, it went badly; that is, it didn't go at all. Youth is fickle and I shall say no more on the subject.

Whether Ganelon suspected that the Fate decreed for his stepson would turn Roland's mind to thoughts of escape, I cannot tell. He was a dark and secret man. Be that as it may, Roland now discovered that he was always accompanied by two knights whenever he rode out to hunt or to hawk his falcon. When he protested their company was neither necessary nor to his taste, he was told that bands of marauding Huns were reported to be advancing up the Danube, and therefore measures must be taken to protect the King's nephew.

Roland said to Benoni, 'I could certainly kill one of these tiresome fellows, and quite probably both, for I am certain I am their superior in swordsmanship. But it is not of their choice that they accompany me, and so it seems wrong to deprive them of their lives merely for following orders. What do you say, Benoni? Am I too nice in my conscience?'

'No,' Benoni said, 'you speak as your father's son and a true Christian. Your sentiments do you credit, but they don't help to solve our problem.'

'As to that,' Roland said, 'I am happy, dear Benoni, to leave the thinking to you.'

'Very well ...'

Winter set in. Icicles hung from the battlements and the Danube was frozen over. All day the sky was a deep blue, at evening touched with red-gold in the west, and at night the floor of Heaven sparkled. The moon was full and in the frost birds fell lifeless from the trees. In the hall at night men huddled in furs and sheepskin while minstrels plucked their strings with icy fingers and sang of old battles and heroic deeds. At the feast of Christ's birth shepherds came down from the Schwabisches Alb and played their pipes to welcome the Christkind into God's cruel world. 'I know that my Redeemer liveth,' sang the choristers of the cathedral. Ganelon drank deep and Irma searched the company with her black gaze. A cold wind blew through the hall, and the air was heavy, threatening snow. The candles guttered. Men wrapped themselves in whatever garments might serve to keep them warm, and slept where they lay.

In the darkest hour before dawn, when even the owl falls silent, Benoni woke Roland by pressing gently with his finger on the young man's temple. He put a hand over his mouth to prevent him from calling out, and whispered in his ear that it was time to rise. He led him from the hall and into a dark passage that opened on the courtyard, where one of the hill shepherds was waiting for them with jackets of sheepskin and low-brimmed bonnets.

Benoni whispered, 'These men have agreed that we may travel in their company as far as their mountain village. There are enough of them to make our passage inconspicuous, and in any case, the guards at the castle gate are either half-drunk or drugged. But you must be careful to say nothing, to remain silent, no matter what you see, until we are free of the castle, for your tongue is not theirs and will betray you of a certainty.'

For a moment it seemed that Roland would resist and refuse the disguise, for it bruised his pride to escape from the castle in such company, as a thief in the night. But good sense prevailed and he trusted Benoni. So they came to the gate, and the leader of the shepherds sang out to the guards that they had done their duty to their master Ganelon and must now be on their way to tend their flocks. The guard did not question them, and they departed from the castle.

They were not long on the march before they heard the sound of hooves ringing behind them on the frozen ground. At once there was agitation among the shepherds, and one called out to their captain that his lust for gold had betrayed them. The captain said,

'All will be well when we reach the hills,' but it was soon evident that the pursuing horsemen were gaining on them, and the shepherds babbled with fear. They were passing by a dark wood, and Benoni, after a word with the captain, took Roland by the hand and forced him to follow him into the wood. The young man would have broken away, even from his only friend, for he was consumed with anger and shame, and was fain to turn back to confront their pursuers. But Benoni held fast and, when Roland still struggled, seized the club which he wore in his waistband, and struck his dearest charge on the head, so that the boy fell down in a swoon. Then he dragged him under cover.

The sun rose to its zenith and then fast declined, and still Roland lay unconscious, growing cold as death. Benoni, fearful that he had struck too hard, lay on the boy, pressing against him, to restore warmth and set his blood flowing in his veins. At some point before the evening fell, Benoni heard the sound of horsemen returning to the castle; soon after, Roland opened his eyes, moaned piteously and gave other signs of returning life. Benoni held a flask to the boy's lips and commanded him to drink the watered wine.

'I dreamed that I was dead,' Roland said, 'and held in a dungeon chained to the wall.'

'Not so, not so. You got a bang on the head, that is all.'

'I remember nothing.'

'A happy condition,' Benoni said, 'given the wickedness of the world. But we must be on the march. In the morning they will scour these woods for us ...'

Roland still looked puzzled, for in truth his wits were still so scattered that he could not recall how they came to be in the wood, nor how they had escaped from Ganelon's castle. Indeed, if at that moment you had spoken the name 'Ganelon' to him, he would not have been able to assign meaning to it. Fortunately, however, he was docile in his befuddled condition, and allowed Benoni to lead him by the hand out of the wood and back to the path.

The moon had risen, throwing shadows such as would frighten women and children, and a keen breeze rustled the leaves. Then, at the third turning of the track, they came upon a man hanging from a tree. The moonlight struck his swollen face, and Benoni saw it was the captain of the shepherd troop.

'Poor man,' he muttered, 'brave man, for he has not talked. If he had he might not be swinging here. Would that I had time to cut him down and lay him in a grave. But peace be his who so nobly died.'

And he hustled Roland on all the faster, though the boy stumbled often and his breath came in short painful gasps, and more than once he made as to fall down and rest. But Benoni was insistent.

They came to a fork in the path, and Benoni took that which led back into the forest and rose towards the brow of a hill.

'We shall be safe when we are in the next valley,' he said, but Roland made no reply.

The climb was steep, the track rough, and it began to snow. Soon they had attained a height where the snow already lay a foot deep, and more still fell, the wind blowing it in their faces. Roland began to weep.

'I can do no more. Let me lie here and die if that is God's will.'

'No,' cried Benoni, and struck him on the buttocks with his staff. 'No, on, on, on . . .'

When Roland stood mute shaking his head, Benoni struck him again, and this time the boy fell to the ground. But Benoni would not let him lie. He seized him by the hair and pulled him to his feet. Then he struck him again and again with his staff, shouting, 'You'll walk, do you hear? Walk, or the Devil will take you.'

So they marched, heavy-legged, Benoni adamant and poor Roland whimpering, as if held in a dark and dismal house of pain, their faces set against the snow, which now blew hard and hostile. It was as though they were alone, the last men in the frozen world; and only Benoni's will defied the elements. At last they attained the summit of the hill and were able to begin the descent into the valley. They had travelled perhaps half a mile – in that harsh night it was impossible to tell – when they came upon a hut or shelter used by the shepherds when they brought their flocks to the summer pastures. Roland was now near to collapse, and when Benoni unlatched the door and pushed him into the dark interior, he straightway fell to the earth floor and lay there sobbing.

In time to come he would recall that night with a strange mixture of emotions. He had never before, or since, experienced such humiliation, such abjectness of spirit. He was reduced to his essence, stripped of all royalty, naked as a beggar, oppressed by images of devils and torture. In himself he was nothing, without will or strength. Yet when he emerged from this darkness and came into light, it was strength itself that he drew from what he then endured. Or so it seemed to him. He had descended into the abyss, into the very pit of Hell where Death approached him as a friend, taking his cold hand and pressing it lovingly; and yet he had not died, he had not surrendered utterly. He had endured.

I see you frown, my Prince, a sneer forming on your lips, and I know what you are thinking: that this is a poor sort of hero I am offering you, a miserable parody of a paladin. Is that not so, Fritzi? You are asking yourself whether presenting Roland to you in this wretched light, I intend to make mockery of all chivalry, by showing this beloved hero of so many noble tales to have been in reality a poltroon.

Such is not my intention, any more than it has been my aim to lead you to despise Charles because I tell you his voice was thin and piping, and show you that he sometimes acted cravenly and vilely, and that his mind was not always firm, but often subject to the persuasion of others, even of unworthy men.

I answer you on both counts, thus.

The Romances in which you delight, in which indeed I have taken delight also, and the songs of the troubadours which sound so sweetly in the ear and which invite us to aspire to noble deeds ourselves, are not false. Not absolutely false. Men do from time to time act nobly; and true heroes are to be found even in royal courts.

But what is a hero?

In the first place, he is one who commands our admiration and whose actions we may long to emulate. But which do we admire the more? Blind, thoughtless courage, as of a fighting bull maddened by the prick of the darts? Or the courage of one who, looking danger and evil in the face, assesses both, knows fear, yet steels himself to the fight? Believe me, the second is the more admirable.

Moreover, delightful as these Romances and *chansons* are, they are not true to life. They offer you an idealised picture. But I, in this history, deal only in realities, in facts, however ugly and brutal. It is my intention that you learn what the world is. Certainly I am happy to feed your imagination with wonderful stories – and you cannot say that I have starved you of such. But – and remember there is always a 'but' in the wise man's view of things – I would be failing in my duty if I did not bring you face-to-face with harsh truth; and courage, I must tell you, is not a constant. Just as even the best of men contain evil within them, so the bravest have their moments of fear and despair. And it is in overcoming such emotions, in recovering from the glimpse of the yawning pit, that man displays his true quality. So, my Prince, do not despise Roland for his collapse. Some day, even you . . .

Morning came on. The storm abated. The sun shone, and Roland and Benoni picked their way through the pine trees that coated the hillside and glittered pink and gold in the morning light. Roland moved stiffly on account of the beating Benoni had given him; and he was at first inclined to sulk. But the glory of the morning revived his spirits.

They descended the hillside, and when they came out of the trees, a lake stretched before them. There was an island in the middle of the water, and a grim, grey castle thrust its battlements and tower above the bare branches of the winter wood that surrounded it.

The path ran alongside the sparkling water, and they were hesitating whether to turn right or left, when Roland saw a boat coming towards them, with two fellows pulling at the oars and a woman sitting in the stern. Benoni took Roland by the arm to pull him behind a bush, but it was too late. She had seen them and was gesturing in their direction.

The boat drew nearer. Roland stood up straight and pushed his hair out of his eyes. The woman was young, scarcely more than a girl, and she was beautiful. Red-gold hair tumbled about

93

her shoulders, which Roland knew at once to be beautiful also, even though they were concealed from view beneath a cape of sleek dark fur. She called out to them in a dialect Roland could not understand. But the meaning was clear. They were to board the little craft.

Benoni hesitated, fearing a trap. Besides, he was eager to put as great a distance between them and Sigmaringen as possible, and to be rowed to an island in the middle of a lake did not serve their purpose. But the choice was taken from him. Roland, his gaze fixed on the lovely face, which, it seemed to him, had swum from his dreams of many a summer night into the light of day, advanced into the water and climbed aboard. Benoni had no option but to follow. Roland settled himself on a cross-spar and began to talk, explaining who he was, both discretion and his troubles of the previous hours quite forgotten. In short, he had fallen headlong in love at the first sight of the lady, who, as Benoni discovered, was in truth no more than fourteen or perhaps fifteen years of age. But she was wonderfully self-possessed.

The rowers set themselves to their task, silently. Benoni turned his back on them so as to be able to watch Roland and the girl, but they seemed oblivious of his presence or were at least unembarrassed by it. Each had eyes only for the other. It seemed for both an enlargement of existence. He knew that, and for the first time felt that his own youth had irretrievably fled.

I sympathise with him, for, as the years pass and one's hair turns to grey, there is nothing so touching and so poignantly painful as to look on the young ensnared by love for the first time, so engrossed in each other that all else is forgotten. What memories, what regrets the sight calls up! In my case these are so alive that I am tempted to describe this girl, whose name by the way was Angelica – and angelic she was indeed – in terms of my own first love, a forest maiden called Alison whom I lay with on the bank of the Yarrow water one autumn evening so many years ago.

And indeed, now I come to think on it, there was a resemblance, for Angelica, like my Alison, had hair the colour of autumn leaves, pale skin, blue-grey eyes and a mouth that any painter would be proud to draw, a curving mouth with lips that cried out to be kissed. Moreover, she was like Alison perfectly formed, her legs long and shapely, her breasts small and round, her waist ... but my eyes grow dim with tears even as I summon up the memory. Alas, she married another, as girls do, and I in despair took Holy Orders and became a clerk before embarking on philosophy. Yet, even now, when I am among the most learned in Christendom, what would I not give to recapture and live again that evening by Yarrow? With love, you see, even too much is not enough. As the wise poet sang, '*Omnia vincit amor, nos et cedamus amori* ...' Is there a happier thought?

When the boat came to shore, Angelica took Roland by the hand and led him to a secluded spot in the little sheltered garden that lay on the west side of the tower. They gazed for a moment out over the lake, now level and tranquil. Silence enveloped them. They looked into each other's eyes and sighed – a sigh of expectation, not of sadness. Their lips drew near and, while the world stood still, they kissed. A long kiss, an exploring kiss, a kiss of love and beauty and youth, a kiss that contained all future kisses, or promise of them, a kiss in which heart and soul and sense moved all in concert, a kiss such as ... but I grow lyrical. You must, my Prince, imagine the rest.

This Angelica was the daughter of one Manfred, a count whose allegiance to Charles was at best dubious. However, it was to Roland's fortune that Manfred detested Ganelon, and had done so since Ganelon played some mean trick on him when they were both but boys. So Roland had nothing to fear from him in this regard. I should rather say, would have had nothing to fear, for Manfred, as it happened, was from home, engaged in some warlike work, the nature and purpose of which has not been recorded. Had he been in residence at the castle, which went by the name of Schloss Prageafels, Angelica would (doubtless) have been less forward.

For weeks Roland and Angelica lived in that state engendered by first love when the world is forgotten, and all cares and anxieties concerning the future are set aside. It was as if they had never lived till this love awakened them from sleep. They were like our first parents in Eden, innocent in pleasure.

Benoni meanwhile looked on them and all they did with a

mingling of tenderness and apprehension. Generous of nature as he was, he could not fail to be moved by the beauty of their love; yet he knew himself, for so long, since Bertha's death, the most important being in Roland's life, to be excluded, and this could not but grieve him. Reason told him it was but natural, yet reason can rarely triumph over the heart. Moreover, he said to himself, it cannot last. One day her father will return. And then what? Or perhaps, now that winter is past and the spring is upon us, Ganelon will send out to seek our whereabouts. He must surely account to the King for the boy's well-being, and what is he to say? Or perhaps he will report that Roland rode off in the dead of winter in the company – I daresay he will add – only of a scurvy knave, Benoni by name, long distrusted. Perhaps he will pretend that I led the boy astray, even into some trap, or that we were both taken by the Huns or made prisoner by the Muslim army advancing through the Balkans. Any invention is possible, and then what?

So Benoni turned such matters over in his mind, and was left in perplexity and trepidation.

Waking one morning, Benoni was aware of an unusual bustle in the castle and sent to enquire the cause of it. His messenger, a pretty, curly-headed page called Rafael, who had formed an attachment to him, and who was on this account sadly jealous of Roland, returned to say that the master, Count Manfred himself, had returned home with rich treasure, the spoils of war or perhaps diplomacy, and also – it was rumoured – with marriage plans for his darling daughter Angelica. Alarmed by this news, Benoni at once dispatched the boy in search of Roland, and was the more disturbed when he came back to report no sign of him.

In truth, Roland was even then with Angelica. She had sent to him as soon as she learned of her father's return, and they had met in a grotto, once the abode of a hermit, deep in the woods. It had long been fixed on as their private trysting-place. They fell into each other's arms and embraced. But when they had kissed – for a long time that was never long enough for either – Angelica drew away, and Roland saw that her eyes were brimming with tears. He asked what so distressed her, on such a lovely May morning, when they were alone together. He could not believe he had offended her; the kisses they had exchanged were surely proof that her love remained as strong and true as his.

'Alas,' she said, 'it is precisely for that reason that I weep. I love you passionately, Roland-Orlando, my darling, and my only happiness is to be with you.'

'Why then,' he said, 'we are as one,' and he made to kiss her again. But she drew away and, laying the palm of her hand over his mouth, said, between sobs, 'Grizel my old nurse used to warn me that the course of true love never did run smooth. I chose not to believe her, but, alas, I now find that she spoke truth.'

Roland took hold of her hand, pressed it a moment to his lips, and said, 'What talk is this? Have you reason to doubt my love? If anyone has been telling you stories that give you cause to doubt my sincerity, I shall tear his tongue from his mouth to prove him a liar.'

'No,' she said, 'it is not that. I have no reason to think you unfaithful, and indeed, seeing that you have scarce spoken to another woman since the day we met – that happy, happy day, for ever to be enshrined in my memory – you have had no opportunity ... but this is silly talk. It is my father who ...'

And here she broke down in an anguish of grief and apprehension; so deep was her distress that she was unable to speak coherently for some time. Instead her sentences were broken and her voice barely audible. To recount exactly what the poor girl said would be wearisome. Therefore, if at the risk of losing dramatic intensity, I shall summarise.

In short, Count Manfred had returned with, as rumoured, a marriage arranged for his darling daughter. The chosen husband was one Suleiman al-Zaquat, Emir of Smyrna – a delightful city on the coast of Asia Minor, famous for currants, and reputedly near the site of Troy itself. There was to be no delay. The Emir was posting hard after Count Manfred, and, as soon as he arrived, the marriage would be solemnised. Count Manfred was triumphant. The marriage was a masterstroke of policy, and though he would be sorry to part from his adored daughter, he could not have arranged a more glorious match for her.

Roland was naturally heartbroken. His first thought was to snatch Angelica in his arms and make off with her. His second to consult Benoni, who said, 'But the Emir is a Muslim.'

'I care nothing for that. He is another man. What am I to do? Advise me, Benoni.'

Benoni knew at once that they were both in great danger and must make their escape from the island immediately. He could not suppose that the love-making had gone unremarked. He could not doubt that someone would lose no time in informing the Count, and then ... it didn't bear thinking on. Manfred might hesitate to have Roland put to death when he learned whose nephew he was, but the fact that he had arranged this marriage with a Muslim ruler was itself an act of defiance, even rebellion, given Charles's inflexible enmity towards Islam. Therefore it was probable that he would hold Roland a prisoner, throwing him into a dungeon to serve as a hostage or bargaining counter, should his alliance with the Emir provoke Charles to attack him.

You, my Prince, bred in Sicily where you have loyal Arab subjects, many of them learned scholars and honourable men, others indeed having formed your saintly mother's most trusted guard, may find it difficult to comprehend how fixed was the antipathy with which the Franks then regarded the followers of the Prophet Mohammed. But so it was.

I myself feel no such antipathy. As you know, I have studied and taught in Spain, at the illustrious University of Salamanca, and also in Toledo and even Cordoba, and I have many friends among Arab scholars. Indeed, in our time and generation, I go so far as to assert that you will find nowhere a richer and more tolerant civilisation than that which flourishes in Moorish Spain, except, of course, here in Sicily. I learned to speak, read and write Arabic, and I rejoice to think that it is by mastery of that language that I have been able to translate the works of the greatest of philosophers, the Athenian Aristotle, which have been preserved for posterity only in the Arabic tongue, into which they were translated by great scholars in Alexandria. By this means I have made my own contribution to the flowering of enlightenment in Christendom. Moreover, I learned there to respect Islam, just as I also learned, in Salamanca, to revere the Jewish faith. We are all – Christians, Muslims, Jews – children of the Book, followers of the same law, which is the word of the one true God. My friend, Ignacio di Perron, Archbishop of Toledo, with whom I have spoken long on these matters, is wont to assert that Islam is no heathen or pagan faith, but a Christian heresy inasmuch as it reveres Jesus only as a prophet, and not as the Christ and Son of God, except in the sense that we are all the Sons (or indeed daughters) of God. Though he did not succeed in convincing me utterly, I respect his argument and concur with his conclusion: that wars between our faiths are foolish, and unnecessary, the Crusades folly, and that the day will come when Christians and Muslims – and, of course, Jews also – shall, as foretold by the prophet Isaiah, lie down together like the lion and the lamb.

Sadly, my friend the Archbishop's opinions caused him to fall foul of the Holy Office, otherwise known as the Inquisition, and he was compelled, after torture, to recant; indeed, even then he was in danger of suffering the penalty of being burnt at the stake, which, as you know, is reserved for heretics. It was painful for me to see so worthy a man subjected to such humiliation and reduced to such abject terror. For which reason I thought it prudent myself to depart from Spain, and to burn the records I had made of our conversations and an essay I had written calling for reconciliation with Islam. Better, I thought, to burn my papers than to risk being burnt myself. Which is how I come to find myself here in Palermo, practising prudence. Nevertheless, in being granted the inestimable privilege of acting as your tutor, I think it my duty to urge you to embrace the virtue of tolerance.

That virtue was unknown in the time of Charlemagne, and there is at least this justification of his hatred of Islam and his readiness to denounce Muslims as infidels: that the Moors had made repeated invasions of the fair land of France. Indeed, soon after the events which I have just related, a Moorish army would besiege Paris; and how this was connected with the alliance Count Manfred was promoting with the Emir of Smyrna, you shall learn in good time.

Meanwhile, enough of this digression, important though it be, and especially valuable to your understanding, my Prince, of your inheritance and the divisions that disturb the peace of the world. Which divisions are unnecessary, and would be healed if those who exercise power were not deaf to the wise advice which men such as myself are in a position to offer. And deafest of all, I say sadly, is your guardian and nominal overlord, the Holy Father, unworthy man that he is.

But let us return to our tale.

We left Angelica in tears, Roland in tears and Benoni anxiously plotting escape.

His first problem was how to convince Roland of the necessity of leaving the island as quickly and surreptitiously as possible. As soon as Roland had dried his tears, the young man was eager to fight for what he called his 'rights'.

'Rights?' said Benoni. 'This is no time to speak of rights, which are in any case usually imaginary, the word being chosen, in my observation, to make respectable whatever people think they want or suppose to be their due. It's a word,' he added, to nettle the boy, 'which is employed only by the weak and foolish. Men have no rights except to what is reasonable, and it is against all reason to suppose that Count Manfred will be diverted from what he regards as a masterstroke of policy merely because you and his daughter declare yourselves to be in love with each other. Love is not a word in the vocabulary of politics. I learned that from my time serving your mother – God rest her pure soul – and your father, the unfortunate Milan, wherever he be now. They were as surely in love as you and Angelica are; and their love came close to destroying them. That will be your fate also, if you don't listen to me, and follow my advice. He will clap you in chains and imprison you in a dungeon where your only companions will be the rats.'

Roland frowned, this being his habit when required to think.

'Certainly,' he said, 'I have no desire to be chained up with only rats for my companions. But what are we to do? To desert Angelica were death to me, no, worse than death. So, if we are to flee, we must take her with us. You will have your Rafael, for I'm sure the boy will follow you to the ends of the earth, and I my Angelica. It remains only to devise the means of escape.'

'Would that matters were so easily settled,' Benoni said.

As he was considering how best to persuade Roland that what he longed for was impossible, the door of their chamber was thrown open, and four guards bearing halberds stood on the threshold. One of them, a sergeant, stepped forward and told them that the Count required their presence.

'Immediately,' he said.

'Certainly,' Roland said, speaking with princely dignity. 'But a simple request would have sufficed. There was no need for this show of force.'

'That's as may be,' the sergeant said, running his finger along the edge of the halberd's blade. 'There might have been two opinions as to that.'

They were led, a halberdier on either side, through the great hall of the castle, and beyond it into an antechamber. The sergeant presented himself at the door that led from the room to the Count's private apartment. Words were exchanged, and they were ushered in.

Roland was at first delighted to see Angelica seated on a stool below her father's chair, but his joy turned to dismay when she lowered her head and refused to meet his gaze.

The Count pulled at his beard, which was thick and black though streaked with grey. He was a heavy, sturdy man with dark eyes and a nose that curved like an eagle's beak. But when he spoke his voice was soft as silk.

'Who are you that have enjoyed my hospitality in my absence?'

'For which we are duly grateful,' Benoni said.

'And which, if I am informed correctly, this young man has abused by seeking to seduce my daughter. But you have not replied to my question. Who are you?'

Roland was about to speak, proudly declaring his royal birth, but Benoni was quick to intervene.

'We are travellers,' he said, 'strolling players, my friend here a minstrel, who lost our way in the forest and were then overtaken by winter. We found refuge here, and would have left by now to seek to rejoin our company, had I not twisted my ankle and lamed myself, then suffered from an ague.'

'From which misfortunes you have recovered?'

'Quite recovered, my lord, I am happy to say, and so we are now eager to resume our journey.'

'I think you an unconscionable liar, fellow. But I am ready to put it to the test.'

He turned to the chamberlain who stood by him.

'Fetch the young man a lute and let us try what manner of minstrel he may be.'

He took a sweetmeat from a silver dish and held it a moment between thumb and forefinger before putting it in his mouth and chewing.

'No doubt it was with your music that you have so charmed my daughter.'

'Indeed it was, Father,' Angelica said, twisting her body so that she could meet her father's gaze, but all the while avoiding Roland's eyes. 'He sings more sweetly than any sucking dove.'

Roland felt the blood rush to his cheeks. His humiliation was extreme, and the temptation to cast aside this play-acting and speak out boldly in his own name was strong. But then he thought of the rats that would be his companions in the dungeon, and he remembered how often Benoni's counsel had held him from acting rashly. So he bit his lip to choke back the proud and angry words he longed to utter, and when the page brought him a lute, he took it and plucked its strings. But even as he did so, he felt the pain of Angelica's denial of their love and of what appeared to him to be the girl's treachery.

So the song he sang was sad and bitter, and told of forsaken love. It went somewhat like this ...

> A shepherd lad lay by an alder tree,
> Making a song of love;
> The summer dawn was fresh and fair,
> The breeze soft as a cooing dove.
>
> 'I met her by the well at e'en,
> Watering her father's flock;
> We gazed into each other's eyes,
> My heart was in a lock.

O, gently, gently did she speak,
Gently I made reply;
Our lips met in a loving kiss;
We parted with a sigh.

Alas, our love was like the rose,
The fairest flower of all;
But which before the day grows dark
Will see its petals fall.'

The shepherd lad lay by the alder tree,
And made a mournful air,
The winter sky was a sullen grey,
And the wind stripped the branches bare.

He laid the lute aside and was pleased to see a tear steal down Angelica's pale cheek. 'She cannot be all false,' he said to himself, 'if my music moves her. It may be that like me she is constrained to play a part. What a foolish and tiresome theatre is this world that we cannot be natural in it.'

Some of the courtiers applauded, but timidly, uncertain whether this was a proper response. The Count fondled the head of a golden mastiff that sat by his right hand, then sniffed, loudly.

'A pretty song,' he said, and Roland bristled to hear the contempt in his voice, 'a mewling whining effeminate piece, a milksop's music. I believe you are what you claim to be, that is, an impertinent pair of rogues, of no moment, scallywags and parasites, corrupters of green girls and children. And you, sir,' he said to Benoni, 'what is your line?'

'Why, my lord,' Benoni bowed low, 'if it please Your Honour, I was a tumbler till I fell from a high rope and lamed myself, and now I am the lowest of the low, a mere storyteller that opens the show and lays our wares before the public. Then I help with the puppets, supplying the voice for Pucinello in our most popular show. Or so I did till we got cut off from our fellows and were lost in the forest till we came here seeking refuge and sustenance. For which we are more than grateful ...'

'Enough,' the Count said. 'A pair of vagabonds.' He turned

to the sergeant of the halberdiers and said, 'Take them to the courtyard, give them a good whipping, and send them on their way. See that the pretty boy feels the lash especially, for his insolence in making eyes at my daughter.'

Roland looked at Angelica, but again she lowered her head and would not acknowledge him. For a moment he was tempted to resist, or again to call out his true name and rank. But he sensed Benoni willing him to keep silent, and perhaps – or so he hoped – that was Angelica's wordless message, too. So he submitted, and even when he was thrown across the bar of the whipping-post and felt the lash bite into his flesh, he uttered no cry. Silence and endurance were his only means of preserving his dignity, of retaining the shreds of self-respect. So, when they were thrust across the drawbridge, to the cries of mockery and execration which soldiers and menials raised to please the Count, he stumbled forward, his back and buttocks all bloody, and never once looked behind. Benoni limped beside him, and they did not speak till they were deep in the forest and came upon a pool where they might wash their wounds. Then they journeyed on and towards evening came to an inn where the boy Rafael, who had slipped unnoticed from the castle and tracked them through the forest, joined them.

Benoni said to Roland, 'You hate me now for the deception I practised and for what you have suffered. But think this, my dear: what we have escaped was more terrible than what we have endured.'

The next day they resumed their journey, travelling eastwards, for Benoni was anxious that they should put as much distance between them and the castle as possible, and was also mindful that they were passing through lands that owed allegiance to Ganelon. So they made haste and scarcely rested till they were beyond the Danube. It was a wretched journey, for Roland was in low spirits, pining for Angelica, and it seemed to him that the fine spring weather mocked his misfortune.

Then one evening they came to an inn where a company of players was gathered, and, since they were made welcome, they joined themselves to the troupe.

XVII

For a little they travelled with the players, but then Roland sank into melancholy and what the Arab doctors have termed depression; which, they insist, is not mere low spirits, but a profound malaise, a weariness of the world. Anselmo, the chief of the players, a genial fellow, but tarry-handed like all Florentines (for he was indeed a native of that proud but close-fisted city), could not understand it.

'Here,' he said, 'is a pretty youth. With his abundant, silky dark hair, his blue eyes, his smooth skin and rosy lips, his figure that an angel might envy, his long legs and well-rounded arms, he could have any girl or woman that he had a mind to having. My own wife – faithful to me for the most part for the last twenty years, if I reckon accurately, calls out to him in her sleep, pleading to be permitted to do things to him that he cannot even imagine. And I don't doubt that my good lady would be as good as her word if His Young Highness would deign even to give her the time of day. And then Lucia, who plays the soubrette in our pieces, and does so, you will admit, friend Benoni, with rare charm and assurance, would prostrate herself before your young friend, and lick him from the toes of his feet to the top of his head. But he will have none of her, either. And that goes also for Gina, who dances so delightfully on the high wire. In vain. At first, friend Benoni, I thought the young man was your catamite, and that you were a lucky fellow to have two, seeing that the boy Rafael can't take his lamb's eyes off you. And good luck to you, friend, thought I; we need such consolation as may come our way on our journey through this vale of tears, and my own tastes have ever been catholic. But I have observed the youth Roland-Orlando closely and I see that, whatever you may feel for him – and who could blame you, friend, if that feeling is desire? – he responds only with a modest friendship, nothing more. And in any case, you now tell me that he is pining for love of a girl, Angelica, who has spurned him …'

'By her father's command,' Benoni said. 'I insist on that. Had she not obeyed him, we – that is Roland-Orlando and myself – were both dead men. There's no doubt as to that.'

'Be that as it may,' Anselmo said, 'his love, if you ask me, is driving him out of his wits, which may not, I grant you, have been of the first quality, for so just is the Lord (men say) that those gifted with beauty are often denied intelligence and wisdom. Nevertheless, should he become raving mad, as I fear he will, we shall have to separate ourselves from you. I don't know how often I have had to lay down this iron law to my troupe of players: there is no place for madmen in our company. I trust, friend, this does not disturb you.'

'Disturb, no,' Benoni said, 'for there is nothing to complain of. A man must be master in his own house and, if our presence makes you uneasy, you are right to say so.'

Soon after this conversation Roland's condition deteriorated. For three days he refused either to eat or to speak, but sat cross-legged, as if he had been a tailor, and stared at a blank wall. And his eyes were as dead as the stones he gazed on.

Then one day he disappeared. Benoni and Rafael hunted for him till night fell and the wolves howled. They searched again the next day and the next. The players moved on and left them behind. They walked for hours day after day, deep in the forest. Rafael's feet blistered and he wept. He cried out that Roland must be dead. In any case, he had deserted them. They owed him nothing, he had always been selfish. Benoni smiled and said, 'I gave a promise to his mother. Do you expect me to break that promise?' His words embarrassed the boy; he felt ashamed. Nobody, he thought, will ever love me as Benoni loves Roland. It was very cold. The wind blew from the wastes of Russia. When darkness fell they lay together and listened to the howling of the wolves. At first light they resumed their search; it was without direction, they were lost themselves. Then Rafael stopped by an oak tree. Someone had taken a knife and carved the shape of a heart pierced by three arrows.

As they were standing there, they heard the sound of a breaking branch and, looking up, saw a woman advancing on them. A bow was slung across her shoulder and a quiver of arrows hung from her belt. The wind blew in her hair, which hung in tresses over her bare shoulders. Her skirt was kilted up above her bare knees, and when she saw that they had remarked her she addressed them thus:

'You have been a long time in coming, for I have looked for you in this place at this hour since the moon was new.'

Her voice was harsh and unmusical, and it seemed to Benoni that she spoke as one to whom words were strange and converse with others unfamiliar.

He began to explain who they were and what their purpose was, but she stopped him with a gesture, and then, putting the forefinger and middle finger of her left hand to her lips, whistled thrice, shrilly, and straightway, two great hounds, milk-white with lemon markings and shaggy coats, bounded from the undergrowth, and came to nuzzle her. So she turned on her heel and led them by a twisting path through the forest till they came to a clearing wherein there was a rude hut. They entered, and the sun, now risen, crept through the leafy branches that were its roof; and they saw Roland lying there, on his back, one arm outstretched and his mouth open. For a moment they thought that he was dead.

As if she understood or divined what they had not put into words, she said, 'He has been like this while the sun has risen and set three times. I found him wandering in the forest, very weary, even to the point of collapse, and so I led him here and gave him water to drink, and then he fell down and lay as you see him.'

'Alas,' Benoni said, 'his wits have fled.'

'Then you must seek them,' she replied. 'For the longer you delay, the further his scattered wits will be blown on the wind, and the harder it will be to assemble them again.'

'But where,' Rafael said, 'are we to seek?'

'In the country of lost things.'

When she pronounced that phrase, which seemed madness to Rafael, who had never heard of such a land, Benoni recalled that the English knight, Astolf, who loved him, had spoken once of

107

journeying there. Therefore he resolved to seek out Astolf first, should he still be alive. And meanwhile he left Rafael to tend to Roland, while the huntress, whose name was Artemis, offered to lead him beyond the forest.

'But there,' she said, 'I must leave you on its borders, for the world no longer knows me, and it is only here in the forest, my hunting-ground, with these my faithful hounds, that I make my abode, who once ranged over all the known world and received the worship of many in great temples.'

'I think she too is mad,' Rafael whispered to Benoni, 'and all the sanity of the world is concentrated in us two.'

Now there are some who assert, my Prince, that this woman who set Benoni on the path which might lead him to Astolf was no mortal woman, but the goddess whom the Romans knew as Diana, she from whose shrine at Nemi Aeneas plucked the Golden Bough that allowed him entry to the Underworld. But this to my mind is fanciful, though the journey she laid open to Benoni was no less arduous. To my mind she was indeed one cast out by men in their cruelty, one who had lived like a hermit-hunter in the woods, and who had taken on the habit of wild beasts. But that she saved Roland's life is certain, and it now remains only to tell you with what success Benoni went in search of Astolf and how the wits departed from Roland.

XVIII

At a village beyond the river Benoni bought a horse, and so travelled eastwards faster. He was seized with urgency, for the woman's warning disturbed him and echoed in his mind. Truly, he said to himself, she may well be mistaken, for men often live to a great age though deprived of their wits, and indeed I have observed that there are dotards who have lived witless beyond the allotted span, and whose bodily strength seems to wax even as their mind grows more vacant. Nevertheless, I fear for Roland, and it even seems to me that he would be better dead than suffered to survive in his miserable condition. What a thing is love that can bring a noble youth to such an extremity ...

It were wearisome to recount every stage of his journey, and indeed it was remarkable for the lack of incident. He was only once attacked by brigands, whom he pacified by the charm of his manners and the gift of an emerald ring; only once seduced by a woman who kept an inn; and once robbed by a priest with whom he shared a bedchamber. He suffered also from an ague which detained him several days in the mountains of Albania, and lost another week when he fell from his horse. But, taking all in all, he was more fortunate than many travellers, and arrived in Byzantium, the city of Constantine, before winter set in. He had directed himself thither because Astolf had spoken of taking service in the Emperor's Varangian guard, which was composed of Norse warriors and Englishmen.

So, having sought directions from a number of citizens (whose answers were, sadly, contradictory and confusing) he came at noon on the feast-day of the Apostle Andrew to the barracks where the Varangians were housed, and inquired of a sentry where the great English warrior, Astolf, might be found.

The guard, a tow-headed Dane, scratched his head, cleared his throat, spat twice, and turned away to consult his colleagues.

One, after a long delay, presented himself to Benoni as Egbert, an English sergeant.

'Astolf?' he said. 'Who are you that ask for him?'

'An old friend whom he will, I trust, be happy to see again.'

'That's as may be,' was the reply, 'or again not, as the case is. Astolf, you see, is not the man he was, and for that reason may not wish to meet again with one who remembers him in the days of his glory. I'm fond of him myself, you know, as a fellow Englishman, and one who has many a night caroused with him till cock-crow. But he is no longer a Varangian, you understand, and, to speak frankly – for I see you have an honest sort of face, even if you are no Englishman yourself ...'

Here he paused, as if to give Benoni the opportunity to deny this. But Benoni merely smiled, and so Egbert continued.

'Like I say, I am fond of the old boy, but the fact is your request needs thinking on, if you don't mind my saying so. And thinking takes time. We English, you must know, are bulldogs who turn things over in their mind before deciding whether whoever accosts them are friends to be welcomed or foes to be bit. Therefore, I say to you: meet me at sundown at the Tavern of the Rosy Garden, and I shall give you my answer there.'

Benoni had no choice but to obey, and was settled in the tavern with a jug of resin-flavoured wine an hour before sundown, for he was impatient. When Egbert at last appeared, he gave him wine, and said, 'My friend, if I may make so bold as to address you as friend, I was foolish to withhold my name, which is Benoni. Once, many years ago, Astolf loved me dearly, and I him, and now I have come seeking his aid.'

'Benoni,' Egbert said. 'I have heard him speak that name in his cups, which I must tell you is the condition in which he passes most hours of the day and night, alas, and this is the reason he is disgraced and was discharged from the Varangians. He is not the man he was, not the man you knew.'

'Nevertheless,' Benoni said, 'I must see him. It is a matter of life and death, and if you will be so kind as to carry a message to him and say it concerns Roland-Orlando, then I make bold to tell you he will see me, no matter what his condition may be.'

'Must?' Egbert said. 'This "must" of yours offends me.'

'Nevertheless . . .' Benoni said again, and waited.

Egbert drank his wine, poured himself another cup, and downed that too.

'Your face,' he said, 'is not dishonest, not absolutely dishonest.'

So, while the candles burned, they fenced with each other, till the second jug was drunk; and then Egbert said, 'Wait here.'

In a little he returned, and beckoned Benoni to follow him along an ill-lit passage that led past several doorways concealed by curtains, and across a garden where women lounged in various states of undress while a fiddler played a thin, melancholy tune, sad music speaking of distant loves and departed hopes, until they came to a hut set against the garden wall. The long, low room was lit by a single lamp, and a man lay on a couch in a recess. A boy in a short tunic fringed with fur sat on the couch and held a cup to the man's lips. He looked round at the intruders and frowned.

'My master is ill,' he said.

But the man in the bed struggled to raise himself to an upright position, and said, wonderingly, 'Is it really you, Benoni? Or am I dreaming?'

Benoni said, 'It is no dream.'

His voice trembled as he spoke. He had come so far, suffered so much, kept going only by hope, and now he did not recognise Astolf in the blear-eyed, hollow-cheeked old man before him. But he held out his hand, and the other's skin felt like parchment, thinly covering bone. Astolf looked at him and his eyes filled with tears. Then he coughed, a violent fit of coughing, and the boy slipped his arm around him and held him as if, without his aid, the thin body might collapse.

Benoni waited till the fit had subsided, then said, 'I have travelled far and journeyed long in search of you.'

'And you find a shipwreck of a man, hidden here lest the world be witness of my shame.'

Saying this, he fell back, whether in sleep or swoon Benoni could not tell. He looked at the bloodless face streaked with dirt which lay encrusted in the deep wrinkles, and he came close to despair. He had pinned his hopes on Astolf, and it had never occurred to him that, after so many years, he would no longer find the bold and valorous knight he had known.

'Oh, the pity of it,' he murmured, and could not tell for whom he felt most pity: for Astolf ruined; for Roland in his vacant lunacy; or for himself who was so weary. So he crouched there by the bed a long while, silent, until his body was wracked by sobs. At last he turned to say something to Egbert, but the Englishman had slipped away.

Then the boy said, 'I do my best for him. What I can.'

'Yes,' Benoni said.

'He should not drink, but it is all he wants to do, it is the only desire that remains to him, beyond the desire to die. And I do not wish him to die.'

'No,' Benoni said.

'He has been kind to me.'

Benoni lifted his head and, for the first time, looked at the boy. He was very thin, with a sharp, peaky face, dark-complexioned, almost black in the dim light cast by the lamp. His bare legs were no thicker than a young sapling and there was a quaver in his high, piping voice.

'When Astolf spoke your name, he smiled briefly – and he rarely smiles, except sometimes when I please him. His smile is always tender as if in spite of the world. Do you understand me?'

'Yes,' Benoni said, 'I remember that smile, but he spoke of shipwreck.'

'He rescued me,' the boy said, 'he saved me. I shan't say from what because it was horrible. It was shameful. And so I love him. But I can do so little for him. He wants to die,' he said again.

'Yes,' Benoni said, 'I understand that. It is something I have seen before, the last temptation, the hardest of all to resist, and, as I have observed, it presents itself most powerfully to men like our friend Astolf, noble men who have achieved much, and yet never been content with what they have done. So the day comes when they long for death. Yes, I understand that. What is your name, boy?'

'I had no name till Astolf rescued me and brought me here. There was no need for one where I was, or at any rate, none thought me worth calling by any name. But Astolf called me

Oliver, why I know not, and so now Oliver is my name and I am proud of it.'

Benoni looked away from the boy, then at Astolf again, who had fallen asleep, his mouth open, breathing stertorously.

'Let me tell you, Oliver, why I have come here.'

So then he told him of Roland's miserable condition, his madness, and harked back to the story of Bertha and Milan, and how Astolf had come to them in the castle high in the mountains. He spoke of the siege they had endured, the terrible privations, and of the love that he and Astolf had come to feel for each other (though he spoke of this in general terms, vaguely, as befitted the boy's youth, even if he could not doubt ... but no matter). As he spoke, Oliver's eyes grew wide with wonder and excitement.

Then he said, 'And this Roland for whom you care so deeply is Milan's son? But that is remarkable.'

'What do you mean, boy – that is, Oliver? What do you know of Milan?'

'Why,' Oliver said, 'it is Milan who keeps this house, or rather, to be exact, it belongs to his woman. Had you spoken of Milan to Egbert, he would have led you straight to him.'

This news astounded Benoni. At first, indeed, the pleasure he felt in learning that Milan was still alive, and to hand indeed, was mixed with disappointment, even disapproval, that he had evidently not remained faithful to Bertha (whom he had so often sworn to be his one true love) but had taken another woman to wife, or at least to his bed. But then he told himself this was ridiculous: Bertha had submitted to her brother the King, and at his command had rejected Milan and married Ganelon. Milan could therefore scarcely be blamed for having made the best of things.

Oliver looked at Astolf.

'He will sleep now for a long time, poor man,' he said, 'and sleep heavily. Come then and I shall lead you to Milan.'

Benoni followed him out of the hut and across the garden, which was now more animated; a number of citizens in brightly-coloured robes mingled with the women who had bestirred themselves to entertain the guests. One of them called out to Oliver to introduce his friend to her, but he answered only with a wave, and hurried Benoni to a door, which led, he explained quickly, to the private apartments of Milan and his lady Euphrosyne.

'It is the hour of supper,' he said, 'when they remove themselves from the company and retire for a little while before the principal entertainment of the evening gets underway.'

With these words he drew aside a curtain and knocked at the door behind it.

In later years Benoni often said that he would not have recognised the man seated at the table as Milan, if he had not been forewarned, and indeed for a moment he thought that the boy Oliver had either led him to the wrong room, or had been speaking of another man who also went by the name of Milan. Certainly Milan, if it was he, was greatly changed, being fat, bald and dull-eyed, in no way resembling the bold cavalier of his memory. But then, he thought, I myself am not what I was, and I would not have recognised my dear Astolf, either. What a sad thing life is, that we are all subject to decay and corruption, even this side of the grave ...

In this, alas, he spoke truth; and yet it is only a half-truth, for, though in outward appearance we do indeed deteriorate as Benoni thought – which, I may observe in passing, accounts for the fervour and passion with which at an advanced age we may yet pursue youthful beauty, seeking to recapture time lost, time wasted, time stolen from us – nevertheless, whoever has followed the arduous paths of learning will find that the desire for knowledge does not grow stale or wither, but continues to enrich and enliven. This, my Prince, is what it means to be a man, and the mind and spirit may still seek adventure even as the body weakens.

When the boy Oliver spoke Benoni's name, it seemed that Milan shed years. His face lit up. He rose and embraced Benoni, and when he spoke his voice was choked on account of the emotion that he felt.

'Euphrosyne,' he said to the woman, 'this is my oldest friend.'

'Is it now?' she said. 'Like that other oldest friend who lies pig-drunk at the end of the garden, I suppose.'

She was a small woman, sharp-featured, and her manner shrewish.

Benoni inclined his head, took her hand and pressed it in courtly fashion to his lips.

'Soft-soap,' she said. 'I'll have none of it. Whatever your purpose in coming here, you'll not persuade Milan to go knighterranting with you. It's taken me years to knock that nonsense out of him, but he is at last a sensible enough innkeeper making his living in a decent and honourable way.'

'That's true enough,' Milan said. 'I've seen the error of my ways and have become a good husband' – here Euphrosyne sniffed loudly – 'and a fond father. Besides, as you see, Benoni, I'm too fat to ride a horse now; pity the poor beast that had to carry me. But what of my other son, my dear Roland? Is he with you?'

Benoni hesitated, uncertain how to broach the matter that lay so close to his heart.

While he remained silent, Euphrosyne bustled about.

'Since you're here, whoever you are, and I won't deny that Milan has spoken your name more than a few times, you'll take meat and drink with us. Never let it be said that Euphrosyne was blind to the duties of hospitality. We may not be rich, but we can put a good bottle on the table – to be drunk in moderation, do you hear, Milan? None of your carousing and giving of toasts – and there's good cold pork with cumin seeds in it, and a salad of radishes and onions and lettuce, which is wholesome food. You're not a Jew, are you, forbidden to eat pig-meat? And there's a noble fish-pie to follow, made according to a recipe my grandfather, a seafaring man, brought back from the Caspian. That's a dish that never fails to find favour with travellers. You, boy, whatever your name is,' she said to Oliver, 'be of some use, don't stand there like a scarecrow, though, by St Athanasius, you're thin enough and gormless enough to serve as one. Jump to it now, fetch the wine and some cheese – it's a good cow's milk hard cheese from the mountains; none of your nasty, foul-smelling and evil-tasting goat's cheeses are served at my table ...'

So she occupied herself, sharply, and not inhospitably, and for a moment Milan and Benoni were left alone.

'Bertha?' Milan said, whispering.

'Dead, alas ...'

'Just so. Make no mention of her, if you please. She belongs to another life, when I was the Milan you knew. And Roland?'

'Living, but ...'

'But ...?'

And quickly, urgently, Benoni spoke of the boy's condition, sparing nothing and explaining why he had come in search of Astolf.

Milan sighed. 'I do not think he can help you. You have seen him? Yes, of course, otherwise you would not have met Oliver, and you will have seen that poor Astolf can scarcely help even himself now.'

Euphrosyne who, despite her activity, had taken a close interest in the latter part of the conversation, now settled herself at the table and told Benoni he was to eat. 'And you, too, wretch,' she said to Oliver, 'skin and bones as you are, child.' Then she said: 'Why I married you, Milan, I shall never know, for you have less understanding of human nature than the cat that lies there by the fire. You have talked often enough, to my great boredom and annoyance, for I'm a hard-working woman with no time for foolishness, of how you long to save that sot from himself and his indulgence in vice, and I have told you often enough that he has no desire for your help, because he hates himself and wants to die. And now this friend of yours – who seems a better sort than I would have expected of a friend of your unregenerate and godless youth – comes here with a proposition that may – note, I don't say "will", only "may" – rouse him from his stupor and dispel his self-pity. But, instead of seeing this as an opportunity, you say he can scarcely help himself. Well, indeed he can't, which isn't to say that he is incapable of helping other people, as indeed – to his credit, for I'm a fair woman, no one dare gainsay that, for I'll do justice even to a drunkard – he has bestirred himself on behalf of this starveling, this limb of Satan, this Oliver here. I'm a good Christian woman, and so I can tell you that even a man who is so consumed by self-hatred that he is guilty of the deadly sin the theologians call *accidia*, may yet be roused to exert himself by the Grace of God to serve another. I say "by the Grace of God" for it is indeed only His grace that can breathe the life of the Holy Spirit into a miserable sot such as your friend Astolf now is. Therefore, if you care for him as you say you do, you would see that Benoni here has come like an angel on a mission from the Lord. I know what's what, and I can't say fairer than that. So the first thing to be done, starting in the morning, is to sober that creature up, dry him out, as they say, and get him in a fit condition to do whatever is required of him. Now, if you've eaten your pork, Benoni, address yourself to my fish-pie. Though I say it myself, you'll never taste better. And you, Milan, one glass of wine is enough for you.'

The fish-pie was indeed all Euphrosyne had promised. Under the golden pastry crust, slices of sturgeon and swordfish, fillets of red mullet and sole, crayfish and mussels and prawns were combined in a rich sauce of white wine and onions, flavoured with saffron and dill. Benoni ate of it with relish, to the woman's approval. He said to himself: Though she has a sharp tongue, she has also, I suspect, a kind heart, as well as a light hand with pastry. For the first time since his arrival in the city he experienced a renewal of hope. But when he retired to rest he saw in his dreams Roland's eyes devoid of understanding and Astolf's ravaged face.

In the morning they set to work on Astolf. Euphrosyne prepared a chicken broth and Oliver held the cup to Astolf's lips, compelling him to drink. Then, at the woman's command, he dipped pieces of bread in the broth and at intervals placed them in his master's mouth.

'Slowly and gently,' Euphrosyne said, 'little by little, or his stomach will rebel. I haven't kept an inn for twenty years without acquiring the knowledge of how to treat his condition. Next we shall let him have a glass of wine, but only a small one, for it is dangerous to cut him off from the stuff abruptly, even though it is what has been poisoning him.'

She then prepared a brew, which was a distillation of musk and hyssop and poppy-flowers, and gave this to Astolf, so that he might fall into a deep and dreamless sleep. And when he woke from this, towards evening, she had Oliver feed him again with the chicken-broth and the sops of bread and another glass of wine, but this time the wine was watered. Then he was given another dose of the drug she had prepared, and slept deeply again. And they continued to treat him in this manner for three days, at the end of which his eye was clear and his hands no longer shook, though he was still weak as a newborn kitten.

Meanwhile, Benoni waited, curbing his impatience, and conversed often with Milan, telling him how even on her deathbed Bertha had breathed his name. Hearing this, Milan wept and said, 'It is so long ago and my life has taken so sharp a turn since those days that I find it hard to believe I was ever loved by another, or that I was once a bold knight, and before that a brigand and outlaw living in the forest.'

'Well,' said Benoni, 'if it comes to that, I should never have thought that such as I, the poor son of a Breton farmer, would ever find himself where I am today, in the city of Constantine.'

Then he spoke of Roland, of his strength and courage and beauty, and of how he was a son worthy of two such parents as Milan and Bertha, though now sadly deprived of his wits.

On the fourth morning Euphrosyne declared that Astolf was now strong enough to be acquainted with whatever was required of him. 'Only,' she said, 'break it gently and carefully to him, for his mind is still fragile, and if what you have to impart distresses or frightens him, then he will, in the manner of drunkards, straightway seek oblivion again in that nasty bottle.'

So Benoni followed her advice, and did so in such a loving and prudent manner that, though Astolf wept when he learned of Roland's condition, he did not relapse, but instead resolved to perform one action, even if it was to be his last, worthy of the noble knight and paladin that he had been.

Raising himself from his couch, he said, 'You shall see, my dear Benoni, what I can yet do. I am an Englishman, and an Englishman never knows when he is beaten. Truly are we called hearts of oak, resolute but never boastful. Now Astolf's himself again. If this be my last adventure, my final exploit, I could not wish for a more glorious one. Therefore, let us be off and slay the dragon.'

XIX

Poets and Romancers, light-headed folk, tell how Astolf, with Benoni and Oliver in train, travelled to the moon to retrieve Roland-Orlando's wits, this being, they tell us, the repository of all lost things. And, if we are to believe them, Astolf flew there on a hippogriff. I would not, my Prince, insult one of your precocious sagacity by retailing such nonsense. The moon is unattainable to man, as it ever will be, and the hippogriff is a mythical beast, to be classed with unicorns and centaurs.

As you know, I deal only in sober fact, and in this instance sober fact is itself sufficiently remarkable.

You may well ask how this error crept in, and how such fancies were devised.

Setting aside for the moment the explanation that the giddy wits of Romancers are always delighted by the fantastic, the truth is simpler, if also the occasion of confusion.

There is in Africa, in the empire of Abyssinia, which was then governed by the famous Christian prince Prester John, a range of mountains so wild and inhospitable to man, that they were long ago given the name the Mountains of the Moon; and like that orb they are often obscured from view on account of swirling mists. Moreover, for six months of the year they are shrouded in rain. High up on a pass through the mountains is found the monastery of Adulabah, dedicated to the blessed St Thomas, who converted the Ethiopians to Christianity. They remain Christians to this day, though their form of the faith is held to be heretical, a rare matter on which the Pope in Rome and the Patriarch of Constantinople find themselves in agreement.

It was to this monastery that Astolf proposed to journey, for, he said, the monks are deeply learned in the art of curing disorders of the mind, and have potions which offer remedies to all forms of madness. If there is to be a cure for our dear Roland, it is there, and there only, that we shall find it.

Hearing this, Benoni was at first dismayed, for, though no geographer, he knew that Abyssinia was far distant, and he feared that, even should they acquire the remedy for Roland's distemper, they would be long in fetching it, and who knew what might befall him meanwhile? However, since he had put his trust in Astolf, he kept silent and did not voice his doubts, merely urging that the sooner they embarked on their journey the better.

So they set off, and if I were to tell you all that they encountered, the dangers they braved, the enchantments they escaped, and the temptations that were presented to them, my tale would stretch out beyond the hundred and one nights of Arabia. Never was there so arduous a journey or one that demanded more of brave spirits. But at last they came to Addisabi, which is the capital of the country and was then the abode of Prester John.

The first sight of the city amazed them, for the walls, extending for some eight and a half miles, were of solid gold, and shone so brightly in the winter sun that for a moment they were blinded. Some chroniclers affirm that these golden walls were but an illusion, the work of alchemists, in whom the city indeed abounded; but since Abyssinia is the great storehouse of the world's gold, with mines that are worked by a hundred thousand slaves, there is no good reason to doubt that the walls of Addisabi were in very fact what they appeared. In any case, they prepared the travellers for the magnificence of Prester John's court.

The Emperor received them seated on a high throne, made also of gold encrusted with precious stones – diamonds, rubies, emeralds and pearls. It was set on a dais which was itself made of silver (for the silver mines of the country employ twice one hundred thousand slaves). Four lions guarded the throne and each wore a necklace of rare jewels.

It is – or then was – the custom in Abyssinia for courtiers and supplicants to approach the throne crawling on their bellies, and inching forward, a procedure that took several hours when the supplicants were numerous, for the hall is vast, as long, some say, as a Roman mile; and the supplicants (and courtiers) were required to crawl very slowly.

But Astolf refused to submit to this custom, for he said it went against the grain for an Englishman to imitate the motion of a serpent. Therefore he marched boldly towards the throne, with Benoni and Oliver following more timidly in his wake; and, as he did so, he eyed the Emperor in a manner that was civil but not submissive.

Prester John himself at first paid no heed and declined to acknowledge their presence. Instead he stuffed himself with candied fruit and other delicacies. His mouth was so large that it could engulf a whole peach or apricot at one bite. He wore a leopard-skin stole and his belly glistened like polished ebony.

Astolf signalled to Oliver to come forward with a gift for the Emperor. It was a silver casket, made in Alexandria and containing a most holy relic: the index finger of St Thomas, the very one he had thrust into the wound made by the sword of the Roman centurion in Christ's side. Prester John took it gingerly, opened the box, touched the finger, took hold of it and sniffed it.

'It would seem,' he said, 'that the saint was unusually well provided with fingers. We have a dozen at least. Nevertheless, this will inspire devotion among the ignorant.'

His voice was low, guttural, indifferent. He laid the box aside, tugged at the mane of the nearest lion, and popped a sugared almond into its mouth.

'There can be no doubt, Your Highness,' Astolf said, 'as to the authenticity of this relic. I bought it in Jerusalem, from a priest of the Holy Sepulchre, and intended to offer it to the great King of the Franks, Charlemagne, but having occasion to visit your beautiful country, it was evident that there could be no more suitable recipient than Your August Highness. I speak as an Englishman, you understand, and it is known throughout the world that an Englishman's word is his bond.'

The Emperor offered no immediate response to this declaration, which apparently made no impression on him, perhaps because in all probability he had never heard of England and Englishmen. He continued to eat his sweetmeats and to toy with the lion's mane. Then he said: 'Why have you come here to spy on us?'

Astolf protested they had no such intention, but the longer he spoke the more ferocious seemed the glowering look on the Emperor's face.

'Why else would you be here?' he muttered.

Then he said, 'We have a custom, time-honoured. When there is doubt, when there is suspicion, when there is uncertainty, we settle the matter by a contest. I shall arrange one. Meanwhile, take these men away, and see they are close guarded. But feed them, and do not put them to the torture yet.'

Guards surrounded Astolf and his companions, clapped shackles on them, and carried them off to the dungeons that lay deep below the palace. They were thrown into a cell from which they could hear the roaring of the lions and the howls of other beasts.

Oliver crouched against the wall, struggling to master his fear and pressing his knuckles hard against his eyes. Benoni experienced a feeling of acute misery; but his thought was for Roland, not for himself. Astolf marched up and down. He said, 'They will discover they can't treat an Englishman like this. Come, Benoni, we have been in tight spots before and survived.'

'If it were only us,' Benoni said, 'but we are here on Roland's behalf, and now we are trapped and powerless.'

Nevertheless, he could not but respond to Astolf's spirit. It was astonishing to think that only so recently his old friend had been a mewling and puking drunkard.

How long they were held in that noisome cell Benoni could never remember. Only a thin gleam of light from an air-hole marked the difference between night and day. They were fed on a thin but lumpy porridge and given brackish water to drink. Astolf fumed. Benoni devoted his time to caring for Oliver, who came close to despair.

They waited anxiously for the day of the contest, and naturally they speculated often on what form this would take and who should be the champion set against Astolf.

He however, refused to submit to despair.

'No matter who I must fight and what form the contest may

122

take, I am confident of victory. That is, always provided the fight is a fair one as it would be in England.'

Benoni was less sanguine, and feared that the odds would be stacked against Astolf. Moreover, with every day that passed, his impatience grew more intense. He could not sleep for picturing Roland mad, wandering the forests of Germany, beset by who knew what dangers. Therefore, he turned his mind to thoughts of escape.

As it happened, this proved easier than he had feared. Their gaoler had a daughter, a comely girl with long eyelashes, who brought them their porridge in the evening and who fell, almost at first sight, in love with Oliver. If you recall my description of the boy, this may surprise you, for he was still scrawny, sharp-featured and, to my mind – and Benoni's – wholly without physical attraction. Yet, if you will permit me a brief digression, I must here remark that nothing more surely proves that – in certain respects at any rate – this world is well and divinely ordered than the fact that even the ill-favoured may inspire love in another. You might suppose that no one would respond except to beauty. Yet wherever you look you will see that even a fat, pasty-faced girl will secure a husband, while I have known a bald, sallow-complexioned hunchback stinking of rotten apples who captured the heart of a well-born, delicately-featured lady, fastidious in taste and manner. Truly, sexual attraction is a mystery, and testifies in its apparent caprice to the benevolence of our Creator.

At first Oliver was embarrassed by the affection the girl showed him and was uncertain how to respond, for this was something he had never experienced before. He could not believe she was sincere and thought she was making mock of him. Even after Benoni had assured him that the girl, whose name was Abora, appeared truly enamoured of him, he remained shy and still did not know how to respond. But, little by little, his uncertainty fell away, and he was happy to withdraw into the furthest and darkest recess of their cell, and submit to her kisses. He tasted delight for the first time in his life, and it seemed to him that no king or emperor was more fortunate than he.

When Benoni saw that the two were well and truly as one, he

unfolded their story to the girl and spoke of the urgency of their mission. The thought of Roland's madness touched her tender heart, and she needed no further persuasion to declare herself ready to aid their escape.

It so happened that they were approaching the Day of the Dead when ghosts walk, and it is the custom in Abyssinia for all to practise self-denial, to fast for the space of the hours of light, to don black garments of mourning and pile ashes, which are the symbol of death, on their heads. But in the days before that solemn date, all give themselves up to general licence and indulge in deep drinking of strong beer flavoured with honey. (Indeed, the beer prepared for the occasion is three times as strong as that which they normally drink, and goes by the name of Plutonian Special Brew.) Abora, however, fearing that even this powerful liquor might not by itself serve their purpose (for the heads of Abyssinians are notably strong) undertook to obtain from her grandmother, a wise woman skilled in medicine and potions, an elixir of poppy-seeds and mandragora, with which she spiked the beer of her father and the prison guards, all of whom accordingly fell into a deep stupor from which, for several hours, it would have required the last trump to awaken them. And in this way she was able to lead our friends out of the prison and to the temporary sanctuary of the inn kept by her grandmother, which was set into the wall of the city.

Since it is forbidden to inter the dead within the bounds of Addisabi, it is the custom on the Day of the Dead for all to leave the city to visit the tombs which line the Great Trade Road that leads to the mountains of the south where the gold and silver mines are to be found. And because they fear lest the Hand of Death should descend and seize them on this journey, the citizens venture forth masked, each mask being formed in the likeness of a beast, according as to whether they belong to the tribe of the Lion, the Jackal, the Leopard, the Hyena, the Wolf, the Fox, the Wild Dog, or other animals too numerous for me to list.

Our friends were now provided with suitable masks by Abora's grandmother, who had been admitted to their secret, and who assisted them because she loved the girl and hated Prester John; he had once had her whipped as a witch and then seduced one of her daughters before discarding her to work as a common prostitute. Moreover, the old woman advised them of the best road to the Mountains of the Moon, and told Benoni the password that would gain them admittance to the monastery where the secret of lost things was held. So they slipped safely from the city, escaping the great peril that had threatened them; and Abora, for love of Oliver, went with them, disguised as a page-boy because no young woman is permitted to pass beyond the ridge that guards the Mountains of the Moon.

XX

The Mountains of the Moon are approached by a narrow pass that rises steeply from the plain. The track is narrow and twisting. A man or mule or ass must be sure-footed to follow it, for it is in places cut into the mountain-side, while on the other flank the ground falls away sharply, first to jagged rocks on which a man or beast may be impaled, and then beyond the rocks to a lake black as pitch. And the path is more treacherous still, for, as I have said, the mountains are veiled in mist some two hundred days of the year, and so the rock is wet and covered often with a thin layer of ice. On the rare days when there is no mist, the traveller is like to be dismayed or alarmed by the sight of purple-backed, bald-headed vultures hovering in the sky above him. Otherwise there is no sign of life, though the night is made terrible by the distant roaring of hungry lions or the howls of famished wolves.

Truly, Benoni thought, this is an awful place, forsaken by God, which is perhaps why men have founded monasteries here in an attempt to call him back.

But he kept this thought to himself for fear that it would dismay his companions.

So they pressed on bravely, and Astolf, whose spirits seemed to rise at the thought of danger, even broke out sometimes in an English drinking song, till Abora begged him to desist.

'My grandmother,' she said, 'advised me that we should travel in silence, for the sound of the human voice raised above a whisper may, she said, set off an avalanche.'

At last, taking a left-hand fork (which is, in the opinion of gnostic scholars, the alternative route to the Deity) they found the gold gate of the monastery of Adulabah. It was flanked by porphyry towers, but the monastery itself was cut into the rock. The gate was guarded by two huge black sentries, their heads shaven and their bodies naked but for a cloak of leopard-skin slung across their shoulders, which cloak did not, however, conceal their genitals from view; and these were of inordinate size. But the Abyssinians do not think this indecent, as we Christians of Europe do, and indeed Jews and Muslims also. Instead they declare that procreation being a gift from God there is no shame in displaying its instruments.

The guards appeared so fierce that Oliver and Abora were at first afraid, but Astolf stepped forward and addressed them boldly and with such a winning smile that they straightway opened the gate, though it was improbable (Benoni supposed) that they understood the English tongue in which he spoke. So they were admitted to the monastery with none of the difficulty Benoni had expected.

Beyond the gate they found themselves in a cavern lit by torches affixed to the walls. The cavern was otherwise empty, and for a little they stood there puzzled as to what they should do, for it seemed to them that the place was deserted. Have we come so far, Benoni thought, only to find that our journey was in vain?

Astolf, however, was undeterred. Commanding them to follow, he marched the length of the cavern, which, they could now see, led to a narrow passage through the rock. As they advanced they heard the sound of distant chanting, and then they came to a door studded with rubies and emeralds. Astolf banged on it with the hilt of his sword, and in a little it was drawn open, with much creaking as if it had remained closed for a long time. A small, very old, very dark man stood before them. He was dressed in a brown habit and his feet were bare. Without a word he turned away and, holding a candle aloft, indicated that they were to follow him. So they proceeded along another passage till the sound of the chanting died away and they came to a door which opened on a chamber, and by now they were in the very heart of the mountain. Oliver clutched Abora's hand; then, remembering that she was disguised as a boy, thought it prudent to release it. As he did so, a tall figure emerged from the shadows and advanced towards them. He was very lean, there was no colour in his face or eyes, and his skin was white as a swan's back. To their surprise he addressed them in Latin. It was not good Latin, but Astolf and Benoni were able to understand what he said.

In reply they offered first the compliments appropriate to the occasion, and then the small, dark, bald man set jugs of honey-beer and little cakes dripping syrup before them, for all Abyssinians have a sweet tooth and shun savoury dishes. So they drank and ate until the moment seemed propitious to explain the purpose of their journey. Astolf undertook this task, being the oldest as well as the best-born, and when he had spoken, the tall man, whom they assumed to be the abbot or at least some senior dignitary, remained silent for so long that Benoni wondered if he had understood what Astolf said. Therefore, to ease matters along, he said, framing his request as politely as he knew how, but still speaking with the sort of hesitation that he feared might suggest incredulity, 'Is it really possible that you have here a repository of lost wits, and can restore them to their rightful owners?'

At this for the first time the abbot – if he was indeed the abbot – smiled. 'How could that be?' he said. 'I fear you have been listening to the stupid stories that old women tell.'

Benoni's heart sank. They had come so far and it was all in vain, a fool's errand.

'The idea that lost wits fly around the world and come here like birds to their nests ... How weary I am of such nonsense,' the abbot said, smiling again. 'It is stuff fit only for those silly enough to believe in the crudest witchcraft, such as suppose that an old woman can, for instance, transform herself into a hare or leopard. I can understand that young people like these boys here should believe such stuff, for it is natural and even proper that the young should entertain absurd fantasies, but that you, sir' – he indicated Astolf – 'who appear to be a man of the world, and you, sir' – he turned to Benoni – 'whose face and manner suggest you are not utterly devoid of common sense, should credit such stuff – why, that amazes me.'

'Then we have been deceived and have come here to no purpose,' Benoni said.

'Deceived, certainly, but as to your journey being to no

purpose, that is a different matter. I see you are puzzled by my words. Let me therefore explain myself clearly. We practise no magic or witchcraft here, and we do not deal in fantastic notions. We style ourselves scientists, which is to say that we study the nature of things, examine cause and effect, and act accordingly. Our business is the chemistry of the brain.'

'I have heard talk of potions,' Astolf said.

'Now that is to the point,' was the reply. 'You say the young man for whom you seek help is mad. That is a statement of fact, and therefore one which I may approve. You say also, however, that he has lost his wits, and when you speak in this manner, you speak metaphorically. He has not lost his wits, for wits can no more fly out of a man's head and go wandering than the man himself can grow wings and fly to the moon. It is an absurdity. The wits remain where they have always been, in his head. But, alas, they are diseased. They are not, as we say, functioning as they should. That is all. They require medicine to be cured.'

'And you can provide, give us, sell us, such medicine that will cure my poor Roland?' Benoni said.

'Why, certainly,' the abbot said.

Benoni was all but overcome with joy; and his joy was all the greater because throughout their long and dangerous journey he had known moments of doubt, times even when he feared that when the woman Artemis advised him to seek Roland's scattered wits in the country of lost things, she herself had spoken the language of madness, and that it was but a delusion. He had even doubted Astolf, for which he now felt ashamed.

'There is, of course,' the abbot said, 'a price to be paid.'

'Naturally,' Benoni said, 'we had not supposed otherwise.' It was folly to suppose that brains came cheaply. 'We have gold enough,' he added. 'At least, I hope so.'

'You mistake me, sir. We do not deal in money or precious stones here. We have no need of such things, seeing that Abyssinia is well provided with them already.' And he extended his hand to draw their attention to the golden walls of the chamber. 'The price is of a different sort.'

He smiled again, and this time it seemed to Benoni that the smile was not friendly, but malicious.

'What can restore a diseased mind? What can re-order dis-ordered wits? The art of medicine we practise – an art which is of our own discovery and devising – goes by the name of homoeopathy: like unto like. To cure the mind we employ essence of mind.'

'What do you mean, sir? I fear I don't understand.'

'It is quite simple. We take the brain from a living man, reduce it to its essence so that it becomes a potion to be fed to him whose mind is disordered. You will understand that it is an operation we perform but seldom, for it is rare to find one whose love for another is such that he will consent to suffer the removal of his own brain in order to cure another's madness ...'

'The removal of his own brain ...' Benoni said.

'The removal of his own brain, which leads inevitably to his death.'

He smiled again.

'Which of you is strong enough in love to make the sacrifice? No doubt you will wish to discuss the matter privately. But be quick. The night of the full moon, which this is, is that most propitious to the operation.'

When they were alone, Abora said, 'It's too horrible. If I had only known.'

Benoni said, 'It must be me. I brought you here. I promised Bertha that I would care for Roland.'

Astolf said, 'Speaking as an Englishman, and therefore not someone who minces words, stuff and nonsense, poppycock, my dear Benoni. You're confused. Your mind's in a whirl, not thinking straight. How can you keep your word to Bertha if you allow that loony doctor to trepan you and scoop your brains out? Simply can't be done. Your duty is to Roland alive and sane. The lad will get into other scrapes and need your help. So we'll have no more of this nonsense. As for you, young Oliver, I'm grateful for all you've done for me. I'd have died in the Tavern of the Rosy Garden if you hadn't been there to slip me a spot of the right stuff on the sly when old Euphrosyne wasn't looking. So nobody's going to lop the top of your head off, lad. No need to look so scared. In any case, I don't mean to be rude, you understand, but, speaking as an Englishman, I have to say

130

that nobody would thank you for your brain, you addle-pate. And, as for you, young Abora, well, you're a girl, even though we have to keep quiet about it here, and there's no point putting a girl's brain into young Roland and turning him into a milksop, no offence meant. I daresay your brain's a good enough one for a girl, but it won't do for him, and that's flat. So cheer up. I'm the one that's for it. Don't snivel, Benoni, and don't look so surprised. You don't suppose I believed all that stuff about catching lost wits – in a net as if they were butterflies – do you? Not at all. I knew what was what from the start, and I'm ready for it. Consider, my dear friends: there I was, a drunken sot, with only the next bottle between me and the horrors, my liver feeling as if old what's-his-name – Prometheus, wasn't it? – had lent me his vulture for the day, and you come along offering me the chance of – I won't say redemption, that's not an idea that appeals to an Englishman – but of performing one last noble action worthy of my ancestors and of the man I was when you knew me in my prime, Benoni. So there it is. I'm happy. This is a far, far better thing I do than any I have done, as the man said. I've had a good life, and now the fire sinks and I am ready to depart. I'd like a last good drink before I go, not this wretched beer, which tastes like horse-piss mixed with some beastly sweetener, but a pint of good English bitter. I'd give my eye-teeth for that. Or that black stuff they drink in Ireland, or a stoup of good French brandy.'

He looked up from his musing and saw Benoni was weeping.

'Cheer up, old sport,' he said. 'My day's done, my life's race run. There's nothing left for me, you see. I'd rather go out in a sort of glory, dying that Roland may live again, than dwindle away or pop off shrieking in delirium, which I would if I was back on the bottle. Now I can say, "Astolf's himself again." But truth is, I've had enough of this battered caravanserai we call life. So there it is. Call the abbot fellow, and let's get it done. I owe God a life, I've often thought. As an Englishman, I'm no great talker and find it hard to put my feelings into words. Don't cry for me, I'll die happy. I too, Benoni, owe something to Bertha and Milan. Bless you all.'

XXI

One day Roland escaped the vigilance of Rafael and fled to roam the forests of Germany, insensible to cold or heat. Some days he was sunk in such deep depression that it was all he could do to raise a cup of water to his lips. At other times he was cast into a frenzy and ran for hours, heedless of direction. Sometimes he cried out Angelica's name to the uncaring moon and stars; sometimes he could recall neither the image of her face nor anything about her. At night he threw himself to the ground under the trees or on a barren rock, but sleep was denied even his exhausted body.

One evening, as the sun was setting, he came to a place where the rocks bent in such a way as to form a grotto. Twisted stems of ivy and the wild vine served as a sort of curtain masking the entrance, and, had he been in possession of his wits, he would have judged it the most charming and romantic of spots. But he pushed through the trailing branches brutishly and sank to the rock-floor, which was wet on account of a little stream that ran through the grotto. To his amazement he saw the name 'Angelica' carved into the rock and below it verses celebrating her beauty. He cried out in horror, knowing this to be a delusion (even in his disordered state). He howled with pain and grief, and attacked the rock with his sword, so effectively, it seemed to him, that he obliterated the verses and the beloved name.

'What have I done?' he cried. 'Surely I have slain Angelica whom I loved before all other woman.'

Then he fled the grotto and resumed his wanderings till he came to a cottage, and saw smoke rising from the roof. He heard the barking of dogs and the lowing of cattle, and was for a moment free of his madness, knowing only a longing for rest. He approached the house, which was certainly mean, the abode of charcoal-burners who shared it with their swine and a single milking cow. When they saw him stagger towards them, they assumed he was a knight wounded in some distant battle, and came forth to succour him. They gave him bean-soup and bread, then cheese and milk, and he took it all greedily, for it was several days since he had eaten. They looked on this strange being with wonder, but kindly and without fear. They asked him his name and he replied, 'Nobody.'

Then one of them, a young girl no more than twelve years old, pulled at her father's sleeve and whispered, 'This wretched man who thinks he is nobody was once somebody, and I think of noble birth, for, ragged and filthy though he is, there is something in his manner which makes me think he is that prince or noble knight for whom the Lady Artemis has been searching the forests. Therefore, Father, if you will watch over him, I shall seek out the Lady Artemis and bring her here.' And so, fearlessly, regardless of danger from wild beasts and brigands, she set off in the gathering dusk.

Meanwhile, Roland, having eaten and drunk, seemed calmer and did not demur when the girl's father suggested he should lie down and sleep. He wrapped himself in the furs they offered, and stretched out, like a dog, before the fire.

But he had scarcely closed his eyes in search of the sleep he so badly needed when the image of Angelica swam into his troubled mind, and now he saw her entwined with her Saracen lover and crying out endearments to him. He leapt up with a cry: 'She has forgotten Roland utterly, and why not, for I am not the man I was nor the man they take me for. Roland-Orlando is no more and I am but the wandering ghost of that unhappy prince, who is now suffering the torments of Hell.'

'Peace, my lord,' said his host, the charcoal-burner, 'you are no ghost, I assure you, for I warrant there is never a ghost who eats bean-soup and the best part of a small kebbuck of cheese.'

But Roland in his despair would not be comforted, and his fury and self-hatred would not abate. He tore at his face with his long nails till the blood ran and the nails were broken, then he threw back his head and howled like a lost dog to the moon. He cursed and moaned, fell into convulsions and made to throw himself into the flames, for he cried again, 'Roland is in Hell —

that Hell which is of our own making – and I am but his wretched ghost condemned to an eternity of wandering.' So, fearing that he was about to do himself an injury, even to death, the charcoal-burner seized a club and struck him sharply on the back of the head (where the skull is thinnest) so that he fell down in a swoon. Whereupon they took his arms and his legs, tied them with thick cord and attached it to their table, which was made of pinewood and very heavy. And they thrust a gag into his mouth so that in his delirium he could not bite through his tongue.

It was past dawn when Artemis and the little girl, whose name was Persephone, came to the cabin. They found Roland still asleep, but now quivering, for it was as if he suffered an ague. Artemis removed the gag from his mouth, and forced him to swallow a medicine that she had brought. Then they bound him to a litter and carried him through the forest back to her abode. He remained all this time in a deep slumber, for the potion she had prepared was a powerful sleeping-draught. The girl Persephone went with them. Despite his madness, she had fallen in love with Roland at first sight on account of his beauty and because, as she said later, she perceived the nobility of his soul.

'How long before he wakes?' she said.

'He will sleep till the new moon lies in the old moon's arms.'

So Persephone watched over him, and Artemis was sad on the girl's account, knowing that Roland loved another and would always love her. But she herself felt tenderly towards the young girl and resolved to keep her by her side.

XXII

If I have said little regarding Charlemagne for some time it is because he was engaged in the routine administration of his Empire. He continued to fight wars against the rebellious Saxons, and, within his dominions, to be assiduous in the administration of justice, travelling for several months of every year to hold assizes. It was on one such eyre (which is the name given to a judicial circuit) that he was presented by a grateful suitor with that soft and creamy cheese called Brie, which he found so much to his taste that he commanded that a round of it be delivered to him every week throughout the cheese-making season; and this is a custom still honoured, which is why every Friday a cart leaves the town of Meaux bearing rounds of cheese to the King, whether he be in Paris or elsewhere. Then he continued to found schools and monasteries, for no monarch was ever more eager to foster learning and True Religion. He hunted several days a week (except in the months from May to August, which he decreed should be a closed season for game), swam whenever the opportunity presented itself, in lakes, rivers and even fish-ponds; took wives and concubines to bed (singly, that is), and fathered several children; but never neglected his Christian duties, hearing Mass every day, confessing his sins (occasionally) and fasting during Lent (a season when no one who knew him presented a petition or sought a favour, since fasting disturbed his temper). He took part in tournaments, but as he aged and grew stiff in limb, preferred to act as umpire rather than sally into the lists himself. In short, he did all that a king should do.

And yet often he found himself weary and sick at heart, oppressed by the loneliness of his great position. Bishop Turpin was now his only confidant. Elgebast, who was accustomed to speak his mind, was now departed from court, gone, some said, on a pilgrimage to the Holy Land, or, as others had it, seeking to win a kingdom for himself in the pagan lands beyond the Elbe.

Charles's nights were disturbed by bad dreams; in one, recurring often, his sister Bertha would appear, upbraiding him for the failure of his love, reproaching him for the neglect of her son Roland. Then his own eldest son, Charlot, was causing anxiety. He provoked a rebellion in Aquitaine which he had been sent to govern, its cause the murder of a daughter of the Count of Bordeaux, reputedly because she had resisted Charlot's attempt at rape. The charge might be false; the King couldn't tell. But the rebels had sought support from the Emir of Saragossa, and made an alliance with the infidel.

In his perturbation Charles sent to Ganelon, commanding him to bring his nephew Roland to Engelheim. For months no reply was received. Perhaps the message had gone astray. Charles sent again. This time he was informed that Roland had fled Sigmaringen, and rumour said, had fallen into madness, losing his wits and wandering the forest like a wild beast, a danger to himself and a violent enemy to all who encountered him. Moreover, Ganelon declared that he could not obey the summons to Engelheim himself, on account of the unsettled state of his province and the danger posed by the alliance between the Emir of Smyrna and Count Manfred, who had impiously given his daughter Angelica in marriage to the infidel. 'Truly,' Ganelon wrote, 'it is a wicked and sinful world.'

The King called Bishop Turpin, who read the letter Ganelon had dictated. 'I don't like this,' he said, 'but then, as you know, I have long thought the trust you place in Ganelon does more credit to your generous spirit than to your judgement of character. The man's a twister.'

'We played together as children,' Charles said. 'But I fear you may be right.'

He looked out over the battlements of the castle. A wind was rising in the east. A raven hopped towards him in search of food. He gave it the last mouthful of the fruit-cake he had been eating.

'I have sometimes wondered if Ganelon murdered my sister,' he said. 'It is time we paid him a visit.'

'He won't like that.'

'So much the better. Again I wonder: is my nephew really mad, or has he been poisoned? Is there a cure for madness, Turpin?'

'Our Lord cast out devils,' the Bishop said, stout in his faith.

'I remember the story.'

He held out his arm. The raven hopped on to it, and nuzzled the royal ear.

Nevertheless, it was some time before Charles set out, and, when he did so, he travelled slowly. This was partly because heavy rains had turned the roads to mud, and violent storms had broken down bridges; and partly because the King was suffering from piles. He was unable to sit on a horse, and instead lay in a litter in a cart pulled by oxen, as if he had been a Meroving himself. This thought depressed him, and rendered him short-tempered.

Eventually, however, he came to the great castle of Sigmaringen, and the sight of this noble edifice enflamed his temper still more. He called Bishop Turpin to him and asked if he did not think it evident that Ganelon had been cheating him. 'How could he have so enlarged and fortified this castle from his own resources? The scoundrel has been keeping back a portion of the tax revenues he should have remitted to me, and employed them for his own purposes. Does he think himself a king, and not my vassal?' Turpin sighed and said it was indeed a wicked world in which few were worthy of the confidence that the King was so ready to repose in them.

Ganelon himself had been alarmed when he learned that Charles was approaching. He had straightway sent to Count Manfred proposing a truce, and warning that Charles was bent on destroying both of them: 'You,' he said, 'on account of your alliance with the Emir, me because he holds me responsible for his nephew's disappearance. Truly,' he said, 'there is no justice in the world. But if we are to survive the danger which threatens us both, then we must lay aside our enmity and act in concord.'

Thus may fear and a guilty conscience sharpen a man's wits.

Manfred trembled to hear the news. The alliance with the Emir had seemed to him a bold stroke of politics while the King was hundreds of leagues distant. But now he saw that he had over-reached himself. The truth was that behind his formidable appearance lay a timid heart; beneath his bluster he was a coward. Moreover, he had another reason for fear. He saw that if he rejected the alliance that Ganelon had offered him, Ganelon, whom he knew to be treacherous as a serpent, would find some means of appeasing Charles, and would join himself to the King once again to make war on a common enemy: that is, Manfred himself and his ally and son-in-law, the Emir. So he sent back in friendly fashion, and a meeting was arranged.

Ganelon said: 'There is only one way in which we can present ourselves as loyal subjects. You must abandon the Emir, hold him prisoner and dissolve the pretended marriage with your daughter.'

'I do not know in what sense you call the marriage pretended,' Manfred replied, 'seeing that it was solemnised by a Christian bishop and a Muslim imam. Would it not be better to kill the Emir? That would dissolve the marriage fast enough.'

'Indeed yes,' Ganelon said, scratching his ear, which was his habit when required to think of matters of great moment. 'Indeed yes, and nobody is happier to see a dead Muslim nobleman than the King. But to kill the Emir is to remove a card from the pack, and it is one, in my opinion, that we may still have need of. As for dissolving the marriage, that surely is easy. No marriage ceremony in which a Muslim imam has participated can be regarded as other than uncanonical. Believe me, my friend, I do not speak ignorantly. I have had my chaplain, Father Peter, examine the matter. He is, though himself a Saxon, well-versed in canon law, having spent some years in Rome where he was a particular favourite of the third Pope before the present one. Believe me, Father Peter has no doubt concerning the question, and nobody is more adept than he at effecting the dissolution of marriages. I have already had him dissolve that which my son Rudolph contracted with a Lithuanian princess after her father failed to deliver the promised dowry. See how Fortune favours us, my friend. Rudolph is now free to marry your daughter, and so to cement an alliance between our noble houses. Joined together we shall be so strong that even the King will think twice about attacking us, and will be ready to come to an accommodation. It will be a powerful point in our favour that we hold so powerful a Muslim prince as your Emir captive. But we shall not surrender him to Charles, but retain him as a bargaining counter. Believe me, my friend, this is our only hope, our only means to save our skins from the royal wrath.'

Ganelon's rhetoric persuaded Manfred. Father Peter did as he was bid. The Emir found himself cast into a dungeon, and Rudolph was quickly married to Angelica, who wept throughout the ceremony, not that she regretted the Emir, but because she still pined for Roland, and indeed ached for love of him.

Even so, Ganelon was disturbed to find Charlemagne look darkly upon him. He remembered that look from the days when they were boys together. Ganelon had then been the leader, the one who devised games and organised play. He was the quicker witted, and often mocked Charles, teasing him with bright remarks, which the prince was slow in understanding. Ganelon also invented scurrilous or scandalous stories about the great men at court. Charles would repeat them and have his ears boxed by his horrible father, who accused him of being a liar. Sometimes he went further and called him an emissary of the devil, and on these occasions he would have him whipped till the boy's buttocks bled. But when Ganelon was suspected of being the source of these stories, his look of injured innocence disarmed the King. Yet things were not as they seemed. It wasn't long before Ganelon learned that there was a limit to what Charles would tolerate. When he passed that limit, the boy-prince glowered. His face resembled darkening thunder-clouds. One day the storm broke. He turned on his friend-tormentor and beat him soundly. That was how Ganelon lost the sight in his left eye. Afterwards Charles felt guilty. The indulgence he granted Ganelon in later life had its origin in that afternoon when his temper snapped.

Now Ganelon, doing his best to ignore the dark look, which might (he told himself) be no more than the product of the piles from which all knew Charles to be suffering, greeted the King with profound respect that did not, however, exclude the suggestion of easy comradeship. Nevertheless, he was apprehensive.

At any moment Charles would ask about Roland, and he did not know what to reply.

Ganelon's wife Irma was also ill at ease. She had been jealous of Roland, and it was on account of her hostility that he had fled. But, saying to herself 'what's done cannot be undone but may be remedied', she set out to charm the King. She sympathised with him on account of his ailment. Her father, she said, had been similarly afflicted. Accordingly she had sought out a wise woman skilled in the art of healing, who had provided her with an ointment most salutary for such conditions. She produced a tub containing a cream of a vile yellow colour, and told the King he must rub himself with it, and then apply to the painful spot a warm napkin, keeping it in place till the pain abated, as she assured him it would. The King looked at it doubtfully, fearing perhaps that the ointment might be poisoned. But Irma spoke in so soft and seductive a voice, urging him to put it to the test, that he felt ashamed of his suspicions. She smiled on him, and her dark eyes seemed to him to be pools of sympathy. He stretched out his hand, touched her soft cheek, and took the ointment. The treatment was effective. For the first time in days the King was at ease, and experienced comfort. So great was his relief that he straightway fell in love with Irma, spoke to her tenderly, and the following night took her to his bed. This, he thought, is sweet revenge on Ganelon. Irma sighed in his arms and covered his face with kisses. 'You are so masterful, my lord,' she sighed. 'All that I have ever dreamed a king must be.'

Charles lay back and she toyed with him. The King was himself again.

XXIII

On receipt of the potion distilled from Astolf's brain, Benoni made haste to return to Germany to seek out Roland, for, as he said to Oliver, 'It were to make mockery of Astolf's sacrifice if we were to tarry here.' At the thought of that sacrifice Oliver dissolved once again in tears, for he had truly loved the brave Saxon knight. 'Besides,' Benoni said, 'who knows how long this medicine will remain effective?' He did not add, 'Moreover, Astolf was an old man, older than I had realised, and it may be his wits were past their best,' but he kept this thought to himself, lest it distress Oliver further. So, taking their leave, they descended the mountain, and, with Abora still one of their company and still disguised as a boy, hastened to the shore and took a ship. Of their voyage there is nothing to relate, for they escaped shipwreck and also the pirates who infested the sea. Thus they came to land – though at which port is now forgotten – and, buying horses with the gold they had brought from Abyssinia, resumed their journey.

At last they came to the great forest, and sought out the hut where Artemis made her abode. Great was Benoni's delight to see her, and still greater when she greeted him warmly and told him that Roland was sleeping within.

'But,' she said, 'his violent madness has exhausted him and I fear he grows weaker by the day. Since the last moon he has taken no sustenance but a little chicken broth and one cup of the elderberry wine I make. I trust you have not come too late.'

Benoni entered the hut, and saw Roland-Orlando stretched out on a truckle bed. His cheeks were hollow, his eyes without expression, and his countenance wore the white shade of death. He gave no sign of recognition, and indeed the only evidence of life he offered was the movement of his long fingers clutching, releasing, and then clutching again the furs that covered him. Benoni spoke his name, but there was no response.

Artemis now joined Benoni. 'Sometimes,' she said, 'he sighs deeply, as if expelling all the misery of the world, and sometimes, towards dawn, he is shaken by trembling, and then he howls like a wolf. I have lavished all my arts upon him, yet he does not revive.'

Benoni said, 'I have travelled too far and endured too much to give way to despair.'

Then he took the potion from his knapsack, and forced some of it into the young man's mouth. For a moment it seemed as if it would be rejected, and indeed a little trickled from his lips. But then, as if with a great effort, he swallowed the liquid, and straightway his hands relaxed. He closed his eyes and slept.

In the morning Benoni repeated the dose, and every day for seven days till the potion had all been drunk. Yet still Roland did not appear to respond, but looked weaker with every day that passed. For two days and nights Benoni did not leave his bedside, and all this time Roland's eyes remained closed and he made no movement of any kind, not even a twitch of his mouth.

He is dying, Benoni thought, and we have been cheated by these rascally Abyssinians.

But at that very moment, as if the spirit of Astolf were rebuking Benoni for daring to question, even in his own mind, the value of his sacrifice, Roland's eyelids flickered open, his lips moved and he uttered the single word: 'Angelica.'

Though he relapsed immediately into sleep and did not wake till the sun had made a full circuit of the sky, from that moment Benoni knew his recovery had begun.

The next day he was strong enough to sit up, and drink soup and wine. A little later he was on his feet, and on the third day, as if he had risen from the dead, he was able to converse. He had no memory of the months he had passed in madness, but spoke, wonderingly, of a journey he had made to the moon.

'I suppose I was dreaming,' he said, and Benoni did not contradict him.

In a little he was able to resume manly exercises, to sit a horse and handle weapons. He did not speak the name 'Angelica' again till it seemed that his strength had fully recovered. Then he said, only, 'It grieves me that I did not defy her father.'

'Had you done so, we had both been dead men.'

'Nevertheless . . .'

There was a resolution in his eye and cast of countenance that Benoni had not known before. Perhaps, he thought, it is not only Astolf's brain that now inhabits him, but his spirit also. But then it may be only that he has been strengthened by his great ordeal, even if he remembers nothing of it.

Benoni had been so occupied with the care of Roland that he had quite forgotten the boy Rafael whom he had left to watch over him, and only now asked Artemis what had become of him.

'That scamp,' she said. 'When Roland slipped away into the forest, Rafael went in search of him, but he soon returned saying it was hopeless, and then, the next day he was gone. My first thought was that he feared your anger because he had failed in the duty you assigned him. But then I discovered that that minx Persephone had gone with him; and what has become of them I neither know nor care.'

Meanwhile, Oliver, at first resentful of Roland on account of the sacrifice Astolf had made, now transferred the devotion he had felt for the English knight to him. This distressed Abora, but fortunately Artemis had fallen in love with her and this love was not diminished when Abora discarded her boy's clothes and revealed herself to be a young woman.

'Matters of gender do not concern me,' Artemis said. 'I love a person, not that person's sex.'

So when Roland, Benoni and Oliver were ready to depart, Abora remained with Artemis. Nothing is known of their subsequent history. One can therefore permit oneself to suppose that they dwelled in happiness.

Why not? There is little enough of that in this sad world, as I fear you may discover, my Prince, as your days lengthen.

XXIV

In honour of the King, and in order also to distract him,
Ganelon announced that a general tournament would be held,
in which all knights who were eager to win renown might
take part. It was only in recent years that tournaments had
become fashionable, originally in Provence and Lombardy, and
this was indeed the first that would be staged in Germany.
The rules governing them were not as well understood as
they are now, and consequently some of these early tournaments
were more akin to real war than to the mimic battles of the
present day. It was then by no means unusual for a tournament
to conclude with several brave knights having been killed or
at least maimed for life.

Ganelon decreed that the tournament should take this form:
he would appoint five knights as defenders, and these would
accept the challenge of any competitor, who would announce his
intention and select his immediate adversary by striking his shield
with the tip of his lance. Should he defeat – that is to say,
unhorse – the first defender, he would then be entitled to renew
his challenge, and any knight who succeeded in unhorsing all
five defenders – which Ganelon thought unlikely – would be
hailed as the Champion.

The king was invited to nominate two defenders, and selected
Elgebast – who had, on receiving word of the tournament,
abandoned his eastern ambitions and ridden post-haste to Sigmaringen – and his own son Charlot. But Charlot excused himself
because, he said, he had injured his shoulder and could neither
ride a horse nor set his lance in rest. There were some who
muttered that Charlot was a coward and his injury feigned, and
many more who suspected this but thought it wise to keep silent,
for Charlot was known to be both malicious and cruel, and was
therefore feared. He now claimed the right to name his substitute,

and selected Ogier the Dane, not because he loved him, but because he hoped to see him humiliated.

Ganelon then invited Count Manfred to nominate his champion, and Manfred, his vanity overcoming a constitutional timidity, declared he would enter the lists himself. Ganelon then chose as the last two defenders a German knight called Hermann, of imposing figure, for in stature he exceeded two yards, brute courage and impenetrable stupidity, and his own son, or, as some have it, stepson, Rudolph, who dared not decline the honour.

The defenders being named, all were satisfied except Bishop Turpin, who delighted in tournaments and had hoped to be named himself; and he was scarcely appeased when the King appointed him chief marshal, being assisted in that role by Charles's bastard brother Gervase of Troyes.

On the appointed day the lists presented a most magnificent spectacle. The tournament was held in a broad meadow by the Danube, which, however, at Sigmaringen is an insignificant stream, grey-green in colour, and offering little promise of its future majesty. Nevertheless, on a fine May morning, it glittered in the sunshine, while its banks were made beautiful by primroses, jonquils and purple flowers whose name escapes me.

The King sat on a dais in the chief pavilion which faced south. Ganelon was seated at his right hand, Irma at his left, while the young squire Alory, who later came to so unhappy an end, settled on a stool by his feet. From time to time Charles leaned forward to fondle Alory, stroking the boy's hair or cheek, and it may be that he did so to disguise the lust he felt for Irma and so to divert suspicion from their liaison.

The heralds blew trumpets, and the chief among them pronounced the rules that would govern the contest, doing so in three languages that all might understand. Then they withdrew. and none remained in the arena save the two marshals, themselves armed cap-à-pie, as the laws of the tournament required in those days, for, on account of the unfamiliarity of the exercise, it was always possible that the marshals would themselves have to intervene to discipline and ride down any knight who contravened the rules. It is to be feared that Bishop Turpin hoped he would find occasion to do so, but the King had named Gervase as his colleague chiefly in order to restrain the Bishop, for Gervase was celebrated as a master of the tournament.

A hush fell over the assembled multitude as the five defenders took up their position at the eastern extremity of the field. Then five knights advanced towards them, and a wild music of eastern origin sounded, a reminder (if such were needed) that the practice of the tournament had originated in the Holy Land where indeed Gervase had himself first won renown. Bells were rung, cymbals clashed and instruments fashioned from rams' horns were sounded. Each of the five knights touched one of the defenders' shields, and then all withdrew and the music ceased.

Bishop Turpin stood high in his stirrups and called out in a loud voice that carried to the surrounding hills: 'Let battle commence.' Visors were lowered, lances levelled and, at full gallop, the antagonists set at each other. The clash was tremendous. Two challengers were straightway unhorsed by Elgebast and Ogier. Count Manfred drove his opponent hard backwards so vigorously that the challenger's horse lost its footing and slipped to the ground. The knight who had challenged Hermann the Swabian champion appeared to lose his nerve, for instead of driving his lance-point against Hermann's shield or helmet, he pulled his horse to the side, so that it swerved away and the lance-shaft caught Hermann across the chest and broke. 'A miserable performance,' Charles was heard to say, and he leaned forward and whispered something to Alory, who at once rose and left the pavilion, perhaps to discover the name of the knight who had so disgraced himself. Only the last conflict between one of Count Manfred's men and Rudolph was held to be even; both splintering their lances in fair fight without advantage to either.

There followed a pause while the defenders withdrew to their pavilion, raised their visors, took each a cup of wine, and composed themselves to await the next challenge.

So it continued till the sun rose to its zenith, and three times the defenders met their challengers and were three times victorious. Among them only Rudolph came near to being unseated, in the second of these encounters; but he too was victorious in the third, driving his adversary from the lists. It was noticeable, however, that, even among his father's vassals, few raised a cheer to greet his triumph; and there have ever since been those to say that this third challenger had been selected by Ganelon in order to ensure his son recorded one signal victory. There were even then a few who murmured that the contest had been 'fixed', this being, my Prince, the term employed by aficionados of the tournament when they believe that the outcome of a fight has been arranged in advance, which is accounted shameful.

Now it appeared that the success of the defenders had dulled the ardour of their challengers, and the pause between bouts was more prolonged than before. Certainly it seemed as if no one was eager to renew the contest. Some in the crowd began to display their disappointment at what they thought to be the premature curtailment of the action. Others took advantage of the interval to stroll in the direction of the booths where food and drink were sold, or to amuse themselves by watching the jugglers, clowns, dancers and puppeteers, who congregate at tournaments to display their abilities, amuse the vulgar and earn money. Even in the royal box, Charles and his immediate companions turned their attention to their wine and to the feast of cold meats, pasties, jellies and syllabubs with which the attendants were ready to provide them. Ganelon began to look nervous when Charles again dispatched Alory either to discover whether new challengers were ready to present themselves or perhaps to encourage any who were loath to do so by informing them of the King's desire to see further action. After a little, however, he returned to whisper something in the royal ear, at which Charles smiled. Raising a chicken leg to his mouth, he tore off flesh, chewed it and said to Irma, 'It seems there remains yet one knight bold enough to challenge the defenders.'

No sooner had he spoken than a single trumpet sounded, breathing, as it seemed, a note of defiance from the western end of the lists. Then the barrier was raised and a knight rode into the arena. As far as could be judged of a man coated in armour, he seemed to be young and slenderly built. His suit of armour was black, and his shield bore the device of a sapling pulled up by the roots, with a single word below it: Disinherited. He was mounted on a dark bay, almost black horse, with one white sock, and as he passed along the lists he sat it so lightly and with such grace that he drew cheers from the crowd, and those in the royal pavilion questioned who he might be. Some of the spectators, whose admiration for the gallant appearance of the young man was mixed with apprehension – for he seemed too slight to withstand the more formidable of the defenders – called out, 'Touch Duke Rudolph's shield,' either because they thought Rudolph the feeblest of the defenders or, in some cases, because they wished to see him overthrown. Hearing the cries, Rudolph flushed with shame and anger, but of course no one could see this since he had pulled his visor down in anticipation of combat.

The Disinherited, however, paid no heed to the advice of the crowd, and instead rode straight to Count Manfred, and, with the sharp end of his lance, struck his shield.

Manfred said, 'Young man, whoever you are – for I take it that you are young, else you would not be so rashly bold – I trust you have confessed your sins and heard Mass this morning, that you venture your life by challenging me.'

But the young man made no reply, merely indicating by an inclination of the head that he had understood the Count's speech. He reined his horse backwards so that, allowing him to keep his gaze fixed on the adversary he had challenged, it withdrew to the far end of the lists to await the marshals' command.

Manfred, meanwhile, read impertinence in the young knight's withdrawal in this unusual fashion, took his shield, which bore the device of an eagle hovering over its prey, called for a new lance from his squire, and likewise made ready for action.

The signal was given and the two charged at each other, meeting with a mighty clash loud as a thunder-clap, and, then, as each rode on, it was observed that both had broken their lances, so that the tips of each were impaled in their respective shields. Furnished with new lances, they charged again, and this time Manfred struck the Disinherited so firmly in the centre of his shield that the lance shattered again and, for an instant, the young knight reeled in the saddle. But, even as he did so, he recovered and, altering the angle of his own thrust, hit Manfred full on the helmet so that he lifted him out of the saddle, and the Count fell to the green sward. But no sooner was he down than he struggled to his feet, and called out to the Disinherited to dismount and meet him on level terms. In no wise reluctant, the young knight did as he was bid, and they stood opposed to each other, swords drawn, waiting to see who should make the first move. But at that moment Bishop Turpin and Gervase of Troyes commanded them to desist: fighting on foot with swords transgressed the rules of the tournament. Whereupon they declared the Disinherited victorious.

Next he challenged the mighty Hermann, and again the crowd hushed, now in anxiety, for the two contestants appeared so ill-matched. Hermann charged forward roaring his battle-cry, as terrible as a maddened bull, but the Disinherited was too quick for him. Even as the Swabian made to level his lance, he met the point of the young knight's spear and was lifted bodily from his horse and deposited on the ground. His helmet flew from his head as he soared through the air, and he sat on his backside looking for all the world like a man suddenly awakened from sleep and ignorant of his whereabouts. I have seen drunkards rise with the same bemused expression from the floor of the hall where they had passed the night.

Resounding cheers greeted this second triumph, and the Disinherited now approached Ogier the Dane, before whom, however, he first inclined his head as if in respect prior to touching his shield. The Dane acknowledged this courtesy by declaring he would be honoured to engage one who had fought with such boldness and skill, and made ready to set to.

This third contest was the most equal to date. Both knights broke their lances at the first clash, but Ogier was thrown back in the saddle and would have fallen to the ground if the Disinherited had not extended his arm to prevent him from doing so. Shouts of acclamation greeted this noble gesture, and Ogier pronounced himself defeated.

There now remained only Elgebast and Rudolph. The former sat his horse serenely, but Rudolph had, since the first bout, been showing increasing signs of agitation. He had sent his squire to try to discover the Disinherited's true name, and when the youth returned to say that no one could provide an answer, Rudolph then turned to Elgebast and said it was intolerable that they should be expected to engage with an adversary who refused to identify himself.

'Who knows who or what he may be? An outlaw? A murderer? A pagan? A Saracen? Why, he may not even be born.'

By which last remark he meant that the Disinherited, despite the implication of the style of address he had adopted, might not be of gentle or noble birth.

But Elgebast merely smiled, and said, 'None of that is any concern of mine. It's all one indeed to me whom I fight, so long as he be courageous and skilful, offering no easy triumph such as any true knight despises, but a challenge worth the name.'

'Spoken like a true chevalier,' said Ogier the Dane, who had ridden up to join them. He removed his helmet, mopped his face with a napkin and called for a cup of wine. 'Whoever this lad may be,' he said in his curious accent, 'he's a brave knight, and I am happy to drink his health. Furthermore, I will lay odds that he is nobly born, and one who has imbibed the principles of chivalry with his mother's milk. He acted towards me like a true gentleman. You look hot, my friend,' he said to Rudolph, whom he now observed to be sweating freely. 'Well, it's a warm day and you may yet have work to do. I wish you well.'

At that moment the trumpet sounded again and the Disinherited walked his horse, very slowly now, across the arena towards him. There was silence except for a huckster on the popular side of the ground calling the odds as to which of the defenders the young champion would challenge next. He paused before them, looking first one, now the other in the eye, and it is said that Rudolph averted his gaze and drew back a little as if inviting the Disinherited to challenge Elgebast. But it was his shield that was touched with the lance-tip. Then the Disinherited withdrew in the same manner as before.

Rudolph now took a napkin and wiped the sweat from his brow. He called for a cup of wine, which his squire fetched and which he drank in one long, convulsive swallow. He sent his squire to beg a favour from his wife, the Lady Angelica, and, to rousing cheers, attached the glove she had given him to his helmet. And all around him later observed that he looked deathly pale. It was a long time before he indicated to the marshals that he was ready for battle, and they passed the message to the trumpeters.

Even then it seemed for a moment that he hesitated, and later some affirmed that they had heard him cry out that a black hand was pressing against his face; but such stories arise whenever something awful or dramatic has occurred, and the speaker wishes to seem important. In truth Rudolph advanced confidently enough, if more cautiously than those who had previously ridden against the challenger. And this was doubtless prudent enough: he had seen Manfred and Hermann defeated by their own impetuosity. He sat his horse firmly and held his lance level. But, as they drew near to each other, he either miscalculated or suffered a failure of spirit, for his lance passed harmlessly over the Disinherited's shoulder, while he received the other's in the neck just where there was a weak link between helmet and breastplate. He fell backwards from his horse, but his feet were caught in the stirrups, and he was dragged round the arena. Then he was thrown free and lay on the grass, blood spurting from the wound in his neck and gushes of blood pouring from his mouth. The marshals called on the attendants charged with the care of the wounded. His squire ran forward to be of such help as he could. Irma also left the royal box, and, in defiance of convention, knelt by her stricken son. Meanwhile, the Disinherited withdrew to his station at the western end of the arena, and sat his horse with an air of placidity and unconcern. It was observed that he looked over to the pavilion where the Lady Angelica was, and all who remarked her said there was no expression on her face, but that she looked as if she had been carved of marble.

Loud wails of lamentation now arose from the arena where Irma and two of her ladies knelt by the fallen Rudolph. The word ran round that he was dead, and this rumour was confirmed when one of the ladies was seen to place a black kerchief over his face. A litter was brought and he was carried from the arena, followed by his mother, who required to be supported by her companions. Receiving this news, Charles rose from his seat and pronounced the tournament abandoned, for, he said, 'It is not seemly to continue.' Then the crowd began to disperse, some disgruntled and muttering that the death of such as Rudolph should not have been permitted to bring the entertainment to a close. Charles sent Alory to command the Disinherited to present himself before him in the pavilion behind the arena, for he wished to know the identity of the knight who had gained so remarkable a triumph. Meanwhile, it was observed that the Lady Angelica had not moved from her seat, but still remained there, her face blank of any expression.*

* Readers conversant with the Waverley novels will doubtless have remarked the resemblances between Michael Scott's narrative and the tournament described in *Ivanhoe*, a resemblance that extends even to the mysterious knight's assumption of the title Disinherited, though in *Ivanhoe* this is given in the Spanish form '*Desdichado*'. This again gives rise to the possibility that Sir Walter Scott was by some means acquainted with Michael Scott's narrative. However, assiduous researches in the library at Abbortsford by the distinguished scholar, Professor Douglas Gifford, Honorary Librarian there, have found no evidence to support this theory. Nor has it proved possible to substantiate an alternative theory that the author of *Waverley*, on his first visit to Paris in the year after the Battle of Waterloo, may have found occasion to visit the *Bibliothèque Nationale* in the Rue de Richelieu, and to have consulted Michael Scott's manuscript there. I am for my part inclined to believe that the similarity between the two narratives must be ascribed to chance, and it is not after all improbable that there should be a close resemblance between two accounts of imaginary tournaments, any more than that there should be similarities between accounts of imaginary football or cricket matches in, for example, Edwardian school stories. This seems to me more likely than the somewhat fantastical suggestion that Sir Walter and Michael Scott drew on the same race-memory (in Jungian fashion) or that the spirit of Michael Scott, the original wizard of the North, temporarily inhabited his near namesake and perhaps kinsman, to whom the same sobriquet was applied. – A.M.

XXV

You are impatient with what you call my 'mysteriousness', my Prince, especially since you declare there is no mystery to be solved. It's perfectly obvious, you say, that the Disinherited was Roland. You are so sure of this that you tempt me to change the plot, and reveal the Disinherited as some quite other knight. I could do so, certainly. The narrator has command of his tale, and my ingenuity is such that I would have no difficulty in introducing a new character at this point, on the grounds that it would enliven the story. This is sometimes necessary; narrative can be obdurate, even when the story being told is a true one, as this is. And the experienced teller of the tale knows the remedy that is ever to hand: have a man enter the hall bearing an axe, sword or some other weapon. This is effective, pleasing the reader, especially when the man who enters is a new character, one unsuspected by audience and author alike.

So, even though I have vowed to adhere to the truth, to serve you history, not Romance, it remains within my powers to introduce a new complication, by retaining, for instance, the incognito of the Disinherited, or by making him perhaps another bastard son of the King, or of the Emperor in Byzantium; and then, at some further point, devising a different means of permitting Roland to enter the narrative again.

The complacency, the smugness, with which you insist in that bored voice that 'of course the Disinherited is Roland, any fool can see that' tempts me to prove you wrong, in order to teach you the invaluable lesson that it is a grave error to leap to conclusions.

But I shan't yield to the temptation. I am too scrupulous an historian to play ducks and drakes with the truth.

Besides, your successful guess – all right, it wasn't a guess but an inference drawn from the evidence, I won't argue the point –

not only does credit to your perspicacity, it saves me the trouble of writing the 'discovery scene', always, in my considerable experience, a bore for the author.

So: take it as written. The Disinherited was brought before Charlemagne and revealed himself to be his nephew – to, I may say, general astonishment, for not everyone there was as alert to the signs as you, my Prince.

Charlemagne himself was overcome by confusion. On the one hand, he was delighted to find his nephew safe and well, and was still more proud that the young man had acquitted himself so nobly. On the other hand, Roland's presence served as a rebuke to the King: this beautiful and gallant nephew owed nothing to him. Charles had forced the boy's mother into a marriage which was, at the very least, unwelcome to her. When she died untimely, the King made no effort to assume responsibility for the boy, but instead left him in the care of his stepfather Ganelon, who, it now seemed, had neglected him.

Roland's manner showed that these were his feelings. It was polite, graceful, respectful – nothing there to complain of – but also distant and reserved. He accepted the praise the King showered on him as his due, but Charles felt that the young man was also profoundly indifferent to his opinion. Indeed, he was only too obviously eager to bring the interview to an end. The King was wounded. He had looked to indulge in a feast of reconciliation – for there was a core of sentimentality in Charles, as there commonly is in men of action who are guided by impulse rather than reason arising from reflection – and it distressed him to be cheated of the pleasure of the 'reunion scene'. Nevertheless, he resolved that he would now keep Roland by his side when he rode back to Engelheim, and there lavish favours on the youth to secure his loyalty and even his love.

In truth, Roland was not utterly indifferent to the King's approval. He knew he had made his mark that day, was proud of his achievement, and, like most young men, delighted to receive admiration. He also recognised that what he might make of himself from this day on depended in part on the King. Benoni had impressed this on him, insistently and cogently. But he was a young man and his immediate concern was pressing. He could not wait to seek out Angelica. He had caught sight of her in the gallery from which she watched the jousting, and she appeared to him more beautiful than ever, as beautiful as when she came to him in dreams. So, shaking off the attentions of the young knights who crowded around him offering their congratulations, promising him their undying friendship and displaying all the eagerness to associate themselves with the ascendant star which is characteristic of courtiers the world over, Roland made haste to the pavilion where he had been told he would find his *inamorata*. (I employ the Italian term of design for there is no word in another language that so finely and justly expresses what Roland felt for Angelica.)

She sat in a high-backed chair such as craftsmen make in the towns of the Veneto, and her maid was combing the long tresses of her hair, which gleamed the rich gold of the evening sun playing on a grove of autumn larches. She had discarded her outer garments and was dressed only in a shift or petticoat of white silk, which revealed the loveliness of her neck, shoulders and the upper slopes of her delectable breasts. When she saw Roland her eyes lit up and her lips trembled into a smile; and it seemed to him as if this moment opened before them a grassy road to everlasting delight. He fell to his knee, and took her hand and pressed it to his lips, and the maid, without a word of command from her mistress, slipped away behind an arras. Words tumbled over themselves in Roland's mind, yet he could utter none. He was speechless with joy and, for a long time, content to kneel before her, holding her hand to his mouth, and resting his own hand on her thigh. How long they remained in this posture, I cannot tell.

Then Angelica said, 'How I have sighed for you ...'

'And I for you. I have been mad with love,' he murmured, 'but now I have come for you, and I must tell you I am not, as you thought, a wandering player or minstrel, but Roland-Orlando, nephew of King Charles himself.'

As he spoke he felt a tear drop from her eye and wet his hand.

'Is it for happiness that you weep?' he said.

'For happiness,' she sighed, 'and for sadness. For happiness that you have returned and have remained faithful to our love;

155

for sadness because you have this day made me a widow by slaying my husband, the Duke Rudolph.'

'But why should that make you sad?' he said. 'Since you love me, and did not, could not have, loved him.'

And now her tears flowed more copiously, as a stream after heavy rain runs freely through a dam which has been broken. Roland was puzzled and begged her to explain, for he did not realise that when a woman weeps in this manner, it is because she has gone beyond language. It had seemed so simple to him, and now he was at a loss. So they remained a long time, their joy turned to misery and doubt, until at last, in a broken voice, she commanded him to depart, for, she sighed, she must be alone to collect herself. Reluctantly, he obeyed, as a true knight must yield to his mistress's demand.

He made his way into the forest to the grove where Benoni had appointed a meeting-place, and there found his friend and mentor drinking wine with young Oliver, who had served him as his squire in that day's tournament. Benoni lifted his head at his approach, and the look in his eyes was that of a faithful dog which fears it is about to be abandoned.

Roland threw himself on the ground and now began to weep in his turn. He seemed so wretched that for a moment Oliver feared that his madness had returned, and moved to assist him. But Benoni laid his hand on his arm and held him back. At last, when Roland's body was no longer heaving with sobs, Benoni said: 'So you have seen Angelica.'

'I do not understand,' Roland said, raising himself up. 'She loves me still, and yet, when I talked of love, she wept. She said they were tears of happiness and sadness, and I do not understand.'

'I might offer you comfort,' Benoni said, 'and say that you do not understand only because you are a man and she is a woman. But though this is true, it would be false comfort. What have you done today?'

'What do you mean? You know what I have done. I have triumphed in the tournament, been hailed as the champion, and I have been praised by my uncle the King, who opens before me the promise of a glorious future. That is what I have done. Can you deny it? So why should I now be wretched? Can you answer that, Benoni?'

'You fought for honour and for love of Angelica,' Benoni said, 'and you fought nobly, my dearer to me than the sons I shall never have. You have won glory, and in one day have been hailed as the most renowned among Christian knights. Be content with that.'

'How can I be content when Angelica is in tears? Tell me what else I have done.'

Benoni hesitated. What he had to say seemed to him too dreadful to utter, and yet the words must be spoken.

'Alas,' he said, and his voice was low, gentle, and loving, 'you have humiliated her father, Count Manfred, who once had us both whipped as vagabonds. Do you think he will forgive you? And you have slain her husband, the Duke Rudolph.'

'But she did not love Rudolph. She could not have loved Rudolph. She loves me.'

'Indeed yes, my child, but Rudolph was her husband, joined to her in Christian marriage.'

'And what does that signify, set against our love?' Roland cried.

Benoni took him in his arms and held him close, as if he had indeed been a little boy.

XXVI

That very night Count Manfred left Sigmaringen with his retainers and took Angelica with him. They rode hard to the east, far beyond the lake-castle where Roland and his *inamorata* had first known love and plighted their troth in true chivalric fashion. They travelled for days and weeks until they came to Thrace, where Manfred had inherited estates from his mother, a Bulgarian princess. Then he sent back for the Emir, who had meanwhile been held in the dungeons of the lake-castle. When he was brought to him, Manfred summoned Angelica, who had long refused to see any but her maids, and had scarce spoken a word since their hurried departure from Sigmaringen. It was given out that she was mourning her husband Duke Rudolph, and that her grief was to be respected. And indeed, though she had cared nothing for Rudolph, she dressed herself in black and wept often. Only her favourite maid, a mountain-girl called Heidige, knew that it was Roland she mourned, not Rudolph, and that she feared she would never see him again.

Now, when she was brought before her father, she was amazed and horrified to see the Emir sitting at his right hand, apparently an honoured guest.

Manfred said to her, 'It is time to leave off mourning. That marriage was a mistake, to be forgotten. I have been most monstrously cheated by Ganelon and that viper, the King, who has, I am told, named me an outlaw and put a price on my head, on account of the alliance I made with my noble friend, the Emir of Smyrna, whom I confess I did, at Ganelon's insistence and as a result of his wiles, sadly mistreat. But that is now forgotten, and the Emir, with the courtesy characteristic of Muslim nobles, has agreed to let bygones be bygones, and is happy to take you once again as his wife. Rudolph being dead, there is of course no impediment to the marriage, which, in any case, he assures me, is still valid by Islamic law, for, he says, he has never divorced you.'

At this the Emir bowed his head gravely, but made no other response; and in no wise acknowledged Angelica's presence.

She herself said nothing. What was there she could say? She had never dared defy her father, courageous though she was. She knew he would never consent to her marriage to Roland, who was in any case now hundreds of leagues distant, ignorant of her whereabouts and unable to ride to her help. Yet every fibre of her being revolted at the thought of being once again bound to the Emir in whose company she had known nothing but pain and grief.

The next day, greatly daring, she sent to her father to say that she could not betray her Faith by marrying a Muslim, and, rather than commit such a sin, she chose to retire to a convent and become a Bride of Christ. And she implored her father, if he loved her, to give consent to her most humble request.

Count Manfred's response was immediate and harsh. His daughter was his to dispose of and her defiance was not to be endured. She would be married to the Emir, and that was that. Sooner than see her retire to a convent, he would throw her into prison and leave her to languish there. Let her see whether Christ or the Virgin would hearken to her prayers. But she must marry the Emir.

You will appreciate, my Prince, with your quick intelligence, that the Count was himself in a state of utter confusion. This is not to be wondered at. He was a man of action and passion, little given to thought, and indeed incapable of coherent reflection. Now two passions contended with each other in his breast: the desire to punish his daughter, and his determination to retain the friendship of the Emir, who had promised to secure him the governorship of a province from the Caliph (nominally the ruler of all Muslim lands). The Count was rash enough to believe this promise and to assume that the Emir had forgiven him for the insults and imprisonment he had suffered. This was foolish, but men are ever foolish when unable to distinguish between their wishes and the reality of affairs.

So now the Count dismissed Angelica's ladies, and had her

waited on only by an old crone named Fricka, who had been his wet-nurse and who had also been accused of witchcraft by Angelica's mother; indeed, there were many who held that Fricka had either cast a spell on her or fed her the poison which killed her. Angelica had always feared and hated Fricka, and shuddered to discover that she was now to be her sole attendant.

'Will you kill me as you killed my mother?' she asked, unable to restrain herself.

Fricka smiled. 'Your father would hardly thank me in this case, for your death would profit him nothing. It's your living body he is determined to dispose of, and you are a very silly girl to think to defy him. What use would you be to anyone in that convent you speak of? My purpose in being here is to make you see the error of your ways. And I shall do so, believe you me.'

'Will you bewitch me then?' Angelica said, indignation for the moment overcoming her fear of the old woman.

'There will be no need of that,' Fricka said, and laughed. 'I have other means of breaking your will, my lass, as you will soon enough discover.'

Yet the victory was not to be as quick as she supposed. Angelica did not surrender easily. First, she refused to eat.

'Do you think I have poisoned your food?' Fricka said. 'How stupid. What purpose would that serve?'

'I don't care whether you have poisoned it or not,' was the reply. 'I will not eat, and that is that. My father will be sorry when I have starved to death, and he will blame you for it. Have you thought of that?'

'If you will not eat, I shall feed you by force,' Fricka said. 'Don't think I won't or can't.'

Meanwhile she sought to break Angelica's will by depriving her of sleep, waking her whenever her eyes closed. Without both sleep and sustenance, Angelica grew weak. She suffered from delusions. She cried out that Roland was riding to her rescue. She placed all her hopes in him until one day she saw on the white wall of the tower room to which she was confined a scene that broke her spirit: it was Roland, taken prisoner, loaded with chains, his head shaved and bowed; and he was led to a gallows by two halberdiers, while her father and the Emir sat on cushions in a pavilion, eating sweetmeats and drinking wine, as they watched the black-hooded hangman slip a noose over Roland's head. A command was given, and her lover swung in the air, while Angelica fell senseless in a swoon. When she recovered she could not tell if what she had witnessed was real, or an image conjured up by Fricka's black arts. But she was terrified, and her spirit was broken. She consented to the marriage.

It is easy to condemn Angelica for weakness of character, and some chroniclers have done so, declaring her submission to be shameful. But to my mind, my Prince, weakness of character, though regrettable, is no more to be despised than physical weakness. We are not all born to be heroes or athletes. Am I, for instance, to be despised because I cannot overthrow some bully in the lists or even in a tavern brawl? The idea is ridiculous. Poor Angelica had resisted to the limit of her bodily and spiritual strength, and when she submitted, it was in preference – however reluctant – to the alternatives, which were madness or death. What more could be reasonably asked of this gentle and beautiful girl? And did it not take a certain courage for her to choose the life to which her father had condemned her, and to resist the temptation of the grave or witlessness? There is a cold courage evinced in accepting the unacceptable. Believe you me.

So the marriage was renewed, with the bride as stony-faced as if carved out of marble. It is said she looked neither at the Emir nor at her father, nor at the priest and imam who conducted the ceremony, but kept her eyes fixed on the ground.

Did she, to the last moment, entertain the vain hope that Roland would ride to her rescue, as the hero is wont to do in Romances, in which she had from childhood taken such delight? Perhaps she did. When we are faced with the worst, we may well seek refuge in dreaming of a fantastic deliverance. But none came. The Emir carried her out of Christendom.

XXVII

When it was discovered that Manfred had slipped away like a thief in the night, taking his daughter and all his train with him, Ganelon was relieved, for he had feared Manfred might reveal their treacherous plots, being stupid. Charles was angry, since it offended him that a vassal should leave his company without permission, and, moreover, he suspected Manfred of conspiring with the Saracens; which suspicion Ganelon was quick to feed in order to distract the King's attention from his own activities. But Charles was not deceived, and continued to have Ganelon watched carefully. 'He is capable of any disloyalty,' he said to Bishop Turpin.

The King's anger and discomfort were nothing, however, to Roland's. When he learned of Manfred's flight and abduction of Angelica, he cursed his ill-fortune with all the curses that sprang into his mind. He bewailed the evil fate that once again conspired to cheat him of his love; he raged through the camp, striking out with the flat of his sword, and terrifying all who encountered him, and it was not till evening, after he had ridden hard in pursuit of the fugitives and failed to find trace of them, that he retired to his tent and fell down on his pallet bed and wept. So shaken with emotion was he that both Benoni and Oliver again feared that he would once more succumb to madness.

But his resolution held. The next morning he announced his intention of setting out in search of Angelica, and would have done so if the King had not strictly forbidden him, saying he could no longer be deprived of his nephew's aid. Roland was tempted to disobey, and Benoni was only able to dissuade him by offering to go himself in search of Angelica.

Charles had good reason to require Roland's presence, for within a month, word came that a huge Muslim army under the command of Marsilion of Saragossa had crossed the Pyrenees and advanced deep into France. To meet such a force, Charles at once declared, would require the mustering of all his vassals and their knights. He could not spare a single man, and now, least of all Roland, whose prowess in the tournament had won the admiration of all his peers, and, being bruited abroad, would make him the hero of all the ardent youth of France and Germany.

Roland could not but be flattered by the praise that was showered on him, and by the trust which his uncle the King reposed in him. And he is not to be blamed for feeling as he did. In the first place, all brave knights seek to win renown; in the code of chivalry nothing is prized more highly than a good name and a reputation for courage and skill in the art of war. Secondly, my Prince, you are to consider what Roland-Orlando's life had been to date. His stepfather Ganelon had denied him any chance to display his prowess, had even tried to force him to adopt the monastic life, and had threatened him with castration. Then, having escaped Sigmaringen, his spirit had failed him, and he had been ready to give up until Benoni rudely compelled him to go on. He had enjoyed a brief, soft interlude of love, but had then been driven from Manfred's lake-castle, but not before he had been subjected to the painful indignity of a whipping. Next he had lost his wits and wandered the forest raving and eating grass like a second Nebuchadnezzar. Restored to health, he had at last been granted the opportunity to display his prowess, and the day of the tournament had been the most glorious of his life. The youth who had been rejected and despised was hailed as a champion. Can it be wondered at that he now looked eagerly to what the future might hold, and that news of impending war came to him as a promise of delight, not an occasion for dismay? He felt himself to be a man made for war, and he responded to the sound of the trumpet with all the eagerness of a war-horse. It was not that all thought of Angelica was dashed from his mind, but what is the goddess Venus to a brave knight in comparison with Mars, god of battles?

Charles now named him master of the horse, which position in the Frankish army ranked as second-in-command. Roland soon proved worthy of his uncle's confidence. His energy was prodigious. Though he had no experience of war, he acted like a seasoned general; neither Julius Caesar nor Alexander could have surpassed the sagacity of his measures. Troops were dispatched ahead of the line of march to collect supplies from towns and villages, so that the main body of the army might advance every day, without being compelled to lose time in foraging. And, even ahead of the troops collecting supplies, he sent out a screen of lightly-armed scouts to bring him information about the movements of the enemy. So, in almost less time that it takes to tell, the van of the Frankish army came within sight of Paris even as the Saracens, or paynim, approached from the south. Never has an army moved with greater celerity than the Franks did then with Roland at their head.

Some day, my Prince, I trust that you will be able to visit Paris. Despite my unhappy experiences there, which were in no wise the fault of the Parisians, who are among the wittiest of people if also impatient with those whose wits are slower, Paris remains for me the queen of cities. Some would award that palm to Rome as the seat of Empire, but to my mind the atmosphere of that city is polluted by the great number of parasitical ecclesiastics there, intolerant blood-suckers, enemies of all men of intellect, tax-eaters, liars, hypocrites, pederasts, slanderers, barrators, simonists, persecutors, and many of them idiots also. Others would hail Naples as the flower of all cities, and certainly the beauty of the surrounding landscape and of the bay, allied to the good humour and vivacity of the people, make a stay in Naples quite unusually agreeable. Yet there is a sad lack of body in the conversations of Neapolitans, and I have often thought that their pleasures are restricted to chattering, gossip, eating and fornication, not to mention a spot of buggery. Naples is a princess, not a queen. Then there is our own Palermo, city of oranges, lemons and the best ice-cream a man may eat, even in Paradise. Moreover, it is a peaceful city, where murder and rapine are rare, which, alas, I cannot say of my beloved Paris. Is there anything more delectable than a summer evening in Palermo when the heat of the day has diminished and the possibilities of amorous adventure seem endless? And yet, Palermo lacks the – what is the word I want? – the *intensity* of Paris. Finally there

164

are those who hail London as the finest of cities, and it is indeed fine on the rare days when the fog in which it is generally enshrouded lifts. But I digress. It is of Paris as it was in Charlemagne's day that I must now speak.

Paris stands in a large plain, in the navel or rather the heart of France, and the district that surrounds it is known as the Île de France, though it is not in truth what we normally mean by the word 'island', and why it is so called I do not know. It stands on the River Seine, which indeed flows through the middle of the city, which is therefore divided, as Caesar said of Gaul, into three parts, and these are called: the Right Bank; the Island of the City; and the Left Bank, which is where the noblemen now have their houses, and where there are many monasteries and convents, and also the university where I studied and taught – oh, happy memories! But there were fewer of these in Charlemagne's time, and the Frankish nobility were not then accustomed to build town houses or palaces for themselves, as many do now, and as the nobility have always done in Rome, Naples and, of course, Palermo. Because it stands in a plain, Paris lacks natural defences, and therefore Pepin, Charles's father (as you will recall), had thrown up a wall on both the northern and southern sides. Entry to the city from the north is by the gate named after the patron saint of France, Denis, but I forget the name of the southern gate. Notwithstanding the walls, the most secure part of the city in the event of attack is the island, which is joined to the city on either bank only by narrow wooden bridges, which may be destroyed in times of extremity and as quickly, or almost as quickly, restored. It is on the island that now stands the great cathedral of Our Lady, but in the days of which I write this was no cathedral, only a mean chapel. The patron saint of Paris itself is St Geneviève, and it was to her church that Parisians flocked when word came of the Muslim advance, and to her that they raised their prayers calling for deliverance from the peril that threatened them, as she had in earlier days saved Paris from the furies of the hordes commanded by the famous Attila the Hun. Her church is situated on the Left Bank, and so acute was the danger that even those Parisians who lived around the markets known as Les Halles and who make it a point of honour never to cross the river did so now.

Marsilion was already preparing to besiege the city on the south side when Roland led the vanguard of the Frankish army through the Porte St-Denis. He at once summoned the mayor of the city and, in a lofty manner that compelled respect, enquired if the citizens were preparing defences or trusting only to the protection of their saint. The mayor flushed and said they would defend themselves to the best of their ability, which, however, was less than it would have been if the King had not the previous year responded to a number of riots by commanding all citizens below the rank of nobleman to surrender their arms – 'as if,' he added, with a contemptuous sniff, 'it wasn't well-known that the riots had originated in scuffles between two armed gangs, the retainers of, respectively, the King's son Charlot and his mistress's husband, the Comte d'Ivry.'

'And is my cousin Charlot in the city now?' Roland asked.

'Charlot in the city?' the mayor said. 'You cannot be well acquainted with your cousin, my lord, to put such a question. He departed with his gang of bullies as soon as word came that the paynim had crossed the Loire.'

On another occasion Roland might have rebuked the mayor for the insolent tone in which he spoke. But he felt ashamed by this evidence of his cousin's cowardice. So he made no immediate reply, then asked the mayor to lead him to a vantage point from which he might survey the Saracen host.

Dusk was now closing in and a mist was rising from the fields. The camp-fires of the enemy stretched beyond the length of the walls, and the horns of the army reached the river beyond them, while the most distant fires at the rear were scarcely more than specks in the gathering gloom, so mighty was the force arrayed against them. But Roland was undismayed. He remembered Benoni's account of the siege his father Milan had withstood in the mountains of Lombardy, and how the English knight Astolf had then declared, 'The fewer men, the greater share of honour', which is indeed a common English saying.

The following morning he had Oliver organise the defences on the southern side, while he himself led a small party of picked knights and men-at-arms up-river by way of the Porte d'Ivry against the Saracen outposts there. Taken by surprise, these were quickly scattered and their tents burned. Roland knew that in military terms there was no great advantage won by this raid, but he calculated it would raise the morale of the defenders; and indeed, when he led his men back into the city, the citizens thronged about them, cheering lustily. Such diversions, while Oliver saw to the strengthening of the defences, were all that seemed possible. They would, he hoped, keep the Saracens occupied till Charles arrived with the main body of the army.

Skirmishing continued, and every day Roland was victorious in some encounter, which raised the spirits of the Parisians who now began to believe that their city would not be given over to the enemy. Correspondingly, Roland's exploits depressed the Saracens, who started to grumble that they were far from home and their loved ones.

Such was the situation when Charlemagne arrived with the main body of the host, and promptly summoned a conference, which was held in a palace on the island. He invited Roland to give his assessment of the strength of the city's defences and of the disposition of the Muslim army, which he did with great clarity and to general approval.

Bishop Turpin then said, 'From our young friend's account it seems clear to me that if we attack the paynim as soon as our men have recovered from their long march, we shall be assured of victory, and I call on St Denis as witness. Meanwhile, let us send out a body of knights every morning under Roland's command to biff the enemy and keep on biffing them, for nothing is so disheartening as to be subject to hit-and-run raids.'

These bold words were greeted with general applause, but then Ganelon held up his hand to indicate that he wished to speak. And this is what he said:

'No one has a greater admiration for the good Bishop's bellicosity than I. Moreover, I approve the dispositions of our defences that my noble stepson Roland has made, and am cheered by his account of the little actions he has undertaken. Yet, my Lord King and barons of the Empire, it is my task, my duty, my obligation to instil a cold note of realism into our deliberations.

Consider the facts, divorced from all rhetoric. Even Roland, though inspired by the nobility of his spirit and the ardour of audacious youth, has been unable to conceal from us the stark reality, that we are heavily outnumbered by the enemy. Our men are also exhausted by their long march, and full half of them are suffering from dysentery. Supplies will not last long, so we are in no state to withstand a siege. The paynim, on the other hand, can draw on all the rich yield of the Île de France. Bishop Turpin calls for a general sally and a frontal battle to be fought. I honour his spirit but question his judgement. Suppose we fight such a battle? We might be victorious, but that is by no means certain, given the disparity of numbers. But suppose we lose? What then? Paris will be sacked and utterly destroyed. The Saracen will be master of the Empire. Is this is a risk to be taken? Better surely to seek negotiations, to discover what grievances have led to this invasion, and to devise what may be done to appease them. It may be that gold will be sufficient to persuade Marsilion to withdraw, his honour being satisfied. Who can tell? No one now, till we have enquired. Let us seek first of all a truce and in that interval see what diplomacy can do to resolve the situation. This may not seem a bold course but it is a prudent one, and in my experience prudence yields more and better fruits than unthinking boldness. For my part, to prove my sincerity, I am ready to volunteer to serve as ambassador.'

Many listened to Ganelon's speech with impatience, Roland chief among those, and it was all he could do not to break out in scornful indignation. Others were less restrained and showered Ganelon with insults. But the King sat there unmoved, stroking his long white beard, his brows furrowed in thought. And indeed there was much to ponder. On the one hand he distrusted Ganelon, his former friend; on the other he respected his intellect, and was impressed by his analysis. The King's silence stilled the clamour. All eyes were drawn to him. Oliver would later say, 'It was then that I first felt his authority and understood what it is to be an emperor, for we were all in his presence as gabbling schoolchildren. I understood how it was that Milan and Astolf and Benoni, though they had such cause to resent him, never spoke of him without respect, even awe.'

At last Charles raised his head, looked around the company and spoke:

'I am a man of war and battles, a soldier of Christ Jesus our Lord, and it is in his service that I have all the years of my long life warred with the pagans, whether they be Saxons or Saracens. My wars have been righteous wars, as the one now looming before us is also righteous. So I understand and applaud the eagerness of so many of you, notably my dear friend Turpin and my dearest nephew Roland, to give battle now. Moreover, if the odds are against us, even though we fight under the banner of King Jesus and his saints, so much greater the glory. And yet, in the days of my white hairs, I have come to recognise that war is also terrible, and that its outcome is ever uncertain. The meaning of the Empire, which is Christ's Empire, is peace. Many wars I have fought to make peace, and no doubt I shall have to do so again, the world being sinful. But I would be happy to avoid this war, so be it that can be done honourably, for it is a war in which, if fought, so many noble men will fall, and who knows which of us will be among the slain? So I say: it may come to war, but we shall first give peace a chance. I therefore empower you, Ganelon, to serve as my ambassador, to conclude a truce, if that be possible, and to enquire on what terms Marsilion will withdraw behind the Pyrenees, so be it he first does me homage and leaves hostages as security. I have spoken.'

Many were dismayed by the King's words, being eager for battle, but none dared question them. Even Roland, whose anger exceeded that of all others, remained silent till he was alone with Oliver. Then he gave vent to his fury, cursing lustily and hurling his helmet at the wall.

Oliver waited till his friend's outburst had spent itself, then said, 'It may well be that Ganelon will fail in his embassy. Why after all should they agree to a truce, let alone to withdrawing beyond the Pyrenees, when they have the advantage over us, as they do now? Moreover, the conditions that the King has set will surely prove unacceptable to Marsilion. So we shall have our battle, never fear. What puzzles me is why Ganelon should have volunteered to lead a mission that is, to my mind, doomed to failure.'

'Because he is meditating some foul trick, that's why,' Roland said. 'You forget I have known him since childhood. He is as twisted as the branches of an ancient olive tree, and as subtle and untrustworthy as a serpent. How I wish I knew what was best to do. How I wish Benoni was here to advise me.'

'When you are uncertain what's best to do,' Oliver said, laying his hand on Roland's shoulder, 'it's best to do nothing. Come what may, matters will resolve themselves. They usually do. Leastways, that's my experience and my opinion.'

So, with gentle words and sage advice, he calmed Roland, as Benoni had urged him to be ready to do whenever the boy's mind was enflamed; and in a little they lay down to rest.

The next day, Ganelon, having sent heralds in advance to declare that he came in peace, rode out beyond the walls and was escorted to the crimson pavilion of the Moorish King. Marsilion received him with that courtesy which seems to be second nature to Muslim princes, though there are those who assert that they are at their most treacherous when most polite. And certainly, a canny man provides himself with a long spoon when he sups with the Devil, as the proverb has it. What Ganelon said, what lies he told, what promises he made, what threats he employed, were never revealed, for, as Ganelon himself was wont to remark, in diplomacy 'silence is wisdom when speaking is folly.' But he rode back at evening to declare that a truce had been agreed for three days and nights, during which time Marsilion would consider on what terms he might consent to withdraw. And those who feared the outcome of battle hailed him as their deliverer.

'It is not yet peace I bring you,' Ganelon said, 'but I believe peace will follow, and, if I read Marsilion rightly, it will be peace with honour and peace for our time.'

When he had heard what Ganelon had to say, Charles laid his distrust aside, and embraced him, as he had done when they were boys together; and he bestowed on him the Order of the Golden Bear, which Ganelon had long coveted but been hitherto denied.

But Roland had Oliver call his chief lieutenants to his chamber, and told them they must be vigilant, for, he said, 'I distrust the paynim, and fear Marsilion has agreed to this truce only in order to cause us to neglect our defences for its period; and if we do so, then he will be ready to launch a surprise attack.'

And to guard against this danger, he continued to ride out with Oliver at his right hand and in the company of a few chosen knights, chief among them Ogier the Dane with whom, since the tournament, he had formed a close friendship, recognising in him a brother in valour.

On the second day of the truce as they rode out in this manner, keeping a distance from the Saracen army but observing its disposition, they came to a farmhouse where they heard the wailing of a woman. They found her crouched by the cold hearth with the naked body of a boy in her arms. For a little she replied to their questions only with sobs and moans, till Oliver knelt beside her and very gently laid his cloak around her shoulders, for she was shivering, but whether with cold or emotion, or perhaps both, they could not tell. Then she showed them the wound in the boy's side, and, drawing aside the cloth that she had laid over the lower part of his body, displayed the vile mutilation inflicted on him. 'Before he was dead, before he was dead,' she said repeatedly, 'for there was still life in him when I came home from the fields and found him thus. And my daughter, his sister, has gone, and I fear that these fiends of infidels have taken her. And my cow also, the red cow that gives us milk. But that is nothing to what they have done to my son and will do to my daughter.'

'And this is what Ganelon calls a truce,' Roland said.

Leaving two of his knights to care for the old woman and bury her son, after which, he instructed them, they were to carry her back to the city, he himself rode there with Oliver and Ogier and the rest of his troop; and his face was black as a sky full of thunder. But he spoke no word to any till they were within the walls, and he ordered them to say nothing to anyone of what they had seen, but to be ready to ride out at dusk.

There were some thirty of them who rode with Roland that evening. He was coated from head to foot in black armour, and was mounted on his dark-bay mare, whom he had called Quattro, for she was, he said, the fourth among his friends, after Benoni,

Oliver and Astolf, who had died that he might regain his wits. All had muffled their horses' hooves, and they rode with the speed and certainty of the avenging angel. When they came in sight of the Saracen outposts, he held up his hand to halt his little troop, and he himself rode on with only Oliver and Ogier as companions. They rode, as it were, negligently, and when the first sentry enquired who they were and what their purpose was, Roland made no reply but, drawing his sword, cut him down with a single blow. Meanwhile, Ogier and Oliver severed the ropes of the guards' tent, which collapsed on those within. Roland now summoned the rest of his troops and they rode through the Saracen camp; and it was as if they were ghosts and the Saracens were struck dumb by the sight. So they approached Marsilion's pavilion.

Now Roland knew, from prisoners he had taken before Charles arrived with the main body of the army and the so-called truce was made, that Marsilion, who was a luxurious man, never travelled, even in time of war, without a company of wives and concubines, and also that he had with him his young son Yusuf, whom he loved with an extraordinary passion. So now, drawing rein before Marsilion's pavilion, he blew a single challenging note on his horn, and at the same time sundry of the knights broke into the other tents and seized the women and also the boy, whom they threw across their saddle-bows. Then Roland drew a missive from within his gauntlet and commanded one of his knights to pin it to the pavilion. And this missive, written in the Arabic script by the hand of one of the prisoners he had taken (on threat of death if he did not comply), informed Marsilion that his women would be given to Christian knights and his son made a eunuch to serve the Christian Emperor if he did not, firstly, surrender the men guilty of the atrocity I have described and restore the young girl to her mother, and, secondly, abandon the siege and withdraw, without conditions, from the fair land of France. And then Roland rode back to the city with his prisoners.

Now I must tell you, my Prince, that there are historians – doubtless worthy men – who question this exploit of Roland's, and affirm that what I have just related is not merely improbable, but frankly unbelievable. How, they say, could a single knight, however bold, at the head of such a small body of men, make his way unchallenged and unmolested into the heart of the enemy camp, seize prisoners and return unscathed?

I have some sympathy with their scepticism, and you know, from what I have often said and written, that I approve the cultivation of a sceptical mind. Nevertheless, the truth of what I have narrated is well attested, not only in the account of Roland's feats of war as recorded by the worthy Bishop Turpin, but also in a narrative attributed to Ogier the Dane which I have myself consulted in the royal library in Paris. Therefore, you must conclude that either the good Bishop and the noble Dane were liars, or that the account I have given you is true.

Which is not to say that there may not be some exaggeration in their writings, or that all the details are accurate. But I have to add that they agree well one with the other.

Roland's raid provoked fury in both camps. Marsilion sent to Ganelon to protest that the truce had been broken and to announce his intention of launching an attack if the prisoners were not returned by sundown. Ganelon complained to the King that his honour had been impugned, and, greatly daring, added that Charles's honour was likewise tarnished, since Ganelon had been his emissary, negotiating in his name. I say, 'greatly daring', for Charles was ever tender of his honour and, in speaking thus, Ganelon ran the risk that the King's fury would be directed at him.

But in thinking this would rouse the King to action, Ganelon miscalculated. Charles stroked his beard, said, 'This requires pondering on,' dismissed Ganelon, and sent for Roland. The truth was that Roland's exploit appealed to the King's warm imagination; it was just what he might have done himself as a young man. Moreover, when Roland told him of the scene he had discovered at the farmhouse, of the murder and mutilation of the boy there and the abduction of his sister, the innate generosity of the King's temper shone bright as the morning sun. Instead of rebuking his nephew, he commended him. He therefore sent to Marsilion repeating the terms Roland had offered for the return of the hostages.

Marsilion, though brave and sagacious, was now alarmed and perplexed. The Christians must be stronger than he had supposed, for it was evident that their King was not troubled by his own threats. So he hesitated: to attack the city and be defeated was to put all at risk, for, as an experienced general, he knew how easily a defeat may be translated into a rout, so he sent again to Ganelon, this time privily, asking him to enquire what terms would be acceptable to the King, short of those demanded by Roland, and promising him a rich reward if Ganelon acted as his true friend, 'For,' he said, 'there is no enmity between you and me.' The request flattered Ganelon, who saw advantage in pleasing the Moorish leader.

Meanwhile, Roland treated the captives he had taken with the courtesy and generosity which were natural to him. He soothed their fears and saw to their comfort. Instead of being thrown into some dark cell as they had expected, they found themselves lodged in a luxurious apartment and granted every comfort they might desire. Marsilion's son Yusuf, a boy of twelve summers, slim, delicate and comely, was dazzled by Roland, and, in the hot-blooded manner of Arab youth, conceived a passion for him.

Roland entrusted them to the care of Ogier, and, with Oliver in attendance, waited once again on his uncle. Charles, who now discovered in his nephew all those noble qualities the lack of which in his own son Charlot sorely distressed him, received him graciously and enquired what he now had in mind. The answer pleased him, and he gave his consent to what Roland now proposed.

Therefore, that evening, while it was between light and dark, Roland, at the head of a chosen body of knights and with Oliver at his right hand, rode out of the city by the northern gate, and made a wide sweep of the country to the east, till they came to a place where the river runs through marshlands. Guided by a peasant whom he had recruited a few days earlier, the troop picked their way through the marshes till they came to a spot where the river could be forded. This peasant, by name François, made his living as a wild-fowler and knew all the secret tracks. So they crossed the river and, still riding to the east, inscribed a half-circle which brought them to the rear of the Saracen camp, where there was a ridge of high ground. They lay up during the hours of daylight, their presence unsuspected by the enemy, and when dusk began to fall, Roland had them collect faggots of wood and furze and the branches of trees with which to make bonfires. Leaving half a dozen men-at-arms commanded by a single knight to tend these, he then led the others further on, where they did the same thing, so that, when it was full night, it seemed to the Saracens that they were near to being surrounded by a large army which had ridden from the east to reinforce the Frankish force. And this so alarmed the Saracens that some of their chief men went to Marsilion and said they were in danger of being encircled and that the road that led south would soon be barred to them. Their agitation communicated itself to Marsilion, bold man though he was. Accordingly, he sought out the soldiers who had been responsible for the atrocity that had so infuriated Roland – or perhaps selected other soldiers to serve as the guilty men – and sent them under a guard bearing a flag of truce, with the young girl who had been taken in their company, towards the city wall, with a herald empowered to hand them over in return for Roland's hostages and the promise that as soon as this was done, his army would begin their retreat to the Pyrenees. He requested only that the road remain open to them and that they might not be molested as they withdrew.

And this was done, though, as Ogier confirmed to Roland, the boy Yusuf was loth to leave, and did so professing his devotion to his captor whom he called 'the noblest of knights'.

XXVIII

For some years there was peace, and it was at this time that Charles came to be known as Charlemagne, which style I have sometimes employed prematurely. He also, as often happens to great men in old age, became eager to have his achievements widely and publicly recognised. I have often observed that old men seek honours even more eagerly than the young.

In his youth he had taken Julius Caesar as his pattern, but now came to have a higher regard for Caesar's great-nephew and adopted son, Augustus, whom he regarded as the true founder of the Roman Empire. Believing that the Franks were the heirs of Rome in the west, he greatly desired to be granted the title of emperor himself. Therefore, he opened negotiations with the Emperor Constantine in Byzantium, seeking to be named as his colleague, and he instructed his ambassadors to say that he himself had extended the bounds of Empire far beyond those set by Augustus. But he thought it prudent to tell them to refrain from remarking that the Empire in the east had contracted, many provinces, including the Holy Land, having been lost to Islam.

Byzantium answered as Byzantium always speaks, in flowery language, lavish in compliments, but evasive and nowise to the point. Nevertheless, Charlemagne persisted, for it had become an obsession with him to secure this title, which might add to his dignity, but not at all to his power.

Many flattering words were exchanged, and presents given by both parties: the Emperor Constantine, for example, sent Charles an elephant, the first ever seen by the Franks, and a beast of great wonder to them. But the title of emperor was jealously guarded, and many around the King feared that his repeated requests impaired his dignity.

So matters stood when that invasion of Italy by the Saracens, which I have recounted in telling the story of Ogier the Dane, caused the Pope to entreat Charles to come to his aid. Which, as you know, he did, despite the foolish counsel and cowardice of the Pope.

The Romans were so incensed and shamed when they learned of the Holy Father's contemptible conduct that two noble families, the Orsini and the Colonna, rose against him. The Pope surrendered on the promise that his life would be spared and his dignity preserved; but the promise was not honourably kept. His eyes were torn out, his tongue severed, and he was dispatched to a monastery in the mountains of Calabria.

Though Charlemagne had no respect for the character of this Pope, he was horrified to learn that the successor to St Peter had been treated in so barbarous a fashion. He therefore sent Roland, whom he had made Duke of Brittany, to Rome to ensure that the election for a new pontiff was carried out in seemly manner, and that a suitable man should be chosen. He had himself selected Hadrian, a notable scholar and abbot of the Benedictine monastery of Monte Cassino.

When Roland rode into the Eternal City at the head of a troop of battle-hardened Frankish knights, with Oliver at his right hand and Ogier at his left, the Roman nobles dared not dispute the matter, and so Hadrian was enthroned. He showed his gratitude by bestowing on Charlemagne the titles 'Patrician of the Romans' and 'Prefect of the City'. Yet these honours made the King still more eager to receive the title of emperor. So he resolved to send Roland to Byzantium to plead his cause.

Events there encouraged him to hope for success. The Emperor Constantine VI, inheriting the crown while a child, had shared power with his mother Irene, who had acted as Regent during his minority. This Irene was a woman distinguished for beauty, intelligence and villainy. Of the first, poets offer ample testimony. Her skin was softer than rose-petals, her dark eyes shone like liquid fire, her breasts were pomegranates and in motion she was graceful as the roe-deer. Of course, poets exaggerate, and it is a poor queen who can find no versifier to praise her beauty. Nevertheless, it is true that Irene, though only the daughter of a tavern-keeper, had as a young girl captivated the Emperor Leo IV, who, not content with having her as a concubine, took her as his legal wife. Very soon she came to dominate the Emperor, and not only by reason of her wit. According to an account written by one of the palace eunuchs, she was the first and only woman with whom Leo was able to achieve climax. But one should not believe eunuchs; they are notoriously malicious and unreliable. Be that as it may, when Leo died suddenly (though he may not have been poisoned), Irene had no difficulty in securing the regency; and the boy Constantine is said to have adored her then.

Now you must know that Byzantium had long been riven by a controversy concerning the place of icons and other images in worship. The Emperor Leo III, called the Isaurian, father, or perhaps grandfather, of Irene's husband, had been converted to the belief that the use of icons and images as an aid to prayer is sinful. So he had ordered them to be destroyed in churches all over the Empire. For this reason historians term the controversy 'iconoclastic'. Leo was guilty of heresy, for Holy Church has ever recognised that icons and images are an aid to devotion. How else or how better can one invoke the intercession of the saints? But Leo had a political motive, too. In commanding the breaking of icons, he hoped to reconcile Christianity with Islam, for the followers of Mohammed abjure the use of images in devotion.

In fact, Leo's policy stirred up civil strife, and Irene, a child of Athens where worship has ever been sensuous and beautiful, was a fierce foe of the iconoclasts. Accordingly, when her son Constantine was converted to the heresy, she did not hesitate to depose him. Then, as is the custom in Byzantium, she had him blinded.

Irene was now sole ruler, but her position was insecure, for the iconoclastic heretics were numerous and longed to destroy her. So it seemed to Charlemagne that the moment was propitious to seek an alliance, his price being his nomination as emperor of the West.

Ganelon objected to the choice of Roland as ambassador, not only because he was jealous of his stepson, but because he thought himself better fitted for the task, which required, he said, a subtlety of mind, and knowledge of philosophy and theology that Roland lacked. But Charlemagne brushed his argument aside: Roland had qualities and virtues that made him well-suited to the undertaking. Besides which, the King had another reason, which he confided only to the faithful Bishop Turpin. The Empress was known to be lascivious, subject to that morbid and scarce controllable sexual desire which, when appearing in women, doctors term 'nymphomania'. She would surely be unable to resist Roland's charms. But Irene had fallen in love with a Thracian girl with dewy eyes and a cupid's bow upper lip, whom, to divert suspicion, she had adopted as her daughter and kept hidden from public view in the innermost chambers of the palace. The girl's name was Tabitha, but Irene called her Eos, for she was beautiful as the dawn.

Nevertheless, Charlemagne was not mistaken in thinking that Irene would experience desire for Roland. From the moment she set eyes on him and took note of his strong and shapely legs, she determined to seduce him. And this she soon did. Roland is not to be blamed for succumbing to her advances. What young man of spirit can resist a beautiful woman skilled in the art of love who is intent on having him, more especially when the woman is an empress? Afterwards Roland wept, for he had been unfaithful to his dream of Angelica, whom, however, he believed utterly lost to him. Yet, despite his self-reproach, he returned to the Empress's bed. As for Irene, her pleasure was great, but her heart was not engaged.

So Roland made no progress with his mission. The Empress was lavish in endearments, but did not dare grant what Charlemagne sought.

'It would be the death of me,' she said. 'I am already surrounded by enemies, and conspiracies threaten me at every turn. Were I to accede to your request, dear boy, they would raise up the city mob and I would be torn limb from limb. Tell the King of the Franks that I am happy to be his friend and ally, but no more than that.'

Then she offered Roland the command of the Varangian Guard, as the only man (she said) whom she could fully trust. It was now his turn to temporise, neither accepting nor refusing.

Byzantium is a city of talk and argument, and Roland took

the opportunity to seek to improve his understanding of the religion of the Saracens, for, as he had once said to Oliver, 'It seems I am fated to fight against them, and it is better, as Benoni used to say, to know your enemy and not wallow in ignorance like a sow.'

There was a learned man at the court, John of Damascus, himself an Arab but also a devout Christian, who took a fancy to Roland and was delighted to instruct him.

Islam, he said, was a perversion of the True Faith, and Mohammed, its founder, a godly man (if given deplorably to sensuality) who had been led astray as a boy. Then he spoke of other heresies such as Arianism (which need not concern you, my Prince, but which resembles the Islamic faith in many respects) and of iconoclasm.

'It is,' he said, 'on account of her pious opposition to this most recent heresy that the Empress Irene is revered by all true believers, and will be forgiven her sins, whatsoever they be.'

And saying this, he looked sadly at Roland, before concluding, 'And yet, my son, you must not think of Muslims and other heretics as devils incarnate, but as errant brothers, led astray by false theology.'

'That is difficult,' Roland said, 'when they are trying to kill you.'

One day, as Roland was wandering through the city, marvelling at its riches, yet sick at heart for no reason that he knew, he heard his name called, and, turning, saw to his amazement Benoni emerging from a tavern. They fell into each other's arms with many expressions of delight.

'Tell me,' Roland then said, 'have you news of Angelica? Is she perhaps even in the city?'

'Alas no,' Benoni said, 'such news as I have is not what you will be happy to hear.'

Then he told Roland how the unfortunate girl had been forcibly wed to the Emir of Smyrna, consenting only when threatened with death, and how he had carried her off to distant lands.

'I followed them,' he said, 'though lagging many months

behind until I lost track of them in the mountains of Asia. There I fell among brigands, fierce men, who held me captive in hopes of a ransom, and who, when they understood that none would be forthcoming, would have slit my throat if I had not escaped thanks to the friendship of a young member of the tribe, a boy called Ahmed. He attached himself to me and guided me through hostile lands till we arrived here in the city, whence I intended that we should take ship to Italy and seek you out wherever you might be.'

Roland said, 'So she is lost to me for ever,' and it seemed to Benoni that, as he spoke these words, terrible in their dark finality, Roland's youth deserted him. There was no expression on his face, and yet Benoni read there what he would look like when death drew near. The pleasures of love, he thought, are brief, but love's pains may endure for ever; and he sighed because he had no words of comfort to speak.

At that moment an Arab boy came out of the tavern, pulled at Benoni's sleeve and told him he was wanted within. Benoni sighed again, touched the boy's cheek in silent acknowledgement, and said to Roland, 'How you come to be here, my dear, I know not, and yet this meeting, though sad, is fortuitous. Sad, not only because of the bitter news of Angelica I have had to impart, but also because ...' Here he paused. 'You may wonder why I have delayed in this city instead of making haste to rejoin you. The answer is in this tavern where your father, Milan, my oldest friend, lies at the point of death. That is why I say our meeting is fortuitous.'

'My father ...' said Roland, who, to tell the truth, had quite forgotten that he had ever had a father and who could therefore scarcely be grieved to learn that he was dying. But it seemed to him now that death lay all about him, for he was downcast and oppressed by a great weariness of the world. So, without a word, he accompanied Benoni and the boy Ahmed into the house.

They were met by a small woman with a wrinkled face and eyes that glistened black as olives.

'He is weaker,' she said to Benoni, 'and gabbling in a tongue I do not understand. Ah well, for all his weaknesses and the drinking, he has been a good man to me, and I shall be sorry to see him slip away. But who is this young spark you have brought into what will soon be a house of mourning?'

Benoni said, 'This is Roland of whom you have often heard us speak.'

'Roland, is it? Well, if his wits have not gone wandering again, you may take him in. If my poor Milan gives him a father's blessing it is all he has to give, for I must tell you, young man, this house is mine and was so indeed before I made an honest working man of your father.'

'I seek nothing from him,' Roland said, 'and even a blessing will, I fear, avail me little.'

'As for you, young Ahmed, you limb of Satan,' the woman, Euphrosyne, said, 'make yourself useful for once in your idle life and fetch the young gentleman wine. Being a Frank, he will not be able to be long without it.'

So Benoni led Roland through to the chamber where Milan lay. Euphrosyne accompanied them. She sat on the bed and took the dying man by the hand, pressing it to her lips.

'Well, my dear, who'd have thought it? Here's your long-lost son – that's Roland, you remember – come to pay his respects. So smile nicely, there's my boy.'

Roland knelt by the bed. Milan extended a trembling hand, parchment skin drawn slack over bone.

Roland said, 'Father ...' a word he had never uttered in address.

Milan's lips moved. Words trickled like slow, heavy-falling drops of rain. 'Bertha ... so long ago ...'

His fingers tightened around Roland's hand, then fell away. Benoni touched Roland on the neck, indicating that they should leave. At the door Roland looked back. Euphrosyne was wiping his father's brow with a napkin soaked in hyssop. The dying man murmured what might have been an endearment; Roland could not be certain.

'He will be gone before it is night,' Benoni said. 'So long ago indeed since I poled your mother across the moat to Milan waiting in the forest, and we rode hard as we could for the hills.'

XXIX

While Roland was thus engaged in Byzantium, Charlemagne resolved to pass Christmas in Rome. In the first place his presence there would buttress the position of the Pope, already rendered insecure since Roland departed by the violence and factionalism of the great noble families, scoundrels one and all in my opinion. Secondly, where better to be than Rome itself when Roland brought word of the Empress Irene's agreement to share the Empire with him?

'You deceive yourself if you think he will succeed,' Ganelon said. 'A raw youth like my stepson, brave and vigorous though he may be, is quite without the subtlety that dealing with Greeks demands. That comes only with experience.'

Charles paid no heed. He still kept Ganelon by his side, on the grounds that he no longer trusted him and that it was better to have him under his eye; but his words fell on the King's ear like the wind whistling through a deserted house.

On the day of Christ's birth Charles crossed the Tiber to hear Mass at St Peter's. His mood was grave and reverent, and some Romans made this cause for criticism, believing that on such a day men should go to worship in light and joyous spirit. But the most part of the Romans cheered the King, being delighted to see that, in honour of the city, he had exchanged his Frankish dress (which Romans still thought barbarous) for the sandals and toga of a Roman patrician. For they regarded this as a tribute to the Eternal City and hence as evidence of their own importance.

Charles knelt in prayer by the high altar. Later he would say that it seemed as if at that moment St Peter himself spoke to him from the vaults where he lies buried (for the high altar of the basilica is placed directly above the sepulchre of the martyred apostle); and Charles averred that the saint addressed him as the 'new rock of Christ'.

But at that very moment, when the reading of the Gospel relating how Jesus was born in Bethlehem of Judaea was ended, the Pope descended from his throne, advanced towards Charles and, in the sight of all, placed the imperial diadem on his head, still bowed in prayer. Then the Pope placed his hands on Charles's shoulders in order to bless him, and called out in a clear loud voice: 'To Charles Augustus, crowned by God, the great and peace-giving Emperor of the Romans, be life and victory now and for ever more.'

All the congregation rose to acclaim the new-crowned Emperor, and the shouts of praise rose to the roof and to the heavens above, the cry taken up by the multitude gathered without.

Then the Pope anointed Charles with Holy Oil and resumed his chair, from which he spoke as follows to the congregation:

'It has long been a sadness and an offence to Almighty God that the city of Rome has been bereft of the imperial presence. Moreover, while some say that the name of emperor has ceased even among the Greeks, this is not so, but the Empire there is impiously held by the woman Irene, who by guile laid hold of her son the Emperor Constantine, imprisoned him, put out his eyes and took possession of the Empire herself, in the manner recorded of the wicked queen Athalia in the Book of Kings. Wherefore, having taken counsel with many worthy men, cardinals, bishops and senators, we, the successor to St Peter to whom our Lord granted the keys of Heaven, and also of that pontiff to whom the first Christian emperor Constantine entrusted the care and government of the Western Empire and the city of Rome when he departed hence to found his new city on the Bosphorus, we have determined to name Charles, King of the Franks, Emperor, seeing that he is a godly son of the Church and holds the city of Rome, which is the mother of Empire, where the caesars and emperors were ever used to sit; and we do this also that the heathen may not mock the Christians saying that the name of emperor has ceased among us.'

Again the Pope's words were greeted with loud acclamation, even though (as you will doubtless have remarked) his syntax was so awkward and involved that few of those who heard him will have been clear as to his exact meaning. But one who had no doubt was Charles himself, and it was observed that the longer the Holy Father spoke, the darker and more stern was the new Emperor's countenance.

Leaving the basilica, however, he played his part with genial dignity, bestowing alms on the poor and even engaging some of them in conversation. So it was not till he had returned to the Lateran Palace where he lodged, and was closeted alone with Bishop Turpin, that he permitted himself to give vent to his feelings; and this was a remarkable example of self-control such as he rarely displayed. But now he strode up and down the long gallery of the palace, his sandals flapping on the marble and his voice rising ever higher, so that to any ignorant of the Frankish tongue it would have sounded like shrill piping. Then he threw off the toga and cast aside the sandals, called for his Frankish garb and boxed the ears of the unfortunate page that fetched it.

'Never,' he said, 'never, and again never would I have entered the basilica had I known or suspected the trick that slimy Italian intended to play on me. He has outsmarted me for the moment but by Christ's blood he shall suffer for what he has done this day.'

Historians, reading the account given by the learned clerk Einhard in his *Life of Charles*, have not hesitated to accuse the Emperor of hypocrisy. They have no doubt that he sought the imperial crown, and in this they are, as I have shown, correct. But, foolishly, they miss the point, which is the manner of this coronation.

The matter has been much argued over, and remains vexed; and yet the true explanation is simple.

Charles had indeed gone to St Peter's that Christmas morning knowing that he would emerge from the basilica as Emperor. I say this with confidence, for I have come upon proof that he no longer hoped to receive the title with the consent and approval of the Empress Irene. And the proof is this: three weeks earlier he had sent to Roland commanding him to leave Constantinople, abandoning his mission, and to return post-haste to Rome where his presence was necessary and where a matter of great moment might be expected. That Charles did not say what this was may be accounted for by his fear lest his letter be intercepted by agents of the Empress's secret service. As it happened, his messenger was delayed by storms, and Roland did not receive the letter, the seal still unbroken, till the eve of the feast of the Epiphany, by which time the coronation in St Peter's had already been reported.

But Charles had had no intention that the Pope should place the crown on his head. On the contrary, he was prepared to take it from the Holy Father, kneeling humbly before him, and then place it on his own head, meanwhile intoning the formulaic words that the Pope took it on himself to pronounce.

Hence his fury. By performing the act of coronation, the Pope made it seem that it was he who created the Emperor, that indeed Charles was his creature, his vassal and dependent. And he emphasised this by declaring that he acted not only as the servant of God but by right of the so-called Donation of Constantine, which, as I have already demonstrated to you, my prince, was an outrageous fraud.

I dwell on this matter because the arrogant assumption of power by that Pope has deformed the history of all subsequent centuries. The struggles between the Empire and the papacy, which have been a sore blot on Christendom, all stem from this day when the Pope so manifestly asserted that the Empire was subsidiary to the papacy, for it has followed, as night succeeds day, that if this were so, then popes are entitled not only to raise up, crown and anoint emperors, but also to depose them. Which is against reason and the principles of good government.

And it is, I think, to Charles's credit that he saw this straight-way on that Christmas morning, and expressed his bitter fury. He did not speak out of wounded vanity, but from the fore-knowledge of trouble to come.

It was in an effort to avert this that, when Roland returned and he had questioned him closely, he did not desist from the attempt to persuade Byzantium to recognise his title as Emperor of the West. He even inquired of Roland whether this might be made possible by a marriage to the Empress Irene.

Roland replied, 'The Empress loves only a girl called Tabitha whom she has named Eos, saying she is lovely as the dawn.'

Charlemagne said, 'That need be no obstacle. We are not, nephew, talking of love, only of marriage.'

But, though Charles sent other emissaries to Constantinople, chief among them his English friend Alcuin of York, to explore the possibility of such an alliance, and even, if they thought fit, to propose marriage, all was in vain. Soon afterwards Irene was deposed and imprisoned, dying before long of starvation. The girl Tabitha's fate is not recorded. Roland always said that she was indeed second only to Angelica in beauty. So we may believe she found some other protector.

As for Roland, all observed that he was a changed being after Byzantium. He dressed always in black, talked little and looked grim. He spoke confidingly only to Oliver, who was now first in such affections as he could entertain. Angelica was, he now admitted, lost to him for ever, and Milan's death had moved him unexpectedly. He said to Oliver, wonderingly, 'I think he was happy. Benoni assured me he was, because he had cast away ambition. And yet it is that ambition which is the hope of glory that moves men. It was ambition that drove Alexander and Caesar and drives my uncle the Emperor. But in the end my father did not care what the world thought of him. I don't understand it.'

Benoni had not returned with him. He remained with Euphrosyne and the boy Ahmed keeping the Tavern of the Rosy Garden. He said to Roland, 'Dear boy, I can do nothing for you now.' Besides, he felt in his heart that Roland had come to resent him, as we resent those to whom we are under an obligation, and those who have known our weaknesses.

They embraced before they parted.

Then, watching Roland ride away, Benoni said to Ahmed, 'There is a doom on him and a fey look in his eye.'

Ahmed said, 'Be that as it may, all will be as the Lord has willed. And now there is much to be done before the clients come seeking pleasure in the garden.'

XXX

Charlemagne was old and now longed for peace. His body had rebelled against him. In cold wet weather his bones ached, his limbs were stiff and he felt the pain of his many wounds sharply. His son Charlot urged him to retire to a monastery and pass the government of the Empire over to him, but Charlemagne would not do so, for, he said, it was God's will he should soldier on; were it not so, the Lord would have taken him.

Charlot was aggrieved and consulted with Ganelon, who had become his most trusted adviser.

Ganelon pulled at his beard and frowned. 'My poor Prince,' he said, 'you will never persuade your father to do as you ask, for he loves power as a miser loves his gold. Besides which, there are those about him who spread calumnies concerning you. I have heard them with my own ears declare that you are not fit to succeed him, and never will be.'

'Who are these liars?' Charlot said. 'Tell me their names and I shall destroy them.'

'There is Bishop Turpin for one,' Ganelon said.

'He has never loved me. When I am Emperor I shall have him put to death, but I dare not now. He is my father's oldest and dearest friend.'

'As he used to be mine,' Ganelon said. 'Then there is Ogier the Dane.'

'That barbarian! When I am Emperor I shall have him hanged.'

'And Elgebast and the young paladin Ivor, who always agrees with him.'

'A brigand and a milksop. I shall lose no time in disposing of them when the Empire is mine.'

'And then there is your cousin Roland, who truly hates you.'

At that name the prince trembled. 'Roland,' he muttered. 'You say he hates me?'

'Certainly. He never loses an opportunity to speak badly of you to your father. I have heard him accuse you of cowardice when Marsilion besieged Paris and you rode away from the city.'

'In search of reinforcements,' Charlot said.

'Indeed yes, but the fact is, my Prince, that you will never be Emperor while Roland lives, for he is resolved to seize the throne for himself.'

The truth was that Ganelon's hatred and jealousy of Roland had reached such a pitch that he was now determined to destroy him. So he said to Charlot, 'You cannot afford to delay till you are Emperor to move against Roland, for while he lives you will never, as I say, sit on the throne which is yours by right of birth, and also of course by merit.'

As it happened, Roland was at this time engaged in suppressing the latest rebellion of the Saxons.

Ganelon said, 'This is your chance. There is an old saying that the absent are always wrong. Therefore, you may seize this opportunity to warn your father that Roland is conspiring against him.'

But Charlot dared not approach his father himself, for as he said, 'The Emperor loves Roland and will not believe me. Moreover, he always hates a man who brings him news that he does not want to hear.'

So Ganelon said, 'Fear not, I shall arrange matters,' and there was a note of contempt in his voice when he said 'fear not', in the knowledge that Charlot dared not do what he longed to do. 'I shall arrange matters,' he said again.

'If you destroy Roland,' Charlot said, 'I shall reward you generously, and give you all his lands in Brittany and Gascony when my father is dead.'

Ganelon left him and summoned his chaplain, Father Peter. Now this priest was a Saxon who also hated Roland, and had done so since the young man was a child at Sigmaringen. He had also, as I have already mentioned – but you may have forgotten since it was some way back in my tale – spent some years in Rome, working in the *curia*, which is, as you must know, the papal secretariat; and he had been the protégé and particular favourite of the Pope of the time. You will understand, therefore, that he was a man well-versed in duplicity and evil.

Moreover, he had now an additional reason to wish Roland brought low, for his brother had been one of the leaders of the Saxon rebellion, and Roland had taken him and condemned him as a traitor to the Emperor. All this Ganelon knew.

'I think you have no secrets from me,' he said to the priest.

'How should I have secrets from my lord and benefactor?'

'How indeed?' Ganelon said. 'For I am not only your benefactor, but also your protector.'

At this Father Peter flushed, hearing menace in Ganelon's words – the threat that this protection, which saved him from the consequences of many evil acts, might be withdrawn.

Ganelon said, 'The Duke Roland has put your brother to death as a traitor. Some might think you complicit with him.'

'Never, my lord,' the priest said. 'I am a faithful subject of the Emperor, and your own most loyal servant.'

'Just so,' Ganelon said. 'But it may be that your brother was no traitor.'

'I should like to think so.'

'I have reason,' Ganelon said, 'to believe that Duke Roland was preparing an alliance with two Saxon earls, who would join him in a rebellion that would enable him to become all-powerful in the State, supplant the Prince Charlot, and compel the Emperor to make him his co-partner in government, with the intention of reducing the aged Charlemagne to the wretched dependency of the last Merovings. Perhaps you have evidence that your brother had threatened to reveal this plot, and that it was for this reason that Duke Roland had him hanged. You have such evidence?'

'Such evidence?' the priest said, and for the first time in the conversation smiled. 'It might be obtained.'

'Might?' Ganelon said. 'Say, rather, "must". I have not forgotten that deposition you made concerning the alleged rape of the young daughter of the Comte d'Ivry. But if you satisfy me in this matter, it shall be returned to you, and I shall see to it that when Charlot succeeds his father, you will be rewarded with a bishopric.'

So, by a mixture of threats and promises, Ganelon induced the miserable priest to concoct a letter purporting to come from his brother which accused Roland of plotting treason; and he himself took it to Charlemagne.

'I scarcely dare,' he said, 'to give you this letter. Its contents pain me indescribably, and will distress you equally. Moreover, I know how unwelcome the bearer of bad news is, and I hesitated, therefore, fearing that your righteous wrath might be turned against me.'

'We are an old and experienced king,' Charlemagne said, 'and know well how to discriminate between bad news and its bearer.'

Whereupon he stretched out his hand, took the letter from Ganelon and read it slowly; and while he did so, his countenance remained impassive.

I ask you, my Prince, to pity Charlemagne at this moment. He had come truly to love Roland and to value him. There was no man, not even Turpin or Alcuin or York, on whom he now placed more reliance. Roland was the lion by his throne. Conscious of the ravages of advancing years, Charlemagne had been content to grant his nephew unprecedented powers. But the nature of monarchy is such that kings can never place absolute trust in any man; they live behind a veil of suspicion. Power makes for solitude, and in the loneliness of absolute power trust is a fragile plant that soon withers. They live in fear of conspiracy, in fear of evil, and so surrender often to the evil of fear.

This was now Charlemagne's condition. He could not believe Roland guilty of treason; and yet he could not believe him innocent. Once the canker of suspicion enters the mind, the faculty of judgement is itself corrupted.

As for Ganelon, cunning and unscrupled as the serpent, he well knew the power of calumny. It is like the ivy that clings to the trunk of a tree and, creeping all over it, hides the ruin that it feeds upon. It is like a fever that spreads through the city.

Moreover, Ganelon was prudent and cautious as he was wicked. Having planted the calumnious seed in the Emperor's mind, he drew back. Of course, he insinuated, he did not believe what the letter said. It was mischievous, or based on a misunderstanding. It was impossible that one so noble and generous as his stepson Roland, the boy he had tenderly reared, could be guilty of such monstrous disloyalty and ingratitude.

And yet he had felt it his duty to acquaint the King with the allegation, just in case ... after all, as the saying goes, there is no smoke without fire. So, now advancing, now withdrawing, now denying, now suggesting, he disturbed Charlemagne.

Then he went to Irma his wife, who had formerly been the Emperor's mistress and who had ever hated Roland. He told her to go lovingly to Charlemagne, to express sympathy with him in his perplexity, to praise Roland and then to insinuate that his temper was nevertheless masterful and jealous. Of course, she was to say, Roland loves you as we all do, and admires you, and is loyal to you; and yet I have often heard him speak rashly – for he is sometimes intemperate and violent – of his hatred and contempt for Charlot your son. I have heard him say that Charlot is unfit to succeed to so glorious a monarch, and that some means must be found to prevent it.

'So it seems to me,' she went on, 'that the conspiracy is aimed not at you, my lord – for who could wish you harm? Certainly not our dear Roland – but at Charlot, and that you yourself have nothing to fear but being made subject to Roland's will, which is powerful. I speak as one who knew him as an ungovernable child, you must remember.'

Then she sought to divert him by talking of other matters, but the more she did so, the more Charlemagne brooded on the matter, and the more he felt the enfeeblement of old age. His former power of decision seemed to have deserted him. He dared not charge Roland, he dared not think him guilty, and yet he could not acquit him in his mind. He passed many hours in prayer, and rose from his knees, his prayers unanswered. He did not dare consult even Bishop Turpin or Elgebast, for fear that they should think him weak. And who knew? They might even be in league with Roland, partners in the conspiracy. Such doubts, extending even to his oldest friends and confidants, were the poisonous fruits of calumny.

At last Roland returned in triumph from the Saxon war, declaring the rebellion crushed. His mood was sunny, his face flushed in victory. He looked for the Emperor's praise, and found it grudgingly given. Charlemagne received him not coldly, but with uncertainty. Roland could not understand it. Was it possible that the Emperor was failing, that he did not grasp the magnitude of Roland's achievement? Could he perhaps be jealous?

Roland found the atmosphere of the court strange, even hostile. Ganelon had been busy. Without saying anything specific, he had been active spreading hints; 'it may be that' and 'if I do not misdoubt me', he muttered in the ear of courtiers. They, sensing the direction of the wind, now shunned Roland. He had been the favourite. If he were now about to fall, it were better to be distant from him. No one knew what was what, but rumour ran round the palace like rats in a store-house. Charlot gathered the young men about him, had them swear oaths of allegiance, hinted that he was in danger, promised them rich rewards when his father was no more. He said nothing of Roland, but spoke often of his enemies, and none doubted whom he meant.

It was Oliver at last who, after diligent enquiry, caught the scent. He came at once to Roland and told him he was the victim of calumny.

'There is a plot against you,' he said. 'What form it has taken and who devised it I cannot discover, but your enemies have the ear of the Emperor, and they are determined to destroy you. I have no doubt of that.'

Roland was first astonished, then anger swelled up within him. His first impulse was to go directly to Charlemagne and demand that he learn what lies were being told about him. But Oliver, who had consulted with Elgebast and Ivor, two friends who had remained loyal, advised against this. Charlemagne, they thought, would prevaricate. 'Elgebast says,' Oliver reported, 'you must take the bull by the horns in another and public fashion.'

So, following their counsel, Roland bided his time till all the Frankish chivalry was assembled in the great hall of Engelheim for the feast of St Michael the Archangel. Roland sat at the Emperor's right hand in the seat or siege which was customarily occupied by Charlot, but he had chosen to be absent, though none knew why.

When they had eaten, and before the minstrels were summoned to renew their music, Roland rose to his feet and stood, glorious as if he had been the Archangel himself, surveying the company.

Silence fell, a silence that was anxious, even fearful. All sensed that some matter of great import was to be disclosed. All eyes were turned upon him, and no man even raised his goblet to drink.

'Is there any knight or baron assembled here who doubts my loyalty to the Emperor my uncle?' Roland asked, and his voice rang out clear and challenging as the trumpet of war.

No man dared lift his voice in reply, but all continued to gaze on Roland as if transfixed.

'I have returned from a mighty war against the Saxons,' Roland said. 'In this war I slew tens of thousands of the rebels, destroyed twenty castles built without the imperial authority, advanced far beyond the rivers, Oder and Neisse, laying waste the lands of those pagan tribes who had given support to the rebellion, and compelled threescore chiefs to submit to Christian baptism. I added new territories to the Empire and restored the land of the Saxons to peace and order. All this for the Emperor's glory and the prosperity of the Frankish realm. And now, instead of being greeted with garlands and songs of praise, I find myself the victim of calumny. I am received with cold looks and muttered words. My friends tell me that I am suspected of treason. Therefore, I say, if any man is bold enough to maintain such charges against me, charges which are vile lies and slanders, let him engage with me in single combat. I throw down my gauntlet, and, three hours after dawn on the morrow, you will find me mounted and accoutred in the lists of the tournament ground, ready to defend and assert my honour against any who consider themselves my enemies and who hold me guilty of treason.'

With these words he turned, bowed low to Charlemagne, and marched out of the hall, followed by his four faithful friends, Oliver, Elgebast, Ivor and Ogier the Dane.

Bishop Turpin crumbled bread and drank his wine. 'Finely spoken,' he said. 'Will any dare to meet the challenge?'

The next morning Roland was ready in the lists as he had promised. He sat his horse from three hours after dawn till three hours after noon. But no man rode against him.

In this way his honour was vindicated. Charlemagne was

persuaded that his fears and suspicions were without foundation and Ganelon and Charlot were left confused and still more embittered, determined to find some other means to destroy the man they now feared as greatly as they hated.

XXXI

Some time after this – but how long had elapsed I cannot tell, for the chroniclers are vague and wandering in their dating of events – King Marsilion, chafing still over the failure to take Paris and the humiliation he had there endured, once more resolved to make war on the Franks. He sent raiding forces first deep into Aquitaine, and many a noble knight was slain defending his castle and his honour. Then he made an alliance with the Basques, mountain folk who inhabit the valleys on either side of the great range of the Pyrenees. These Basques are a sturdy, high-mettled people who are loth to accept any man as lord, and, because Charlemagne had made Roland Duke of Gascony, a title that carries rights of suzerainty over the tribes who dwell on the northern side of the mountains, they felt a particular ill-will towards their new master. Nor was this diminished by Roland's firm rule, for the Basques declare themselves to be a free people. There is indeed much to admire in them, but they make for uneasy neighbours, and not only because they speak a language that no other Christian can understand. Nevertheless, they are reputed to be devout in their faith, if also of a heretical disposition. They refuse to acknowledge any bishop appointed by pope or emperor, but insist on electing one of their own; and some of their priests deny the realities of Purgatory and Hell. This is known as the Pelagian heresy, and its attraction is evident, for if there is no Hell, then nothing is forbidden and all permitted. Accordingly, the Basques think it no sin to break their word when that has been given to a foreigner. But their high sense of honour ensures that their loyalty to each other is fixed as the Polar star.

When winter came, Marsilion retired to Saragossa, his stronghold, well pleased with his summer's work. But some of his barons came to him as he sat in his orchard, and one, Blancandrin, upbraided him.

'My Lord King,' he said, 'I am told you are pleased with your summer's work, and indeed I read satisfaction in your eye. But consider: is it wise to twist a lion's tail, or to dance before a fighting bull, enraging it? That, I fear, is what you have done, my Lord King, and all that you have done. Your little raids into the fair land of Aquitaine have delivered no mortal blow to your enemies. You have merely pricked them, as if with a pin, not buried your sword deep in their belly. Do you think Charlemagne will not seek revenge?'

Marsilion smiled. 'Blancandrin, Lord of Valfonda,' he said. 'There is no one whose counsel I value more than yours, but in this case you are wrong. Charlemagne, the Emperor, is old, his beard is white as the snow on the high mountain-tops. He is weary of war and content to amuse himself with his mistresses. Moreover, I did not embark on this expedition without seeking allies from among the Franks. There is the Emperor's son, Charlot, who has engaged to grant me Aquitaine when his father dies in return for the tenscore gallant knights I have promised him to secure his throne. And there is the Duke Ganelon, a noble man and one who sees no cause for dissension between Christendom and Islam. Should Charlemagne speak of war, Ganelon will be the voice of peace that dissuades him. And he knows he will be well rewarded, and that the many presents I have already sent him are but a token of the riches I am ready to lavish on him. So there is no need to be afraid.'

Blancandrin nodded. 'All you say may be true, my Lord King, but, from what I have heard, Charlot is a poltroon, and Ganelon may have less influence over Charlemagne than you suppose. The truce we made at his instigation when we were camped before Paris did not hold. Have you forgotten that? And have you forgotten the Duke Roland, who is so mighty in war and so implacable a foe of the True Religion? You have suborned the Basques, whom he counts as his vassals, and made an alliance with them. Do you suppose he will not seek revenge? And Roland is the leading man among the Franks.'

So the argument raged among the Saracens, some backing

Marsilion, others Blancandrin. But even the former group were apprehensive, wondering what the Franks would do when spring touched the trees with green.

Even before the snow began to melt on the lower slopes, there came word that a great army was being assembled to cross the Pyrenees. Charlemagne, it was reported, had bestirred himself, and, though unable to sit a horse and confined to a litter, was coming by slow stages from the north. Meanwhile, Roland led raiding parties against the Basques, defeating them in several skirmishes, killing many and taking prisoners. It was said that he had demanded hostages – a son from every Basque chief – and would not be satisfied till all were delivered.

'Do you think the Basques will hold true to their alliance?' was the question anxiously put among the Saracen nobility.

Not even Charlemagne had ever led a more mighty army than that which now crossed the Pyrenees. The Basques, cowed by the ferocity of Roland's raids, and mindful of the hostages he had taken, dared not resist. They retired into the uttermost depths of their valleys like men who take shelter in a cave to escape the fury of a thunderstorm.

The Franks themselves were jovial, riding gaily, eager in the hope of winning renown and acquiring much booty. It is, my Prince, one of the strange quirks of human nature that, though every man knows war is terrible, and that even the bravest of knights will one day be as the dust, the first stages of a campaign are days of song and laughter. And yet it has always seemed to me that no commander is entitled to be light-hearted when he launches war, for, in the course of battle, many men will go to a horrid death, some unshriven, women will be made widows and children left fatherless. Bear in mind, my Prince, that the monarch who embarks on war must charge his soul with a load of responsibility that weighs heavy as lead. It may not always be possible to avoid war, but no war should be fought that is not just.

There are many learned doctors who affirm that any war fought against pagans or heretics is by its very nature just. But I cannot agree, and not only because I have a regard amounting to affection for the followers of Mohammed, whom I do not scruple to call my brothers. For are they not mortal men as we are? Do they not feel pain and experience joy as we do? Is it not a fact that they love their wives and children, and may be as brave and loyal friends one to another, as any Christian?

Truly, my dear Prince, we should live in peace, side by side, each ready to honour the other's Faith, and to learn one from another. For if we have any purpose in this world, it should be to pursue knowledge and wisdom, not to fight and slaughter. I am an old man, my Prince, who has seen much and pondered deeply on all manner of questions, and in my travels and hours of study I have learned this: that if we are to escape from the desolate landscape of injustice, if we are to rise from the pit, shaking off the slime that has coated us, we must first pull down vanity.

Let me dwell a moment on that word, vanity. It has two meanings. The first is that of the preacher who cries out, 'Vanity of vanities, all is vanity.' In this sense it means emptiness. Now, what is this emptiness? It is firstly the feeling or conviction that there is nothing worth attempting; but secondly, if I may coin a phrase which will come, I fear, all too easily to the lips and tongues of future generations, it is a moral vacuum. By that I mean it ushers in a world in which right and wrong have lost all meaning, in which there is no place for that simple and soiled word 'kindness' (the word is soiled but not the thing which remains the expression of the best there is in our nature), a world (to conclude) in which there is no law but the law of power. There has never been a monarch, I fear, who has not felt the attraction of this sort of vanity. Was it this vanity that now drew Charlemagne and Roland across the mountains into Spain?

The other meaning of vanity is the common one, or, as some would say, the vulgar. (Never, my Prince, come to despise something simply because it is called common or vulgar; all that means is that it is judged good by the majority of men and women.) In this sense vanity may be defined as excessive self-regard. Note the qualifying epithet. Self-regard is good to a degree, for the man who has no regard for himself will have no sense of honour, no sense of shame and, as I have observed, no regard for others. But the excessive self-regard, which I call vanity, is dangerous and destructive. He who surrenders to vanity finds his judgement destroyed. Blinded by his self-regard, he can no longer see others as they are. They exist only in relation to him, and it is to his mind proper that they be subjected to his will. If they resist, he experiences resentment, which corrupts his judgement further.

Were Charlemagne and Roland subject to this vanity also? I see you are impatient, eager for me to resume my narrative. But nevertheless, I implore you, my Prince, to consider this question: was their war in any true sense of the word necessary?

Certainly they had been sore provoked by Marsilion, himself a victim of this foolish vanity. But would it not have been enough to garrison the passes through the Pyrenees, and so to have prevented any future incursion? Charlemagne talked, you will recall, of the beauty of peace, and indeed said, often, that the meaning of Empire is peace. Yet now his sword leapt from the scabbard. He revered the Emperor Augustus. Yet the proudest moment in that Emperor's reign came when the doors of the Temple of Janus, the two-headed god, were closed, denoting that there was peace throughout the Empire and even on its frontiers. It was also the wise Augustus who established the limits of Empire, even though his poet, the noble and magnificent Virgil, tells us in his epic poem how the god Jupiter had promised Aeneas (father of the Roman people) and his descendants 'empire without limits'. Forgetting the example of the emperor he admired above all others, Charlemagne now blundered into a terrible war.

At first all went well for the Franks. Moving with a speed that took the Saracens by surprise (even though the Emperor in his litter lagged several days' march behind the vanguard commanded by Roland), the Franks attacked the Saracen army outside Burgos while it was still mustering and awaiting contingents advancing from the south and from North Africa beyond Spain. The Frankish chivalry did great execution that day and scattered the paynim as the autumn gales blow leaves from the trees. They encamped on the battlefield. Bishop Turpin sang the *Te Deum* and the minstrels – young troubadours – made verses in praise of the mighty and glorious Roland, numbering the Saracen chiefs who had fallen to the strokes of his sword, Durendal, which name means 'enduring', the sword that was never blunt, and which that evening shone red with paynim blood. 'Leopard or lion was never fierce as Roland,' they sang. 'Golden is his fame. Even as the deer before the deerhounds flee, so also before Roland the paynim reel.'

In his tent Roland lay at ease. One squire polished his armour, another rubbed his limbs and back with oil. He smiled to hear the voices raised to salute his deeds. 'A good day's work,' he said to Oliver, and sent to Charlemagne to acquaint him with news of the victory gained in his name.

The next morning the Franks entered the city and looted it. Some took women to themselves. Others loaded mules with plunder and sent them under guard back to the main body of the army, and thence to their estates in France. They set fire to the mosques, but, at the urging of Bishop Turpin, Roland commanded that the great library of the famous scholar Ahmed bin-Iskander be preserved.

Towards evening, the six richest Jews of the city, who had been found taking refuge in the catacombs below their synagogue, were brought before Roland. Charged with collusion with the Saracens, they found no excuses but the truth that they had been constrained. Caught as they wretchedly were between the Scylla of Mohammed and the Charybdis of Christ, they appeased the Franks by opening their treasure to them (but, prudently, it is said, reserving in case of future need, the greatest part of their gold, silver and jewels which they had buried in a secret place).

Some commanders might have tarried in Burgos, relishing their victory, speaking of the need to consolidate and waiting for the main body of the army, with the Emperor himself at its head, to reinforce them. But this was never Roland's way. If anyone proposed such a delay, pointing out that the Saracen army would itself now have been strengthened by the arrival of the African levies, Roland merely shrugged aside such objections. 'The essence of war,' he said, 'is speed.'

He called a council, if only for form's sake, knowing that the pride of the great barons would be sore offended if they did not believe they had been consulted, and when he had listened to what they had to say, which he did with a patience that was foreign to his noble and impetuous character, he said simply, 'An army withers and stagnates if it does not fight. The enemy is before us. They will have been dismayed by the first encounter. Therefore we attack and attack and attack.'

To the troops mustered to march south from Burgos, he spoke as follows:

'Soldiers! You are far from home, and we march against an enemy we have shaken but not destroyed. I make no promises to you, but I tell you that yonder below us lies the rich land of Spain that once was Christian and is now under the heel of the Infidel. I offer you the hope of glory and I shall lead you over harsh and dangerous country until we descend to the land of orchards and olive groves and great wealth. That wealth will be yours for the taking.'

So, appealing simultaneously to their love of glory and their greed, he mounted his horse, and ordered the standard to be raised.

And, to the sound of trumpets and the beat of drums, the Frankish army marched out of Burgos.

For three days they traversed a barren land, brown and rocky. The villages were empty, for their inhabitants had fled before the approach of Roland and taken refuge like the coneys among the hill-places. Even Christians, as many of the peasants still were, were stricken with fear of the Franks, and hid, for they believed that Roland was marked with the sign of the Devil; and some among them held that the Franks were man-eaters.

Meanwhile, Marsilion had assembled a great army at the city of Vascos, which is in Castile, and when he drew it up in battle array it was a wondrous sight, for all the chivalry of Islam from the deserts of Arabia and the rich pastures of Morocco had been summoned to Spain to resist the Franks. The line of battle stretched a Roman mile, and the air was bright with the fluttering of silk pennons and the glint of sunlight on steel. The Barbary horses and pure-bred Arabians pawed the earth and neighed, scenting the battle. Marsilion himself sat on a high ivory throne before the city gate, and he smiled to see the grandeur of his army.

He said: 'They told me this Duke Roland was a mighty man of valour, and so indeed he may be. Yet I am happy to discover that he is also rash and unskilled in the art of war. Else he would not have pressed so hard upon us, but would have awaited the arrival of Charlemagne with all his host. A wise man once said that a king should learn to divide his enemies that he might rule them. Our enemies have divided themselves. So we shall surely conquer. Three generations back my great-grandsire invaded France and was driven back, his army destroyed, by that other Charles whom the Franks called "the Hammer", on account of the execution he made among the faithful that awful day. This morning shall see my great-grandsire revenged and the Franks utterly defeated.'

With these words he retired into his tent to pray to Allah, and was assured, men say, that victory would be his.

Roland sat his horse surveying the scene, so still and calm that man and horse looked as if they had been carved by some noble artist from a block of marble. The sky was a deep blue and there was no wind. Two falcons hovered overhead, and on the roof of the great bell-tower of the city a pair of storks, indifferent to the impending conflict, were building or repairing their nest. The Frankish knights had dismounted, both to rest their horses and to check their accoutrements and harness, especially the saddle-girths, for every knight was aware that the breaking or slipping of a girth might cost him his life. Women, camp-followers, moved through the ranks of the army dispensing water and wine, and some of them kisses also to the men-at-arms and archers who took their fancy. Bishop Turpin raised his mighty voice in prayer, and, as he did so, a solemn hush fell on the army, and even the bravest commended their souls to God in whom they trusted.

'Aye, very fine,' Elgebast said to Ivor in an undertone that others might not hear. 'Very fine, but for my part I trust to iron and my good horse Jubilee.'

'And I to my Moll,' Ivor said, 'for I have never had a braver or more sure-footed beast.'

'And I observe,' Elgebast said, with a wry smile, 'that the Saracens pray no less earnestly than we do, and I do not think that God can answer the prayers of both.'

Ivor smiled again, for he had often heard Elgebast speak in this vein, but another Frankish baron, Tibbald of Rheims, who had overheard the last part of this conversation, said sternly, 'Not so, Elgebast, for ours is the One True God and ours the

True Religion, while the paynim worship a false god devised by that camel-driver Mohammed.'

'So you say, Tibbald,' Elgebast said. 'So you say, but for my part I have ever found that battles are fought by men, not gods.'

At this Tibbald grew heated, and his hand flew to the pommel of his sword as if he would have challenged Elgebast, but Roland now called them to him where he stood with Oliver, and gave out the order of battle. Elgebast and Ivor would lead their regiment against the Moorish horse-archers, for, Roland said, 'They must be driven from the field early in the conflict. It is a rule of war that archers be not permitted to hold their ground. You, Tibbald, will command the reserve, while I, with Oliver at my right hand, will charge the centre of the enemy line where I observe Marsilion has drawn up his veterans.'

Tibbald, who feared that he would be denied the chance of glory, said, 'Duke Roland, Marsilion himself, as I observe, commands his army from the rear in order that he may respond to the course of the battle by making rapid dispositions. This to my mind is the proper place for the general-in-chief, and indeed it is that which Charlemagne himself is accustomed to occupy.'

'My uncle is old and his beard is white,' Roland said, 'but I am young and in the prime of life, and I lead from the front. Moreover I trust you, Tibbald, to be able to make any necessary – what did you call them? – dispositions.'

With these words he raised his horn to his lips and gave the signal to advance. Then he pulled down his visor and rode forward at the head of his knights. Never can there have been a more glorious sight than the bold array of the Frankish army as, firm in line and gathering speed, it crossed the deserted ground between the armies and launched itself at the Saracens.

(I say 'glorious', my Prince, even though I have, as you know, a deep loathing of war, and look forward to the day of universal peace that shall surely dawn, if not, alas, in my lifetime, so wicked is the world.)

The force of the Frankish chivalry struck the Saracen line like a mighty torrent rushing down a steep valley carrying rocks and torn-up trees before it. Never was there such an onslaught as that which Roland delivered that day. He himself stood high in his stirrups, calling on his men to follow him, to strike hard and give no quarter, and strike hard they did, terrible to behold. The first charge broke the Saracen line; it was like nothing the battle-hardened veterans of King Marsilion had encountered before. Brave men though they were, they were scattered like chaff. The few who formed themselves into a square and tried to resist were all cut down. Roland himself did great execution; his sword was red with Moorish blood from point to hilt.

In another part of the field the Saracens fared no better. Their archers fled even as Elgebast broke through the ranks of paynim knights and led the charge against them. Some few, turning in their saddles, loosed their arrows, before seeking safety in rapid flight. By ill chance, one arrow struck Ivor in the eye and he fell from his horse. The gallant Moll stood over her fallen master, protecting his body, little knowing, poor beast, that Ivor's life was ebbing away.

Marsilion, watching from his high vantage point, was over-come by despair and seized by terror. He fled into the city and, pausing only to mount a horse and snatch up a sack containing his jewels, rode off by the southern gate.

It is said that the great battle lasted no longer than a quarter of an hour, and that evening one of Roland's minstrels sang that its duration was as brief as the flight of a swallow through a hall.

'All Spain is ours,' Roland said, 'but where is Elgebast and where is Ivor?'

They found the old brigand kneeling by the body of his friend, cradling his head and weeping. Moll stood by him, not restless as horses are when they smell death, but still and reverent as a mourner. Now Roland and Oliver wept also, for Ivor had been the gentlest and most courteous of knights.

Only when they had laid him to rest by the light of the summer moon did Elgebast stay his tears.

He said: 'He was so afraid when the King sent him with Yves to seek me out in the forest so long ago, and yet he conquered his fear, which is the true mark of courage.'

XXXII

The Saracens had escaped like rabbits (as Roland put it to Charlemagne). They were dismayed, desolate and perplexed. Why had Allah permitted such misfortune? Allah the merciful, Allah the all-powerful. For what backsliding, what sins, was this disaster the penalty?

Men think like this, Christians and Mohammedans alike, ever more ready to attribute misfortune to divine displeasure than fortune to God's favour. It is natural, I suppose. Our successes are our own, but failure rarely our fault. The ability to look reality in the face, and accept it for what it is, has been denied to the common run of man.

The Saracens withdrew in confusion to Cordoba, city of gardens and fountains, orange and lemon groves, of arcades and palaces, of mosques, synagogues and even a handful of Christian churches. (For the emirs had not then outlawed the practice of our religion, believing it must wither in the blazing truth of Islam.)

Marsilion called his councillors together.

'You know, my lords,' he said, 'how sore afflicted we are. The Franks have proved too strong for us, and men say that Allah has abandoned our cause. This I cannot believe, for my faith in Allah the ever-merciful is strong and pure, firm as the great rock of Gibraltar. Nevertheless, whether we are being punished on account of our sins, as the mullahs allege, or not, the fact is that we have suffered two terrible defeats and our men daily desert and seek their homes. What shall we do? Who will propose that which will save me from death and the loss of my renown?'

For a little no man dared speak, all being afraid to say what was in their mind: that Marsilion himself was responsible for the disaster and his renown already lost. But then at last

Blancandrin, Emir of Valfonda, cleared his throat and called attention to himself.

'It were vain now,' he said, 'to remind you of how I argued that it was folly to provoke the Franks and draw their army into Spain to avenge themselves for our raids across the mountains into France, and for our actions in inciting the Basques to rebel against them. It is no satisfaction to me that I have been proved right. But at least this permits me now to speak with some authority. Therefore, Marsilion, my Lord King, this is my counsel.

'You should seek to appease the Frankish Emperor's wrath and wounded pride by promising him your faithful service and your friendship from this day on. Prove your sincerity by sending him rich gifts: lions, bears and hounds, camels and mewed hawks – for he is devoted to falconry, and all the world knows that there are no hawks to match those of Spain. Send him also pack-mules laden with gold and silver, and a wagon-train of treasure so that he may offer his soldiers rich rewards which will cure them of the itch to make war on us. Submit in all humility and you will find that Charles himself will be satisfied. He is an old man and will be eager to return to Aix and his palace of Engelheim. Promise that at Michaelmas, which is his most favoured Christian feast, you will present yourself there, as vassal to the Christian lord. Yes, even promise that you will henceforth be subject to the Christian law.'

At these words a murmur of discontent ran round the company. Though none dared call for continued resistance to the Franks, yet equally few were prepared for the humiliation the Lord of Valfonda argued must be theirs. Some cried out in defiance, 'never', or 'for shame', but Blancandrin, magnificent in stature, silenced them with uplifted hand.

'It may be,' he said, 'that this will not be enough. Charles may demand hostages. You must let him have them, even our own sons. Believe me, my Lord King, I swear by my right hand and my long beard that if you do as I say, the Franks will turn away, eager to be home. Charles will take his ease at Aix, far from Spain. Then, at Michaelmas, the trysting-day, either you present yourself and swear to be his liege, or you send no news, no message, to him, and he kills the hostages. That is for you to decide, but all I have further to say is this: better the hostages, even our sons, should die, than that Spain should be subject to the Franks, and the Faithful be oppressed.'

For a long time Marsilion pondered these words, delaying an answer in the hope that some other means of escape might present itself to him. But there was none. Therefore he commanded Blancandrin, as the author of the proposal, to go to Charles and speak as he had advised.

'Carry an olive branch,' the King said, 'bedewed with my bitter tears.'

So Blancandrin rode out of Cordoba with other Saracen lords that the deputation might seem impressive; and among them was Yusuf, the King's son, who admired Roland.

Charlemagne received the Saracen envoys, sitting on a throne beneath a tall pine-tree. His manner was both courteous and haughty, displaying his high and noble breeding, but also his distrust. When Blancandrin had spoken, which he did eloquently and in a fashion that impressed all who heard him, the Emperor said, 'I know you, Emir of Valfonda, as a brave knight and one with a high reputation. But why should I believe your master, who has broken his word before now, who invaded the fair land of France in despite of his promises, and raised up my vassals in rebellion against me?'

Blancandrin said: 'My Lord Emperor, I should wish to believe that my Lord King Marsilion's word was enough warranty of his good faith. And yet, I know that you Christians are ever distrustful of us who follow the law of the Prophet Mohammed – though I regret this and assure you that you are mistaken in this distrust, for our word is as good and worthy of honour as yours, saving Your Majesty. Yet, as I say, I understand you, and so does my Lord King Marsilion. Therefore, as surety, we shall surrender hostages, all of noble birth, my son and the king's son Yusuf here among them. And if my Lord King Marsilion does not present himself at your palace in Aix come the feast of the Archangel Michael, and there submit to you as your vassal, swearing allegiance and being baptised into your Christian faith, even though such apostasy is sore humiliation, why then the hostages' lives will be forfeit. And I can say no fairer than that.'

Then Charles asked Blancandrin to step aside while he consulted with his council.

There was much argument among the Frankish chiefs, with some saying one thing and some another, and so they debated while the sun rose high in the heavens and passed its zenith. And Charlemagne listened patiently to all that was said, for, in old age, this had become his custom, to let argument exhaust itself before he pronounced. At last he said, 'You have all spoken well, and given me much matter to ponder. But there are two among you who have remained silent, from whom I would wish to hear: you, Roland; and you, Ganelon.'

Roland first rose, beautiful as the morning, and when he spoke there was scorn in his voice.

'I have not spoken till now, uncle,' he said, 'because the argument is vain, the matter scarce meriting debate. What it comes down to is this: we are invited to trust Marsilion and retreat from Spain at the very moment when we are poised to become masters of this rich land and to regain it for Christendom. And what does he offer in exchange? Merely a promise that, come Michaelmas, he will present himself at Engelheim to swear allegiance to you and to accept Christian baptism. And, as earnest of his good faith, he will surrender hostages. But why should we believe him? Marsilion has proved himself a liar many times. By Michaelmas, when we are long gone from Spain, he will have repaired his defences and brought new armies from Africa. In my opinion his word is worthless, and when he breaks it, as he surely will, we shall find we have gained nothing by this war in which so many noble men have fallen, among them Ivor, beloved by all. As for the hostages, never doubt, my uncle, that Marsilion does not give a docken for what becomes of them. He will see their heads lopped off and will not care, so long as he himself is secure in Spain. This at least is my opinion and my counsel which you demanded. Refuse his offer and let us smite him again and make our conquest complete.'

Roland's bold words evoked a murmur of agreement, but Charlemagne listened impassively, then called on Ganelon to speak.

He said: 'Sire, your nephew, who is also my dear stepson, speaks as we would expect him to speak, and the course he advocates is certainly bold. But it is also reckless. Certainly the war has gone well for us – so far. Roland has won himself great renown, and, because he loves war, he is eager to pursue it further to gratify his own ambition, his love of glory. That is all very well. But I am an older man who has seen more of the world than Roland, and I know how abruptly the fortunes of war may turn. Unlike Roland I am learned in history, and I know that no man can be assured of success for ever. The great Persian King Xerxes was confident of victory when he made war on Greece, but was defeated by an inferior force. Likewise, the Romans knew Pompey the Great as the darling of Mars, their god of war, but he was brought low and was ignominiously slain.

'Suppose, however, that Roland is right in thinking that one more battle would give us mastery of all Spain. What then? Think you the Saracens will be content to see Spain lost to Islam, that they will submit to subjection? I say no, for they are a proud people. We should be faced with rebellion after rebellion, and then the emirs of Africa would proclaim a *jihad* or holy war against us, and this war would be terrible, perhaps perpetual. It would drain us of our life-blood. Moreover, while we were constrained to fight for years on end as it may be here in Spain, is it likely that the Saxons would not seize the opportunity to rebel yet again and this time perhaps successfully? My lord, it is not wise to push fortune to the extremity. Marsilion's offer is fair and good, and one that does you great honour. The man who urges you to reject it cares nothing for the general good of the Franks or the prosperity of your Empire, but only for his own glory. Therefore, I say, turn deaf ears to reckless counsel. That is my opinion.'

Charlemagne, in the wisdom of age, sensed that Ganelon's words had persuaded even many of those who had applauded Roland's bold speech. Therefore, he gave approval to the proposal and asked his councillors who should be chosen to lead the embassy to Marsilion.

Roland again stood up.

'Because I distrust the Saracen King,' he said, 'I am the man to be your ambassador. One thing is certain: Marsilion fears me, and will not dare to try to pull the wool over my eyes.'

But others said no, believing that Roland was too high of spirit and quick to take offence, that he would land himself in some quarrel and the embassy would founder.

Then several others proposed themselves, or different candidates, but the Emperor approved none of them.

At this point, my Prince, I part company with the noble and eloquent author of the *Chanson de Roland*, my principal source for this debate. He says that Roland now proposed his stepfather Ganelon for the task, and that Ganelon flung back his great furred robe of marten and burst forth in fury, declaring that he would not trust himself in Marsilion's camp and that Roland had named him in order to destroy him. Our poet has him say, 'I am thy stepsire, and all these know I am, yet me thou namest to seek Marsilion's camp' – as if, being in that relation to Roland, his life would be endangered.

But this is ridiculous, and not only because in the summer heat of Spain it is improbable that Ganelon would have been wearing a furred robe of marten. It is ridiculous because Roland hoped that the embassy would fail, and therefore cannot have proposed Ganelon as its leader, since he was the man most eager it should succeed.

It is, of course, possible that the poet is right and that Roland did indeed propose his stepfather, thinking that Ganelon would suspect a trick and so try to decline the honour, as the poet says he did. But this seems to me too subtle and duplicitous for Roland. And so I think the poet was confused, as poets often are.

Be that as it may, Charlemagne approved the choice of Ganelon, and he set forth the next day in company with Blancandrin and the other Saracen lords.

XXXIII

Blancandrin and Duke Ganelon rode side by side through the fair land of Spain, and as they rode, they talked, and as they talked they came to understand each other.

'I marvel at your Emperor Charlemagne,' Blancandrin said.

'And you are right to do so, for he is truly the wonder of the world.'

'So old,' Blancandrin said, 'so infirm that he cannot now sit a horse, so replete with glory. Will he never desist from war? Will he never weary?'

'That's as may be,' was Ganelon's reply.

'You and I,' the Saracen said, 'are men who have seen much of war, and done great execution in it.'

'Indeed yes,' said Ganelon, and so they rode on through the groves of olives and cork oaks.

'When you are young,' Blancandrin said, 'war seems glorious, but do you see these birds hovering high above us, and do you know what they are? They are vultures and they love war, too, for they feast on the bodies slain in battle. That is the meaning of war, that we become carrion to feed the birds of prey. I wonder that your Emperor in his wisdom still loves war.'

'Charlemagne is old, as you say, and his beard is white as the snows on the high mountains. Truly I think that he would wish to be at peace.'

'And yet he pursues war. I know that you Franks are worthy men. Yet those dukes and counts who urge Charles to make war do him wrong if, as you say, he would have peace.'

'Charles would have peace,' Ganelon said, 'but he is old, and as his will is now infirm Roland commands it. Why, my friend, we would have made no war in Spain but for Roland. It was he who came one day to Engelheim with a golden apple in his hand, presented it to the Emperor his uncle, and said, "Take this apple as symbol of the riches of Spain which I shall win for you if you consent that we make war on Marsilion, the Lord King.""

Then they stopped at an inn to refresh themselves, and drank wine and ate bread, olives and the good cheese of La Mancha, and as they ate, they continued their conversation, Ganelon slowly drawing the Saracen to his point, as a fisherman who has hooked a salmon plays the great fish and at last draws it in. And so engrossed were they in the plot they now devised, they did not remark that Yusuf, Marsilion's son who admired Roland, sat by them and overheard what they were saying.

'Truly this Roland is a villain,' Blancandrin said.

'Just so,' said Ganelon. 'He is my stepson, as you know, and from infancy has been a thorn in my flesh, for his temper is so high that he is ungovernable, and he slew his half-brother, my own dear son.'

'How you must hate him,' the Saracen said, speaking very gently.

'As the shepherd hates the wolf that devours his flock.'

'If Roland was no more ...'

'Then there would be peace,' Ganelon said.

'Can you contrive that?'

'I shall devise the means.'

So they rode on, and Yusuf marvelled at the wickedness of men, being himself but young and ignorant of the world.

(How I pity him, my Prince, torn as he was between duty to his father and his faith on the one hand, and the love and admiration he felt for Roland on the other. For Yusuf had never known so noble a knight; he was dazzled by Roland's radiance, and his heart went out to him.)

They came to Cordoba where Marsilion received them.

'What terms will Charles offer me?' he asked, and bit his nails to the quick in shame and indignation while Ganelon, speaking boldly, expounded the conditions Charlemagne laid down, and put no varnish on them.

'This is the Emperor's word,' he said. 'You must accept the Christian faith and be baptised in it. Then Charles will grant you the southern half of Spain to hold as his vassal.'

'But half my kingdom, half to be reft from me?' Marsilion

said, and turned away to hide the flush of shame that suffused his cheek. 'What,' he said, brokenly, 'what of the other half?'

'That he will grant to his nephew, Duke Roland. He'll prove a bold neighbour to you, I'm afraid, a bold and troublesome one.'

'Roland to have half my kingdom. What if I refuse?'

'Why then,' Ganelon smiled, 'the war shall be renewed. You will be seized and fettered, carried off to his city, Aix, not riding a noble steed as is your wont, but on a mule, with your feet tied by ropes, and there you will be put on show to the common people that they may mock you and behold the shame and degradation of Islam.'

Marsilion wept and tore his clothes, and howled in his rage and misery like a woman whose children have been snatched from her by brigands.

Then Blancandrin said, 'My Lord King, you have heard but one part of what my friend Duke Ganelon has to say, and that the worse one. Now compose yourself and hear the better.'

'If there is another part', Marsilion said, 'to Ganelon's speech it must be better, for it cannot be worse than what has gone before. Therefore, speak on.'

'When you have accepted these terms,' Ganelon said, 'the Emperor will rejoice and be eager to quit Spain. He is old and weary and longs to lay his head in his palace of Engelheim. As soon as he has the treasure you've promised and the hostages, among them your son Yusuf, he'll be off. Now I shall contrive that Roland commands the rearguard. Do you therefore send to the Basques, who hate him, to block the pass once the main body of the army has crossed over into France, while you yourself, with all the chivalry of Islam that you can muster, come hard on Roland's heels. He will be caught in a trap. No doubt you will lose many men. I won't try to deceive you about that, for Roland and his companions, among them chiefly Oliver and Elgebast, will fight bravely and do much slaughter. But they will fight to the death; yes, to their own death. Victory will be yours and peace, too, for, with Roland dead, Charles will have no heart to renew the war.'

Marsilion said, 'Is it possible? Can you contrive this?'

Ganelon replied, 'I can and shall.'

Then, one by one, the Saracen chivalry advanced and took Ganelon by the shoulders and embraced him and kissed him on the lips, so moved were they by what they had heard.

But still Marsilion hesitated, till Blancandrin said, 'Trust in Duke Ganelon, my Lord, for a nobler and more honest man never walked the earth, nor one more devoted to your welfare.'

He said this to convince the King, though he well knew that it was hatred of Roland that provoked Ganelon's treachery.

Then the King said, 'Will you swear an oath to do as you have promised?'

'On my good sword and on your Holy Book,' Ganelon said.

Then Marsilion promised him eternal friendship and wealth untold.

Ganelon smiled and said, 'Time is precious as a rich jewel. I must be on my way.'

So he mounted his horse and rode back to the Frankish camp.

XXXIV

It was not yet light when Roland stood by the open flap of his tent and smelled the windless air. This was ever for him the best time of day, when others slept and the world was his alone. The grass was wet, even among the tents where it was scuffed and trampled. Roland looked across the valley, but the hills were still dark and shrouded in mist or cloud. He felt his limbs stiff and there was an ache in his back as he descended to the horse-lines. There was no place he liked to be more. He put his arm about Quattro's neck, cupped an apple in his other hand and let her find it, and then she nuzzled him and he breathed in the warm, fleshy horse-smell that is sweet as new hay. Yes, he thought, this truly is the best time of the day, and there is no one better to share it with than your horse. Then, not waking the stable boy who had charge of Quattro, he bridled her and, not troubling with a saddle, vaulted on to her back, and rode away from the camp towards the hills. He loved the long, slow, lazy walking-stride of the horse and the proud carriage of her head. In a little the hills turned blue-grey, and then they were dappled with light, and soon after that the world was no longer his alone, but a place of danger, uncertainty, perplexity.

The previous night, after their supper of lamb cutlets baked on charcoal and the good red wine of the region, Roland had stretched himself out on his camp-bed and said to Oliver, 'Benoni used to speak longingly of the salt-marshes of Brittany and of how his father would set him to watch the sheep, and he once said, "It may be that when you come to old age, you are once again like a little boy watching the sheep in an empty land where the air is keen with the sea-breezes and sharp with the scent of the salt-water and thyme and camomile. And you are at peace because you are at one with all around you." I remember his words exactly because he seldom spoke like that. Indeed, he rarely spoke of himself except to remind me that he was the son of a poor Breton peasant, and therefore, he would say, a simple man. Which wasn't true, unless to be a good man is simple, which I think not the case. Dear Benoni, I wonder if he is still alive, keeping that inn with Milan's widow and that Arab boy whose name I forget. And if he still thinks of me. He must do, I suppose, for I was for so long the centre of his life. Indeed, he made his life over to me, and when I was young I did not understand why he did so, and, to my shame, often resented him.'

Oliver said, 'You speak strangely. It is not like you to dwell on the past.'

'No,' Roland said, 'it is not like me, I know that. For a long time it has seemed to me that the past is another country where they do things in a different manner, and where I was indeed another person, foreign to the man I am now. Is this foolishness to suppose that it was not I, Duke Roland of Brittany and Gascony, who loved Angelica so madly, and that the youth who did so is now dead? Perhaps my madness wiped him out, and yet I loved Angelica when I was restored to sanity, or, as may be, the image of Angelica. And now I ask myself on such a night as this, when the bird that is called Philomel sings its sad song in these soft gardens of Spain, whether Angelica was not perhaps a girl I had dreamed, for she still comes to me while I sleep and vanishes with the light.'

Oliver said, 'Are you disturbed that you speak like this?'

'Disturbed?' Roland said. 'Or suddenly at peace? I cannot tell. I have passed my life in action, furious action, fuelled by the ambition that men call noble, the ambition to win glory and renown. But then I think of Benoni the boy among the salt-marshes and now, it may be, the old man tending the inn and eating that fish-pie of which you have said my father's woman was so proud, and I think: is my renown in war and battle of no more import than that fish-pie?'

He laughed, and Oliver read bitterness in that laugh, the acrid fruit of disillusionment, and said, 'I think you are fey, my dear.'

Roland said, 'I am certain Ganelon is plotting some treachery to destroy me. Why then should I not be fey?'

These words came surging back to him as he sat his horse looking over the valley as the hills acquired their firm shape. 'Why should I not be fey?' He leaned forward and spoke them into Quattro's ear, and then he pulled, very gently, on the rein to turn the horse's head, and rode back to the camp.

XXXV

When Ganelon returned to announce that Marsilion had accepted the terms offered him, a cheer rose from the Frankish camp. Even those who had been most ardent for war were now happy to go home. They had all got themselves rich booty, and now Marsilion's mules, laden with treasure, were led into the camp, and barons and knights competed to divide the spoil, keeping the best for themselves (as is natural) but setting some aside for their retainers.

Ganelon presented the hostages to Charlemagne, who addressed them graciously, assuring them they would be well cared for and their lives safe, unless their King broke his word. Hearing this, Yusuf, Marsilion's son, flushed in shame, for he knew his father well. Moreover, he had overheard Ganelon and Blancandrin hatch their plot, and this was cause for still deeper shame.

He was a noble youth, but now sore perplexed. On the one hand, as a true Saracen, it pleased him to see the Franks prepare to depart from the fair land of Spain, which was his by right of inheritance. Even so, he thought, I shall not live to sit on my father's throne, for, when he breaks his word, I shall be the first of the hostages to be slain. But this thought distressed him less, so noble was his nature, than the other matter that weighed heavy on his mind. And this was the need to find some means to warn Roland of the conspiracy.

So that evening, when a boy brought him his supper – a lamb stew and good wine, for Charles had ordered that he be treated royally – Yusuf asked whether the lad would carry a message from him to Duke Roland. 'Tell him,' he said, 'I seek an audience, and I have matters of great import concerning his welfare to impart.'

This the boy promised to do, but, instead of going to Roland, he went to Ganelon, whose servant he was, and reported Prince Yusuf's request.

Ganelon said, 'Carry this message back to the young man: the Duke Roland does not deign to converse with infidels, and therefore he denies him the audience he seeks.'

And Ganelon then ordered that a close watch be kept on the Saracen Prince, and that he be prevented from speaking to any but those whom he, Ganelon, trusted.

In a few days the Frankish army was ready to march. Charlemagne called his council together. The Emperor smiled and the mood was cheerful. Then he said, 'Which of you will command the rearguard? Believe me, it is a post not only of honour, but of great importance. Marsilion has accepted our terms, but till we are all safely quit of Spain and beyond the mountains, there is still danger, for it is not wise to trust the word of an infidel.'

Roland said, 'Uncle, I was the first to ride into Spain. I shall be the last to leave. Give me command of the rearguard.'

His words were greeted with a loud cheer. Though none of the peers of France would have declined the command, yet none but Roland was eager to assume it.

But Ganelon pulled at his beard, and said, 'Much as I admire my stepson's ardent spirit, I have to advise you, sire, that he is not the man for that post. We all know his virtues – and his faults of character. If you give him this command he'll find some way to engage in battle. We know he is not committed to this truce, or rather peace. Therefore, I fear that he will so stir things up that King Marsilion himself will find excuse to break his oath.'

Ganelon had two reasons for speaking like this. First, as a precaution, lest some suspicion of his conspiracy should be aired. Were that to happen, he could argue that he had tried to prevent Roland from assuming this command, and therefore could not be guilty of plotting against him. But second, he knew full well that his opposition would make Roland the more determined to maintain his right to be the last man through the pass of Roncesvalles.

It fell out as he expected. Roland commanded the rearguard, and Ganelon smiled secretly in the knowledge that the stepson he so hated would never set foot in France again.

The next day, in the white dawn, the army marched. Men sang and cheered. Only Charlemagne was ill at ease, for his night had been disturbed by evil dreams.

XXXVI

For days they marched over the ridges of little hills following the great Roman road that leads westward to Pamplona. With every day the gap between the main body of the army and the rearguard lengthened, and there were several reasons for this. In the first place stragglers fell behind, some of them wounded, others merely footsore and weary; and these delayed Roland and his men. Then the way was blocked often by wagons that had lost a wheel or stuck at a crossing. There were many places where the road itself was in disrepair, some where it had sunk into marshland, or the mountain streams had washed bridges away; and though such accidents had hindered the main body, too, they impeded the rearguard more. Yet even this was not the worst of it, for the rearguard had to be on the watch for clouds of lightly armed skirmishers, horsemen mounted on nimble hill-ponies, who pressed hard upon them, loosing their arrows and then darting off to invite pursuit. These did not appear to be regular troops. It seemed that Marsilion was observing the terms of the agreement, and there was no sign of the Saracen host. Yet these skirmishers delayed them further, and made it necessary to pitch camp well before dark, and post sentries.

So by the time they came to the crossing of the roads, where that to Pamplona meets that which leads north from Burgos, this city being now well to their backs, the rearguard was a full day's march behind Charlemagne. Nevertheless, few were anxious, for they trusted in Roland and in their own strength. They were not a rabble in retreat but a victorious army retiring in good order.

On the seventh day, towards noon, they came in sight of the great pass that led across the mountains to France. They halted for their midday meal, but only briefly. All were now eager to be out of Spain. For some hours they marched under a hot sun over a wide plain rising gently to the north, and, ahead of them, like a mighty rampart guarding a sacred city, they saw the great line of the Pyrenees. Between them and the mountains there rose on either side of the road a noble wood of beech and oak, and they were happy to enter into its shade. Beyond the wood was a little col, which goes by the name of Roncesvalles. The sun declined as they made their way through the wood, and then they were again in open country. From this point they were able to look beyond Spain and see France, and even the weariest were cheered by the sight. Some even supposed that they could discern the long line of the main body of the army far in the distance, but they were probably mistaken.

Roland called a halt, and the men refreshed themselves from the mountain streams. Those who still had wine in their leather bottles diluted it with the cold water so that they might quench their thirst. Roland, with Oliver and a couple of squires, now rode forward to the head of the army, to survey the road they must follow, winding down the mountainside and, even as he watched, disappearing from view in a deep pass. For a long time he gazed on the valley in silence.

No one now can tell what his thoughts were. Doubtless his heart lightened to see the Gascon plain spread out before him beyond the pass. For days now he had borne a heavy load of responsibility, and he was very tired. Did he ask himself if they should halt for the night, and not risk the pass in the gathering gloom? He must surely have been aware that the Basques who so hated him, and were eager to revenge themselves on the Franks, might be lurking on the heights above the pass. But there was silence, of that we may be sure, a deep silence, the silence of a great church at dead of night, and there was no sign of life on the hillsides.

So he wheeled his horse, and, outlined against the sky, gave the signal to advance. Then he himself took up his place at the rear, with Oliver and a band of his most trusted and experienced men-at-arms. Far behind he could now hear the whoops and cries of the skirmishing horsemen, but there was nothing to fear from them.

The pass narrowed and the column moved more slowly, as men and wagons jostled for positions. The shadows lengthened, and every now and then a soldier cried out that he could discern shapes moving on the hillside among the trees.

Then Oliver, mounting a ridge, looked back to where the light was dying on Spain, and cried out that he saw clouds of dust rising and the red sun glinting on armour.

'We are betrayed,' he said. 'This is no little band of skirmishers that snaps at our heels like little dogs, but the panoply of Islam. We are betrayed, my friend. Marsilion's treachery is clear to see, and either we make a stand in this narrow defile, or make speed to make for France.'

Roland said, 'Never in my life have I turned tail and fled, whether from Saxon or from Saracen. We'll stand and fight, and drive them back to Spain, and then I'll follow and seize the treacherous King and slit his lying throat.'

Brave words! But, even as he spoke, there came the sound of huge boulders crashing down the hillside, and then the wood awoke, pouring forth fierce, ragged mountaineers, howling their war cry: 'Death or Liberty.'

It was impossible for the Franks to deploy. The Basques were among them, and the narrow valley rang with the clash of weapons and the cries of the wounded and dying. It was a general mêlée, without order or form; but still more Basques charged down the steep flanks of the hills until it seemed to the desperate Franks that they were numerous as swarms of bees, and indeed their sting was sharp.

Oliver cried out to Roland to blow his mighty horn, that Charlemagne, far ahead, might hear it and turn back, and come to their aid. But Roland smiled, sadly, and said, 'He will not hear,' and, even as he spoke, the first force of the Saracen cavalry fell upon their rear. Straightway, Roland and Oliver rode hard against them into the heart of the mêlée, and, rising high in the stirrups, did great execution. For a moment the Saracen line wavered, but then the second line came up at a sharp canter and pressed hard upon them so that the Franks were submerged as rocks are in a high tide. For many hours the carnage continued until the Saracen commander, even Blancandrin, sounded the recall. Then the mountaineers, having stripped the slain of their weapons and jewels and plundered the wagons, disappeared, silently now, silently as they had waited in ambush, back up the hillsides and into the deep forests.

The moon rose and its pale light shone on the faces of the slaughtered Franks. How many brave men died that awful day, I do not know, and nor does anyone else.

But the name of Roncesvalles is never to be forgotten, and Roland lay dead with Oliver by his side where the battle had been fiercest.

XXXVII

When, my Prince, you have mastered Old French (for the tongue has changed since those heroic days), you will delight in the poems called *Chansons de Geste*, and especially in the noblest of them, the *Chanson de Roland*. And you will read there of the many brave and noble speeches that Roland and Oliver made in the course of the battle, as well as the list of the Saracen lords who fought them. But you will hear nothing of the Basques to whom the honour – if honour there was – of the victory belonged, but only of the Saracens, and I must tell you that men do not make long speeches in battle. The poem is magnificent and brings tears to my aged eyes whenever I read it. It is magnificent, but it is not war as war is fought. That is grim and brutal and there is no glamour to it, though there is heroism.

It is enough to know that Roland died as he had lived, bravely. May we all be in death what we have been in life.

And if you say, as I see you are about to say, that my version is not without fancy, I submit to the charge, except that I insist I have employed imagination, which is a penetrating and enlightening faculty of the mind, whereas what I call fancy is mere decoration.

XXXVIII

The next day the few Franks who had escaped the slaughter limped in to Charlemagne's camp, many wounded, all blood-stained and begrimed, their eyes eloquent of the horror they had seen and endured. Many were also shamed because they had survived while all their comrades had been killed. But in truth they had no cause for shame, since they had fought their way out of the battle and had not fled.

When Charlemagne heard what had befallen Roland and his peers, the glittering chivalry of France, he wept and cried out, 'Roland is dead, you say? Roland that was so valiant? Roland dead? And Oliver? And all the peers? Alas, fair France, now are you desolate indeed ... would I had fallen with you, nephew Roland.'

And for a long time, as the sun mounted the sky, he spoke in this vein, repeating himself again and again in his shock, his voice high and piping, and its sound as thin as the mountain air. Some say he seemed like a widow woman, keening by her husband's corpse.

'Ganelon, my friend,' he said at last, 'what shall we do without our Roland?'

Ganelon shook his head, as if in sorrow, pulled his beard and said, 'A brave knight, no one doubts that, but I must take leave to wonder what he did to bring this battle this disaster, on to himself and all of France. Whom did he provoke, and in what manner? You will recall, sire, that I advised against giving him command of the rearguard because, I said, he was so rash and warlike by nature, so little given to prudence, that it was wiser to give that command to a more cautious and temperate general. But let us speak no ill, but only nobly and honourably, of him now that he is no more. Rash youth, rash youth.'

Then Charlemagne dispatched a company of knights to

Roncesvalles, that fatal field, that they might seek among the dead for the bodies of Roland and all the peers of France. And they numbered Roland's wounds, which were thirty-seven in all, so that men marvelled at the strength and courage he had displayed, fighting so long when grievously wounded.

His face, they said, was beautiful in death and strangely content.

So they took his body and carried it into Gascony, and laid it to rest in the church of Saint-Romain-de-Blaye, and Charlemagne commanded that thirty-seven masses, one for each wound he had suffered, be sung for his soul.

His tomb has long been a place of pilgrimage, and I myself have knelt there to pray, for though I abhor war, I honour the brave, and Roland is numbered among them with Hector and Achilles, heroes of antiquity.

XXXIX

When, my Prince, you come to read the *Chanson de Roland* in
the Old French, you will learn that Ganelon's treachery was
discovered and how, after a trial by combat in which his
champion was defeated, he was sentenced to death by torture in
the antique Frankish manner. Moreover, before this the poet
told us how Charlemagne rode back into Spain, defeated the
Saracens in a great battle and slew the treacherous King Marsilion.

All this is as it should be in a work of art, for it is proper that
it takes a perfect shape and that the wicked do not go unpunished.

But, as I have often told you, I deal in history, which is life,
and not in art, and I do not recount things as having happened
merely because it is fitting that they should.

Therefore, I have to tell you that things fell out differently.

The Emperor did not return to Spain, but retired to his place
of Engelheim in Aix. He was old and weary and sad, and soon
fell into a decline.

Ganelon's treachery was not made manifest. Instead he
reminded everyone of how he had advised against giving Roland
command of the rearguard. If any thought he protested overmuch,
they prudently held their peace, for Duke Ganelon was a great
power in the Empire, the close confidant of Charlot, the heir,
who now assumed much power, his father being so weak. Only
the Saracen prince, Yusuf, was witness to the Duke's treachery,
but Ganelon requested, as a special favour, that he be entrusted
with the keeping of the boy, as the most noble of the hostages.
He carried him to his grim castle of Sigmaringen, and cast him
into a dungeon. History knows no more of the youth. Some say
he was strangled, some that he was starved to death. In the inn
below the castle they will tell you, when fortified with wine, that
on St Stephen's day each year, the night sky is disturbed by

sobbing and a boyish voice calling on Allah for mercy. But the common folk love such legends, and though I once passed the feast of Stephen in the little town, and walked in the market-place below the castle wall at midnight, I heard nothing.

Envoi

Yet there are other ghosts.

Many years ago, when I was studying in the city of Constantine, I would repair in the evening to the Tavern of the Rosy Garden, where the wine was good and the company agreeable if also louche.

The old woman who kept the tavern had learned of my interest in the heroic tales of Charlemagne and Roland, and one evening led me into her private chamber and told me this story.

'You must know,' she said, 'that this tavern has been in my family for many generations, for my great-great-great-grandsire was an Arab called Ahmed who was received into the Christian faith and took the name Orlando. He was a favourite of the old woman who kept the tavern then and of one Benoni, a Breton who had been the friend of the old woman's husband, whose name I forget. It was this Benoni, I have been told, who insisted that he take the name Orlando when he was baptised a Christian, for Benoni had been the friend and tutor of the Frankish hero you speak of who went by the name of Roland or Orlando.

'It so happened that one day, when Benoni was an old man and Ahmed (as he still was) had attained the prime of manhood, there came to the tavern a woman, heavily veiled in the Moham-medan fashion. Only her eyes were visible and they shone with brilliance and intelligence, but there was sorrow in them, too, that sorrow which comes from too much knowledge of the world. She spoke for a little with Benoni without revealing her name, and he did not recognise her, because in his old age he was near to being blind. Then she said, "My poor Benoni, I am Angelica, and I come here because I have escaped my husband the Emir, and now that I am in a Christian land again, I wish to find my beloved Roland."

'Benoni sighed, and said, "Alas, I have heard that our dear Roland is dead, fallen gloriously in Spain."

'"There is nothing glorious in war," she said.

'"I know that," Benoni said.

'At that moment Ahmed, my great-great-great-grandsire, came into the chamber, and she looked at him, and said, "But he looks like Roland, a Roland at peace with the world. Is he Roland returned from the grave?"'

'"No," Benoni said, "he is not Roland but he is a good boy."

'So they talked for a long time, recalling the past, and Angelica, who had suffered much, grew easy in their company. When Benoni died soon after, Angelica married Ahmed who was now Orlando. She did not love him as she is said to have loved Roland, of that I am certain, but she loved him because he had no desire to go adventuring, but was content to keep the tavern.

'Yet, though they lived in peace with each other, and prospered, Angelica never forgot your Roland, but delighted to hear travellers speak of his glory, and would herself often recount the great feats he had performed in tournaments on account of his love for her.

'In old age she would wander the gardens calling his name, and sometimes, when the nightingales are silent, I myself have heard her calling at dead of night. But her husband, who had been Ahmed and was now Orlando, was not distressed or perturbed, saying it was foolishness to be jealous of dead loves. For his part he never enquired into Angelica's past, being happy to live in the present. They had five children, but I am the last of the line and have never married or borne children myself. So when I die, Angelica will be forgotten here, and if her ghost still wanders in the garden ... well, who knows?'